T0157075

Letting Go *of* Forever

When You Lose Someone You Love

Jim Rule

iUniverse, Inc.
New York   Bloomington

Copyright © 2009 by Jim Rule

All rights reserved. No part of this book may be used or reproduced by any means, graphic, electronic, or mechanical, including photocopying, recording, taping or by any information storage retrieval system without the written permission of the publisher except in the case of brief quotations embodied in critical articles and reviews.

All Scripture quotations, unless otherwise indicated, are taken from the Holy Bible, New International Version. Copyright © 1973, 1978, 1984 by International Bible Society. Used by permission of International Bible Society.

Other Bible versions:

Verses marked TLB are taken from The Living Bible, copyright ©1971. Used by permission of Tyndale House Publishers, Inc., Wheaton, Illinois 60189. All rights reserved.

Scripture taken from THE MESSAGE. © Copyright by Eugene Peterson, 1993, 1994, 1995. Used by permission of NavPress Publishing Group.

Scripture taken from the NEW AMERICAN STANDARD BIBLE®, Copyright © 1960, 1962, 1963, 1968, 1971, 1972, 1973, 1975, 1977, 1995 by The Lockman Foundation. Used by permission.

Scripture quotations marked "NKJV™" are taken from the New King James Version®. Copyright © 1982 by Thomas Nelson, Inc. Used by permission. All rights reserved.

The Scripture quotations contained herein from the New Revised Standard Bible, copyright 1989, by the Division of Christian Education of the National Council of Churches of Christ in the U. S. A. Used by permission. All rights reserved. Scripture quotations marked as RSV are from the Revised Standard Version of the Bible, copyright 1946, 1952, and 1971 by the National Council of the Churches of Christ in the USA. Used by permission. All rights reserved.

iUniverse books may be ordered through booksellers or by contacting:

iUniverse
1663 Liberty Drive
Bloomington, IN 47403
www.iuniverse.com
1-800-Authors (1-800-288-4677)

Because of the dynamic nature of the Internet, any Web addresses or links contained in this book may have changed since publication and may no longer be valid. The views expressed in this work are solely those of the author and do not necessarily reflect the views of the publisher, and the publisher hereby disclaims any responsibility for them.

ISBN: 978-1-4401-8988-3 (sc)
ISBN: 978-1-4401-8986-9 (dj)
ISBN: 978-1-4401-8987-6 (ebook)

Printed in the United States of America

iUniverse rev. date: 1/13/10

In Loving Memory
of
Peg Rule

Born Margaret Ann Ricca – August 30, 1946
Died – August 8, 2003

Contents

Acknowledgments

I am grateful to God for my friend, Karen Moore, Christian writer, speaker, and author, whose encouragement, insight, skills, and knowledge helped shape and bring this book to completion, and whose gentle spirit touched a lonely heart. (Visit her website at www.karen-ann-moore.com to read her inspiring daily devotionals and to learn more about her books in print.)

I am grateful for my friend, Joan Daughenbaugh, who did meticulous proofreading in the final stages of preparing the manuscript, correcting errors in writing and structure. Joan's confidence in the book has been reassuring and she became another of God's blessings to its production and to me personally.

I am grateful to grandson, Joseph Rule, for all he did to prepare, improve, and format the pictures for publication, amazing this former photographer.

I give thanks and praise to God for all who grieved for Peg with me and who grieved for me following her death.

For family who, in their own grief and loss, listened to mine, especially my son, Mike, his wife, Becky, children, Joseph, and Rachael, and my sister, Nancy, who have also allowed themselves to become exposed in these pages.

For friends Steve and Bob, who made sure I wasn't personally alone in grief and loss, who let me talk and weren't afraid of my emotions.

For a church family who loved Peg and missed her deeply too, and loved me enough to allow me time to find my way back to ministry.

For associate pastor and staff member, Rev. Jaye Reisinger, who while coping with her own sense of loss, capably took over my pastoral responsibilities during my leave of absence.

For a denomination, the United Methodist Church, that was generous with support through leaders and colleagues in ministry, and with time to grieve.

For Dr. Gary Smith of Midland Family Physicians and the staff of MidMichigan Medical Center of Midland, who did all they could to preserve Peg's life and for their tender care while her life ebbed away instead.

For the Comforter, the ever-present Spirit of Christ Jesus, who has brought me along in my great loss, giving me a way to express, through these pages, my struggle that not only sustained me but now stands to sustain others in theirs.

Preface

For many years I had a copy of C. S. Lewis's book, *A Grief Observed,* in my collection of books-to-read-someday. But each time I finished one and returned to that collection I passed over that book. Though the author was the reason I had picked it up in a used book sale—anything by Lewis must be worth reading—whenever I would look at the description I would put it back on the shelf again. A book about the death of a spouse from cancer and the struggles of the surviving spouse, even if he was C. S. Lewis, never sounded as appealing as one of the others. Then after my own wife, Peg, died of cancer and I found myself overwhelmed by grief and loss, that book zoomed to the other end of the interest scale. My sudden immersion in its subject matter made all the difference and impelled me to read what I had previously shunned, and even to write about it myself.

The death of someone close, especially a spouse, induces thoughts, feelings, and experiences that stress logic, faith, and even relationships. Harold Ivan Smith said about his book, *Once In a Lifetime: Reflections Upon the Death of a Father,* "It's one son sharing his road map with other pilgrims who have lost their father and are desperately trying to make sense of the experience."[1] This book is one husband's experience—my road map of the journey I have been on—trying to adjust to the loss of my life-partner. But the writing hasn't just recorded the journey, it has been part of the journey itself, taking me from one place to another.

I feel confident that anyone in close contact with grief and loss will recognize many of the features of the landscape in what David, the writer

---

1   Harold Ivan Smith, *Once In a Lifetime: Reflections Upon the Death of a Father,* (Originally published by Thomas Nelson, Nashville, TN, 1989; © acquired by Augsburg Fortress Publishers: Minneapolis, MN).

of the Bible's Twenty-third Psalm, called "the valley of the shadow of death." Those who have not yet traveled into its deepest shadows themselves will discover what some of the prominent features are and their impact on the sojourner. The impact on this sojourner may be unsettling for some people who have an image of what a "good" pastor's faith should be like and how any Christian should regard death. I discovered early-on that it's one thing to hold certain rational beliefs, and it is another thing to live them out emotionally and spiritually in the depth of that valley—the distance between head-level and gut-level is much more than mere inches.

To provide structure I have written under three headings: *Illness*, *Aftermath*, and *Individuation*. Chronologically illness belongs first because that was where my grief experience began. But from my experience previous to Peg's death, as mentioned, I realized I probably wouldn't read very far if the book began with the morbid details of a woman's illness and death from cancer. Because some summary and enough details are included in the main text to provide understanding of these things when needed, I have included that as *Appendix A: Illness and Death*. Anyone who begins to wonder about the shadows of illness that reach forward to aftermath and individuation can leave the main text at any point and read the story in more depth. With that desire satisfied the reader can then return to the main text with a better sense of how the preceding illness, not just the death of someone we love, carries over into *Aftermath*.

The essence of this journey is under the two broad headings of *Aftermath* and *Individuation* which constitute the main parts of the book. Aftermath is the phase that immediately followed Peg's death and burial. This is what I began to deal with as a result of her death, the things that any surviving spouse must face in our society, as well as things I had to face in my own unique circumstance. It began with arrangements and business consequential to her death starting very shortly afterward. (In general, half of the married population will eventually have a similar experience with one partner preceding the other in death.)

Individuation is what I call the process of moving from being a twosome to a solitary individual once again. I naively expected the line of demarcation to be fairly distinct between the two; that once aftermath was complete, I would begin individuation. It was not distinct. There is an overlap in the timeline for both with a gradual shift, most of the early writings under *Aftermath* being previous to most of the later writings under *Individuation*. Grief does indeed involve oscillation between various phases.

The tone of some of the episodes may seem maudlin or depressing. That is because some of this writing is lament, which is something that our society avoids. I did not understand lament is what I was doing when I began. But this is an ancient and universal human way of dealing emotionally with grief, loss, and sorrow, a way of mourning that is practiced ritually in many societies. Lament does not always make rational sense and often seems to conflict with faith, but it is an important part of the grief process. It is a genre of literature found in the Bible significant enough to have a book by that title, *Lamentations*.

In our society, when lament is expressed in social settings, it is often not accepted and even discouraged. Those who continue to express it beyond the immediate context of the funeral and burial are often perceived as being stalled in their grief and needing to move beyond it. Actually they may be right where they need to be because healthy expression of grief is normative. In truth, many are so deeply stunned at first that they are incapable of deep mourning until some time has passed. In our society that is so devoted to comfort, those around us often want to spare us the pain and try to take it away, but their attempts to circumvent it often drive it inward, and instead of release, there is withdrawal, internalization, and despair. Besides that, I have found a curious need to experience the pain which is related to the meaning and significance of the relationship that is its cause. It hurts so much because it means so much. Lament is there in these writings and you might identify it in your own experience if you have encountered a significant loss.

I began this writing with a momentous purpose, one expressed by Mark Twain in his autobiography. He lost a son, who was not quite two years of age, to death. Then in later years, a daughter, Susy, who was just age twenty-four. In chapter three, he recalled the telegram he received notifying him of her death and the circumstance of it, observing, "It is one of the mysteries of our nature that a man, all unprepared, can receive a thunder-stroke like that and live. There is but one reasonable explanation of it. The intellect is stunned by the shock, and but gropingly gathers the meaning of the words. The power to realize their full import is mercifully wanting. The mind has a dumb sense of vast loss -- that is all. It will take mind and memory months, and possibly years, to gather together the details, and thus learn and know the whole extent of the loss." Twain went on to reminisce about her personality and character. Then he wrote little detailed stories about her as a child, in all of it, I'm sure, sensing the vast loss he spoke of.

As Twain suggests, time and the details of the past have helped me to sense the loss—not only my own loss, but the loss of others, in Peg's premature death. The writing of it has allowed me to experience this tragedy more profoundly, to discover and work out many things that I believe would never have been revealed to me otherwise. And so I see the urge to write through the grief as a blessing inspired by God for my comfort and consolation and I am extremely grateful.

However, having all this in written form means the journey in the shadowy valley can be shared, and that God may have given it not just for me, but for others. That feels both risky and compelling. It is pleasing to offer these pages as public tribute to Peg in her memory. It is appropriate to offer them in praise and thanks to God for the blessings of married life he granted to both Peg and me for thirty-seven years. It is encouraging to think that someone else on the same journey in the shadowy valley might be blessed through these pages in their encounter with grief over the death of a loved one. But there is still the feeling that putting so much of private and public life under the microscope has its risks. I'll take that risk for the great consolation there is in believing that reading of what happened to Peg and me might serve some useful purpose for others and for God.

PART I
AFTERMATH

Chapter 1

Solitary Life Begins

Today has been my first day alone. The last of my family has gone home and I am now facing the grim reality of life on my own, without Peg. I expected this to be difficult, but I had not reckoned with God. Why God does what He does, I cannot comprehend. He did not choose to spare Peg's life and cure her cancer or even send it into remission for some years. Yet He sent someone to ring my doorbell just as my lunch finished heating in the microwave.

I answered the door and found a man standing there with a book in his hand—one of those people whose religion compels them to interrupt lunches and other important things while they pedal their publications and their faith, I assumed. He introduced himself and said he had learned from his pastor that I had just lost my wife. He had come to bring me a copy of a book I might find helpful, C. S. Lewis's, *A Grief Observed*. It had been helpful to him since his wife's death at age 53 just a month ago. My whole demeanor changed in an instant.

I was going to begin reading that very same book as soon as I finished my lunch. I had found my copy the night before among my collection of books-to-read-someday. It came to mind shortly after Peg's death and I was sure it was my reading assignment as soon as I would be on my own. But when I went to look for it, I couldn't find it where I thought it was among my unread collection in the parsonage. So I searched for it in my library at the church office. But it was not there either. Perhaps I had disposed of it the last time I thinned out my over-growing prospects. I remember looking at it several times and thinking, why would I want to read about someone else's misery? Now I knew.

Knowing that it was now a must–read book, I went to a Christian bookstore hoping to find a copy, and since their last one had been sold earlier that day, I ordered one. But after I got home that evening, further thought sent me back to the bookshelves, and there it was. On closer scrutiny, I found it in a color and size I had not pictured in my mind's eye on the earlier search.

My visitor was now bringing me the copy the bookstore had sold earlier that day, to him. I declined to accept it suggesting that someone else might benefit from it since I now had one in hand and another on the way. But I invited him in and we talked for awhile about the illnesses our wives had suffered and what our experiences of grief had been like thus far. We parted, both a little encouraged, with names and phone numbers leaving me with the hope that we might talk again.

But the widower with the book wasn't the only one God had lined up for the day. About noon a phone call from my son, Mike, had been the first contact from the outside in my now empty world. I talked longer than necessary about the arrangements we were making to schedule an appointment for the following day to consider a gravestone and about things that could easily have waited until we were together. Mike thoughtfully let me ramble filling some of the void of the day.

In the late afternoon another phone caller was a parishioner-friend, who asked could he stop by and drop off some videotapes of Peg's funeral service. When he arrived, he could have handed them to me at the door, but he accepted my invitation into the family room. Our conversation struck a rhythm between events surrounding Peg's death, my future, and events in his own life and family. It was therapeutic to delve into the hard things I was facing, then periodically withdrawing into the reality of on-going life.

A few moments ago my sister, Nancy, called to let me know she and mom had arrived safely after traveling the nearly 500 miles home. And now my first day at home alone without Peg is nearing an end. I didn't accomplish much—just a few household chores and a little reading. It had a few difficult moments, but not as many as I imagined there could be. God has ministered to me through the people who came and called as well as in the reading of the book, which I did begin. There will be days that are more difficult, I suppose, even if someone comes or calls. But the Lord has launched me into this new existence with some assurance. I just can't say I'm pleased He didn't prevent it in the first place.

Grief is so unpredictable. Wednesday proved it. For the first time since her burial, I went to Peg's grave. I had driven the 60 miles from the tri-city area where I continue to live, to meet with my son, Mike, his wife Becky, and their local funeral director to select a gravestone. With that completed, the three of us went the additional dozen miles to the little rural township cemetery we have all chosen for family burial, which is near one of the first churches I served and the family farm where Becky grew up.

I had imagined it would be difficult emotionally to visit Peg's grave for the first time. But it wasn't—at least not in the way I had expected. There was, of course, the fresh sand mounded over the grave mixed with stones of assorted sizes. I could visualize the wooden casket below the ground in the vault and her body, as I last saw it, inside. But any surge of horror was immediately overruled by the realization that the real person she had become was no longer there and the fact of her physical burial stirred more dull resignation in me than anything.

What disturbed me most were the remains of the flowers cast upon the center of the gravesite, probably by the cemetery workers as they finished their task. The flowers were now withered and disheveled and seemed like a comment on the final sum of the meaning of Peg's life and my regard for her. I was extremely disappointed that I had not thought to bring something fresh and vital to put in their place—something that would make a statement that there was still beauty, life, and love above ground and above earth. Becky was coming to the city the next day, and she offered to pick out something appropriate for the season and see that it was put in place when she returned. Though I was very thankful for Becky's intentions, I left the cemetery feeling more than anything vaguely depressed and disappointed with myself.

As we left the cemetery, I was thinking the most difficult part of the day was behind me, but it was still to come. We returned to their home where I would stay for supper. After visiting for awhile, we gathered at the table. Everyone sat in their usual places where we always sat when Peg and I came for a meal, except a friend of our grandson's was also coming for supper and he was to be seated where Peg usually sat. But when time came for the meal, we learned he had already eaten, and so he went home to do some chores until we were finished. His clean dishes were picked up and put away. Alone on my side of the table, Peg's absence was conspicuous to me. Besides that, for me to be at our son's home without her was something very rare. She never missed a chance to be with them and would have envied my being with the grandchildren without her.

The meal and the visit were good but the ride home was lonesome. Not only was the passenger seat empty, but so would the house be when I arrived at home. Previously those rides home meant more than an hour of time to talk over our visit, appreciate our family, and enjoy our companionship. I missed her desperately as I drove alone through the farmland that had become so familiar to both of us. The tape of Christian music I listened to ministered to me but the reason I needed to be ministered to was all too real. I hadn't expected the difficult things of the day to come from where they did.

"She's gone!!!" I find myself saying that out loud every now and then. "She's gone!!! I can't believe she's gone!" During Peg's illness things kept going wrong. She was diagnosed with lymphoma, but before she could begin chemotherapy, she needed to be treated for bone cancer. She received fourteen radiation treatments over a large area of her spine and pelvis. She seemed to be coming along OK, considering all she had been through with three previous hospitalizations, one for a severe reaction to a pain medication, and the other two for unmanageable and escalating back pain. After the radiation, she was beginning to keep her food down without the help of medication. But then she got so very tired and felt extremely crummy. After a phone call to her radiologist, she went for blood tests and we found her hemoglobin was down to 6.2 when it should have been at least 10. She received two units of blood.

Then her stomach began bothering her more. She couldn't lie on her left side and it was getting uncomfortable to be on her back as well. She began to feel generally worse and she never did find the recovery everyone predicted the new blood would give. She was admitted to the hospital and tests revealed she had fluid on the lungs. She was put on oxygen to ease her breathing, and after removal of nearly two liters from one lung, she was totally exhausted.

Then her kidneys shut down and her doctors tried treating that with medication to get them restarted. But there were signs that there was fluid in her abdomen area as well. When the subject of other procedures was broached, she said adamantly, with somewhat slurred speech because she was getting so weak, "No more! Every time I have something done, something else goes wrong." And she was right. She had reached her limit. She'd never have been able to stand more invasive procedures. If the medication didn't work, she'd had enough. It didn't and within two days, she died.[2]

Twice during the whole ordeal she said to me, "I just want to go home." One night she said it while she was laying on the bed we had set up for her

2   For a more detailed account of Peg's illness and death, see Appendix A: Illness and Death.

in the family room so she didn't have to go upstairs, which eventually she was unable to do anyway. She was in obvious distress, struggling to find a comfortable position. Her tired soulful eyes got a far away look in them that scared the wits out of me, as she said to me, "I just want to go home." I never saw that look again after that and I sometimes wonder if some part of her didn't begin leaving that night.

We talked. She was worried about me—if I would be OK. Of course I wouldn't without her! But I couldn't tell her that. With tears that betrayed my feelings I struggled to tell her I loved her and if she needed to go, it was OK. We hugged and cried. That was the hardest thing I ever said because I knew if I said it I had to mean it. With my mind I knew I needed to say those words and let her go but I'm still trying to say them with my heart.

So I'll try to say them again! It's OK. Peg, it's OK that your body, which hardly ever slowed you down—even with occasional aches and pains—it's OK that it no longer has you sidelined just trying to survive and to keep from suffering with the illness and side effects of the treatments and medicines. It's OK that your legs that once took you scurrying about the house and the church doing all that you managed to do, that pedaled your mountain bike over miles of back roads and old railroad beds—it's OK that they are no longer so weak that they could no longer support you to get you off your bed in order to conduct your bodily functions. It's OK that your hands that once played beautiful organ solos for worship, contemporary keyboard in the Praise Band, and made the keyboard of the office computer chatter at speeds no one else could come close to—it's OK that they are no longer cold and pale and unable to carry even a few ice chips to your mouth to soothe its dryness. It's OK! You needed to go home, and it's OK!

But she's gone! She's gone!!! The Lord has been reminding me to say, when that realization strikes me unawares which it can at any moment, not just that "She's gone," but that "She's gone home!" She's gone to be with her Lord and He has saved her, not from her disease, but out of her disease.

At Peg's funeral, my district superintendent, Rev. Tom Robinson, talked about things that cancer cannot do like destroying love, hope, and faith, that it couldn't harm all the memories present at that moment. And he assured us it couldn't stop resurrection.

So Peg is not just gone, she's gone on to the new life our Lord has promised. And I'm trying to say, not just "She's gone!" but "She's gone home!!!" I pray that saying that will somehow lessen the pain of her absence and give me a sense of her presence where one day I shall be present too, by the grace and mercy of God![3]

---

3   After I finished writing this, I opened sympathy cards that were delivered during the

After his wife died, C. S. Lewis said everything had this vague sense of wrongness about it as though something was amiss. Even when he wasn't thinking about her, there was this sense that things were not right. I agree. Peg has left a hole in virtually everything, even the things that we did not do together.

Late yesterday afternoon I cut the grass in the front of the house. I could sense something wasn't right even while I was absorbed in the mowing. Often I would cut the lawn before supper and so I would be conscious of needing to finish in time to be ready to eat when Peg would have the meal on the table. But yesterday there was no meal being readied while I cut the lawn—there was no one preparing it. That's what was amiss.

After worship this morning, church friends invited me to join them for lunch in a local restaurant. The topics of discussion around the table were various and I was grateful for the companionship. Though no one mentioned Peg until later in the mealtime, it just didn't seem right to be there and I'm sure it's because I was without her.

This afternoon I went for a bike ride. I used to do that by myself, a half-hour ride, just for exercise. That's what I did today, and though I've often done it before, it just wasn't right somehow. Of course, we often biked together on Sunday afternoons and some summer evenings just for the joy of it, using our headset communicators to talk to each other as we rode. Maybe that had something to do with things not seeming right on today's exercise run.

I suppose, in part, all this is because she had become a factor in every action, every decision, every nuance of life, even though I sometimes didn't give her conscious consideration. How my life effected hers needed to be taken into account. After all, we had become one as God said we should. "But from the beginning of creation, 'God made them male and female. For this reason a man shall leave his father and mother and be joined to his wife and the two shall become one flesh.' So they are no longer two, but one flesh," (Mark 10:6-8 NRSV). In fact, it wasn't so much our becoming one by our own doing as God's making us one because we were married. When God said "the two shall become one flesh" He wasn't giving an instruction so much as pronouncing an outcome of living together in daily interaction and intimacy.

It seems to me extremely unfair to put two people together in a

---

day. The second one I opened had this printed message. "May you find comfort in the thought that your loved one is now enjoying a beautiful new life with Jesus."

relationship that will bond them together at the deepest levels of their being, and to then tear them apart leaving the survivor stricken and in despair. God warns *us* not to do such things. "Therefore what God has joined together, let no one separate," (Mark 10:9 NRSV). Evidently God intends to reserve that prerogative for Himself, however unfair it may seem.

If it is intended to teach us about intimacy, it works. Of course, God desires intimacy with us too, intimacy that will never end through Christ, which is expressed in the language of marital intimacy in the New Testament—the Church is called the bride of Christ and Jesus is described as the bridegroom coming for His bride. Then perhaps there is some redeeming quality to this separation if God's intent is to impress upon us what real intimacy is. But it seems like a painful lesson on the human level that most people don't really get anyway.

This much I do know. A husband or wife cannot be god for the other—only God through Jesus Christ can meet the ultimate needs of our souls. I have been reminded of that through this experience. There is so much stress on marriage these days because couples expect a partner to fulfill their every need and no husband or wife can do that. Perhaps I had become more reliant on Peg than I realize with my sense of well-being dependent upon her. But if I did not hurt when she hurt, suffer when she suffered, or die in some sense when she died, where is the oneness? It does seem unfair to put us into such deep intimacy that operates at levels we hardly grasp until we are wrenched apart simply to make us aware of our own lack of self-sufficiency or the other's insufficiency for us.

Back to this matter of things being amiss, perhaps living long enough with this sense of it I will begin to adapt to it and it will seem normal. I know I have heard some people say you never "get over" a significant loss but you do learn, in time, to live with it. Perhaps I will acquire a new sense of normalcy. And maybe the sense of things being amiss is God's way of reminding me they are. This is not yet heaven though the Kingdom of God has come in part wherever the Holy Spirit lives and reigns on earth, as I believe the Spirit did in Peg and in our marriage.

There is a small single serving container of cranberry juice in the refrigerator I cannot bring myself to use. I brought it home from the hospital along with a small container of green Jell-O. Both were left in Peg's room when she died. I ate the Jell-O a few days ago without any problem. Peg didn't like green Jell-O—that's why it was left. But within the last week of her life, she developed a special love for cranberry juice.

When she had a yearning for it, we would go to the nurse's station and ask for some. They would go into their little supply room, open the refrigerator and hand us one. On one occasion when they were out, I explained that apple or grape wouldn't do. She really loved cranberry juice. So one of them made a raid on the supply room of the other unit on the floor and Peg had her cranberry juice. We would put some ice in a Styrofoam cup, pour in the juice, insert a straw, and Peg would enjoy the tangy flavor immensely.

Eventually the point came where she could not drink liquids. She was taking ice chips, however, to keep her mouth moist, especially since the oxygen tended to dry it out. Finally even ice chips were out and all we could do was give her ice water on a swab to moisten her lips and mouth. Then I asked her, "Would you like some cranberry juice?" Her eyes that had begun to look so tired opened wide, an expression of delight came over her face and with great enthusiasm that surprised us all, she said, "Yum! Yum! Yum!" We made sure we had cranberry juice on hand after that. She got it on a swab and would suck it vigorously until she was no longer able to respond when we asked her if she'd like some.

Whenever I open the refrigerator and see that little container of cranberry juice, I remember her on the verge of death, with that surprising expression of great delight coming over her at such a little thing. I hope the clothes she wore, the books she read, and all of her other personal things are easier to deal with than that little container of cranberry juice.

Today, August 30th, is Peg's birthday—it would have been her 57th. She died three weeks ago yesterday and missed it by 22 days. I didn't want to spend the day feeling sad because she only lived to be 56. I wanted to do something that would celebrate the 56 years she did have and 40 years that we knew each other. After all, birthdays are supposed to be about happiness—about celebrating life.

Frankly, I was a little puzzled as to how to do that now. We had agreed years ago to not spend large amounts of money on expensive gifts adding to our accumulating stuff. Instead we provided some kind of gift to open as a way of saying I remember it's your birthday, I want you to enjoy your special day, and I love you. So I always gave her a birthday gift of some sort—in these later years, clothes or sometimes certificates to do things she liked to do. One that she enjoyed at Christmas was a trip to Barnes & Noble that included coffee and dessert of her choice as well as a new journal and a book. But now other than in some token way, I was uncertain as to how to give her a gift.

Usually Peg made a special meal for me at home on my birthday and we went out to eat for hers but that didn't feel like something that would make me feel closer to her. Eating birthday cake by myself didn't seem appropriate either. In fact, we often didn't have cake for her birthday unless someone else made it. None of these things seemed appropriate now.

I decided this celebration was really for me rather than her, to help me deal with her first birthday since her death. After all, there's nothing on earth that she needs or would even desire any longer given where she is and who she's with. Therefore it needed to include whatever might help me to celebrate her life. I decided to take out some of our old pictures and look through them. Some are in albums but others are gathered in boxes still in the envelopes from the photo labs. I took out some of each. They might help me to appreciate her and the past we shared.

It was pleasant to hunt through them looking for her in the pictures. Sometimes she was simply one in the crowd, but I focused on her in each one where she appeared, even if she was just incidental to the rest of the picture. It brought back memories of things she did, places she'd been, and people she knew and enjoyed, many of them things we shared in common. As I looked through them, I was once again impressed with her winning smile and her attractiveness over the years. No wonder I married her!

One picture in particular caught my attention. It was a picture of her on her bike taken back in the early '70's with the Escanaba water tank in the background. She was arriving in Escanaba after biking about 80 miles from Negaunee to Escanaba in Michigan's Upper Peninsula where we were living. We were serving as leaders for a youth group that did a bike-a-thon and she rode with them. She biked that 80 miles on a single speed bike along with the youth and wasn't the last one to arrive at the destination either. She loved to bike and we were still doing so last summer with our longest trek being 26 miles, though we now had mountain bikes with 21 speeds. Actually, we were planning some longer expeditions for this summer and were working our way up to 40 miles a day to see how well we could handle sustained biking.

The picture brought back that memory and other connected ones I had not thought about for some time. So I decided to run it through the scanner and make an enlargement of it that I can put in a prominent place to look at for awhile. That was perhaps the outstanding memory that came out of all the pictures I looked at.

Both my sister and my son called today, as well as one of Peg's friends who remembered it was her birthday. It was much harder to talk about it being her birthday than it was to look through the pictures. I suppose conversation brought me back to the present while the images of the past took me away from painful reality. Both must have their place and need to be integrated into a healthy outlook.

Peg arriving at Escanaba after biking 80 miles.

On a 20 mile jaunt.

So I can't say that I've come to the end of this birthday full of joy, but at least I can say I'm thankful for things that we were able to do together and things that I know were significant to her. Somehow it seems important to think that her life had joy, accomplishments, achievements, and fulfillment. I know there are many things that she was aspiring to yet. Some of them I regret she never experienced because I know I wasn't inclined to pursue them, at least not to this point, and she was content to forego them. Some of them I like to think we would have fulfilled if life together had continued longer.

As a result, if I have any pertinent advice to give to husbands and wives it is this. Live together in such a way that if your partner should pass away unexpectedly you can look back and feel that you made it possible for her or him to have at least some significant dreams and aspirations come true. Peg had some of hers fulfilled. That's probably more significant to me today on her birthday than it is to her.

It's six o'clock in the morning. I have just awakened to the most pleasurable feeling, though at first I couldn't decide if it was real and a blessing or a cruel reminder of my situation.

Finally I am dreaming again. I used to dream a lot. Not vivid, elaborate dreams that I would remember well. I would just wake up, realize I had been dreaming, and be able to recall some of the dream, if I would focus on it right away. Then Peg's illness came along and began to intensify. As soon as I would begin to wake up, my immediate response was to check on her to see if she was OK. Or I might wake up because she was awake and I had responded to her slightest movement or sound. Often it would be after only a few hours sleep and so I would not remember dreams. Instead I was attuned to the immediate reality of her situation.

Now I am dreaming again. Perhaps it is a sign of coming out of that intense occupation with her illness and needs. It did strike me, though, that Peg wasn't much in my dreams thus far. I was thankful, however, that I had not been dreaming horrible dreams about her sickness and suffering. Still I wondered if I should be concerned about her almost total absence in them.

Tonight, however, she came. I was dreaming that we were swimming, or perhaps I should say that we were in the water together. I don't recall motions of swimming per se and the sounds and feel of the water. What I do recall is coming together, embracing, and then floating backwards, me on my back and she lying against me. It was the way we would often embrace after we got in bed, arms around each other, cheeks together, holding each other for a few moments. Usually, she would be the first to say "Have a good rest," or

"Have a good sleep." I'd say, "You too," we'd kiss, say "I love you," and then separate to find our books and read until we were ready for sleep. Still there was always the sense that we were near each other, sometimes laying lightly against each other. We might even snuggle up back to front with an arm over the other to sleep.

In the dream, we floated together using our feet, I guess, to keep us moving and afloat—dreams seem to need some plausibility. As the dream began to give way to consciousness, I could clearly sense our arms loosely around each other, her body against mine, and her cheek against my cheek. Then I began to gradually realize it was a dream. Still the sense of her nearness continued. I could still feel her near in my arms, our bodies and faces lightly touching. I was, however, becoming more aware that I was laying in bed. I realized I was on my left side facing toward her side of the bed, slightly turned on my back and the covers were held loosely in my arms and pressing against my cheek. But in that state of half dream, half wakefulness, it didn't matter. The pleasurable sense that I had was of her presence with me, and I lay there enjoying the moment.

Then my mind began to question whether this was really something to enjoy or just a cruel reminder of my being alone. It wouldn't take much to go down that trail of thought and acutely feel her loss. Something in me pushed such reasoning aside, preferring to embrace the feelings that were just as real as if Peg had been physically there. I also began to be aware that I needed to get up and use the restroom, which is the reason I commonly wake up early in the morning, something that has become more common with increasing age. Again, something in me kept that at bay and I was able to remain in the dream, if in fact dream it was. Whatever it was, the physical sensation of Peg's presence was real enough for me. It was only reluctantly, knowing I couldn't postpone getting up a lot longer, that I finally gave in. But even then the physical and emotional sense of having been together continued with lingering pleasure.

As I write this, a part of me wants to dissect what happened and bring it down to earth, but I've decided to squelch that in favor of appreciating the thoughts and feelings that continue, even as I write this an hour later.

What I will say, in order to satisfy the "thinker" in me, is that I believe we are all emotional beings, made by God in need of intimacy and contact with other human beings. We need to touch and be touched physically, emotionally, and spiritually to counter the sense of isolation and aloneness that arises in every solitary soul. It is the way God has made us so that we are inclined toward social interaction with others and with Him. For most married men, especially in our younger years, much of that need for intimacy and touch is met in our sexual interaction with our partner. It is less so for women who need more intimacy and affection that is distinct from sexual intimacy and affection.

I am acutely aware that in the loss of Peg, I have lost one whose touch satisfied my need for intimacy and affection in sexual and non-sexual ways. Through her my primary needs for contact with humanity were met. She rubbed my back if it hurt and sometimes even when it didn't. She cut my hair and shaved my neck afterward. (It has been an adjustment to let a total stranger do that now.) She examined rashes, lumps, or marks on my body in places I couldn't reach or see, and sometimes even those I could. Likewise, I touched and caressed her body as she had needs and desires. During the time when her back was hurting so terribly I spent hours rubbing it to try to give her relief from the pain and to distract her nerve endings from distress. In the last days of her life, when she didn't have the strength to move, it felt so good to her to have her legs rubbed, and Becky and I would take turns gently rubbing and massaging her.

I watched her body, over a period of weeks, go from a healthy 135 pounds to a depleted 110 pounds, which I'm convinced would have been even less were it not for the fluid that was accumulating in her torso, keeping her body weight up. At the last, she could not even raise her weakened arms for even the slightest hug, arms that she previously used to hug anyone, no matter how long she'd known you, if she thought you would accept. How hard that was to see her decline, physically and otherwise.

Losing her now means a whole reorientation of body life because truly we had become "one flesh." But her flesh was buried a month ago yesterday and so also a part of mine. (How interesting that this dream came one month later.) Perhaps the dream was part of God's "reorienting." No, I've decided it was more than a "dream." Whatever you call it, Lord, any time you're willing to put Peg back in my arms again, I'm more than willing!

One of the things Peg had often said during her illness was that she hated to be the center of attention. She preferred to be the one who focused attention on others, who served their needs, who helped them accomplish their purposes. On several occasions when there were nurses clustered around her bed, or doing some procedure with her, she said she hated being so "high profile." The irony in that is that the Lord made her "high profile" at the conclusion of her life, to her credit and to His glory.

Several of the nursing staff surmised that she was a Christian, though she had said little about it. They could tell by the way she was interested in and responded to them, and the way she handled all that she had to go through. She and the nurse who held her through the removal of the fluid on her lungs developed an instant bond and when she happened to be nearby on Tuesday, her day off, came in to see Peg just to see how she was doing. The same nurse told us how several of the nursing staff had mentioned in a gathering the impression Peg had made on them. The sharing at her funeral service gave testimony to the ways that she touched the lives of others in her own "low profile" way. In her message at that service, Becky said, "In talking to so many of you over the last few days, I have absolutely marveled how one ordinary person can be so extraordinary and leave such a big hole in so many hearts and lives...Peg gave to each one of us very comfortably and very effortlessly, seemingly. It was more difficult and more uncomfortable for her to receive. She intensely disliked what she called being 'high profile.' It occurred to me this morning, and the more I think about it the more I have to laugh because, the joke is on her. She was high profile all along and she didn't know it, because it was high profile one person at a time."

We literally received hundreds of letters and cards of sympathy, with hand written notes. One of those letters from a former district superintendent said, "Peg was a person of remarkable positive energy and hope. She understood other people very well and responded to them so appropriately that I sometimes wondered, in observing her, why she never thought to seek out a pastoral role for herself. She is a clergy spouse who truly was a pastor with you."[4] Peg did not have the formal education, credentials, and laying on of hands of the institutional church for ministry. God called me to that. But He called her to ministry as well and He laid His hand on her and anointed her with His Spirit to serve Him by serving and caring about others.

Like many of those who served Him faithfully and best, He did not spare her suffering, trauma, and pain. Perhaps she is better remembered in her untimely death than she would have been had she lived into her nineties, outliving those whom she loved and served. I can only speculate hoping there's some redeeming factor in her death at only 56. I do know this. Had she lived to old age, I would not have been driven to read the books about grief and death I have read, nor to write the things I am writing now. As I write, I believe God is using this to minister to my grief and I pray he may use it to minister to someone else's as well. I know that simply because she has died, death will not stop claiming other wives or husbands prematurely. If her ministry continues on through her illness and death, she will once again be "high profile" to God's glory. Amen!

---

4   Letter from Rev. Ken Ward, pastor of First United Methodist Church, Dearborn, Michigan, dated September 4, 2003.

Like all families that practice traditional burial, when the time came, we had to decide what objects placed in the casket for the visitation would be buried with the body. We left very little with Peg. My own belief is that material things are only for this world. Unlike the Egyptians who buried provisions and many other things with their dead, we do not need to bring anything with us into the next reality, nor can we. So the things the grandchildren made, Joseph's cross and Rachael's bracelet, along with her flowers, and the Pepe Le Peau pin that Rachael selected to be displayed on the casket headliner, were all removed before the casket was closed. (Pepe was Peg's favorite cartoon character and the pin was a souvenir gift of Santa Barbara, California.) We left her turquoise earrings in place, but I had her wedding ring removed.

In his book, *A Severe Mercy*, Sheldon Vanauken said he and his wife, Davy, saw themselves as two stones grinding together until they became one new stone in a perfect fit with each other. Something similar happened to Peg and me with our wedding rings and our marriage.

Peg and I decided to marry when I was home from photography school in Chicago for Thanksgiving of 1966. Then we picked out our wedding rings when I was home again for Christmas, anticipating our wedding the next month. Peg had looked at several in Ray's Jewelry on Fifth Street. They were in the window and we stood there not minding the cold as we looked them over. We both liked the ones with white and yellow gold. The ones we agreed on are a wider yellow gold band with a smaller band of white gold overlaid at the center. The white gold has lozenge shaped facets cut into it—about ten of them completing the circle. The edges of the yellow gold band and the lozenges on the white gold were very definite when we saw them there in Ray's window.

37 years of daily wear has worn down the sharp edges so that, at a glance, you might not even realize there were facets in the white gold. And thirty-seven years of daily interaction ground away some of the rough edges on each of us as well. I know there were stresses and strains in our relationships throughout the years, especially within the first ten years of our marriage while those edges were most distinct and sharpest, although at this point, I don't remember what most of them were.

I know that while we were at seminary in Kentucky, which was the 13th through the 15th year of our marriage, we would often walk and talk when Peg got home from work (I was a full-time student then). She talked about being a secretary in the agriculture department at the University of Kentucky, a job she truly loved, and I shared with her about many of the subjects I was studying in school, among them Bible study, theology, spiritual issues, and counseling. With more time together than we had back in Michigan, we applied those things to ourselves, realizing the influence that our family backgrounds and the world had on our values and ways of doing things. I believe this was one of many ways God worked in our relationship for deeper discovery of ourselves as well as of Him. Just as stones tumbled together in lapidary work need grit for the polishing process to be most effective, so the Lord Jesus became the grit in the tumbling that life and each other were providing. After 37 years, we fit together rather well in a functional working relationship that I believe both of us valued and enjoyed, and I often took for granted.

Someone has said that marriage is perhaps the best school there is for growth in character and personal qualities, and I believe that's true. There's plenty of homework and once it begins, it's never out of session, except that one of us graduated and, so for me, classes have been suspended. Of course, there's still plenty to learn and appreciate from the course of study completed. I'm continuing to wear my ring, at least for now, like others might wear a class ring signifying the school they attended.

That brings me back to our rings. I do not want them buried with us. My sister has our grandmother's wedding band and it is very meaningful to her. Some day, members of our family will have ours and I pray those who receive them will be reminded of these truths. If they will look at them from time to time, remember us, and remember these things, they will do much more good than if they're buried in the ground. So to any who happen to come into possession of our rings, I say: Let the Lord Jesus become the grit between you and your partner in marriage so that you may grind the sharp edges from each other becoming, more and more, who the Lord wants you to be, as a blessing to each other and to those around you.

I find myself on two sides of a coin about Peg's continuing existence. It's not that I have a conscious flip-flop of thought about her afterlife, sometimes believing that she still lives and other times that she doesn't. It's simply this intense feeling of sadness because she is gone that is not easily consoled by the belief that she is alive forever.

C. S. Lewis had similar experience after "H," his wife, died. In his book, *A Grief Observed,* he said after the death of a close friend he felt certain that his life continued. But he had no such certainty about "H." In fact he begged for even a fraction of such conviction about her, but none came. I hardly dare to venture an answer where C. S. Lewis had none, but I do observe that Peg's death has made visible a wide gap between the faith of my intellect and the faith of my heart's feelings.

What I have grasped and embraced with my rational understanding through Bible study and theology is not always held as firmly with my emotions under the influence of life experience. It is one thing to say that I believe there is life after death. It is another thing to surrender a dearly loved life partner to the death in this world that transports her to that new life. Faith of the intellect requires only persuasion of the mind; faith of the feelings requires persuasion of the heart which gets at the root of love.

Peg and I knew love was at the root of our relationship, even before we became Christians. Like most young people attracted to and increasingly fascinated with each other, we had very personal ways of expressing that. Early on in our relationship one would say to the other, "I love you." The other would reply, "I love you too." The first one would then say, "Forever, and ever." To which the response was, "And then some!" Although we still said "I love you," we hadn't said that to each other for years, but it came back to me while she was dying in those last few days. She couldn't reply, so I said both parts to her—"I love you, forever and ever, and then some!"

It must have been the emotional trauma of those final days that brought back to me the basics of our earliest relationship, which was also very much emotional. We wanted to believe that what we had together was and would become so special it would never end. But it did end, and it does end for all who love. As do all married couples, we acknowledged that in the marriage vows and concluded them with these words, "Until we are parted by death."

Before H's death, C. S. Lewis wrote a letter to Sheldon Vanauken wondering about the transition that couples go through from the happiness of young love to mature love in their advanced years. He thought that perhaps bereavement was the least difficult way to lose that earlier love, which cannot be retained forever. He said just as there must be crucifixion before resurrection so there has to be death of the earlier love for there to be re-birth of this new love.

I think what Lewis is meaning, in part, is that until the natural self-serving love of youth between a man and a woman dies and becomes a genuine mature love for the other person, there is no real happiness and fulfillment in marriage. The happy old couples he refers to are those who have found their love for each other moved from superficial attraction and desire to genuine love. It moves the lovers from being in love with love in an idealized other, whom they do not really know because they have not yet had enough in-depth life experience together, to being in love though they *have* come to know that other person, even at all costs. It is the way that Jesus loves

His followers. "Husbands, love your wives, just as Christ loved the church and gave himself up for her..." (Ephesians 5:25).

As our Creator, God said He loved us, even though He knew that we were sinners, before Jesus was ever born. But when He lived among us in the flesh and blood person of Jesus and experienced us as we are, He still loved us enough to give Himself up for us in death. Such love did not die on the gruesome cross but lives on beyond the empty grave. He had to die to the natural in order to live to the eternal.

The disciples were overcome with grief and sorrow at Jesus' death because they had seen Him suffer and die. There is no doubt they loved Him and were grieved by His agony, this One they had grown to know and love in their years together. Besides that, they had such hope in Him. His death left them lost, disappointed, and bewildered. It took the resurrection, and for some the proof of bodily existence after death, to move them on to hope, faith, and joy. Of course they had the benefit of seeing, hearing, and touching Him tangibly. So Jesus said to Thomas, and to us as well, "blessed are those who have not seen and yet have believed," (John 20:29b.).

I have never seen Jesus the way the disciples did, in the flesh or in His resurrected body. Yet I believe that He did live on earth and lives now in His resurrection. The Spirit of God has persuaded my mind and heart to that conviction. But I have seen Peg in the flesh. In fact, I have lived intimately with her as her husband and lover and I have known her as a real person. Though she has been dead now for close to two months, I have not yet seen her in the resurrection, nor do I expect to in this worldly reality.

It seems to me, the more closely we are bonded with another person in this life, especially as husband and wife are in the "one flesh" of marriage, the harder it is to grasp the other's continuation after death, even though such faith may never have been difficult in regard to others. I have preached the message of resurrection and new life in countless Sunday sermons and funeral messages. I have never doubted the resurrection and new life of those "saints" of the churches it has been my privilege to know in this life and commend to the next in services of memorial and celebration. But it is a whole different matter to go home after a meeting or a worship service to an empty house and rejoice that Peg still lives.

Yet, because Jesus lives, I do believe that Peg lives. The God of my faith has convinced my intellect. I pray now that He will convince my heart in consoling ways when those feelings of sadness at her loss weigh heavy upon my heart!

Chapter 2

Return to Work

Wednesday, October 8th, two months to the date of Peg's death, I will be going back to work. But it has really been longer than that since I was active in ministry on a regular basis. Getting Peg through her illness became all-absorbing. As her condition deteriorated, I began to retreat into the ever narrowing world into which her illness was taking us until it became a 24 hour a day, every day of the week existence. I thank the church I serve for letting me do that. Graciously and lovingly, the people of the church picked up every rein of ministry I let fall and kept things going. In the same spirit of love and care, they gave me time to grieve and rediscover myself in God.

As I face driving back to Freeland tomorrow, I wonder just how ready I am to resume. I have about a six-hour ride to ponder and prepare. Although I am not in touch with the situation there in detail, what I do know does not make it very inviting. I know that two members of the congregation are seriously ill, one elderly woman with kidney failure, and a young man with a relapse of leukemia. No one has yet been hired to fill Peg's position in the office, something I had hoped would have been finalized during my absence. In addition, our meeting with the district superintendent for annual business will be in less than three weeks. Then the holiday season is coming, the most stressful time of the year with its mix of personal and church activities.

How I will keep personal life together and ministry functional, I do not know. I am wondering if I have the wherewithal to handle it without half of the ministry team and my helpmate to keep personal life together. I have long said, God provides. But He has provided through Peg, I know.

Besides the need to sustain high levels of activity, I wonder about the emotional stress. I know I am emotionally raw. It is a fearful thing to honestly deal with grief. It involves feelings and doubts toward God that, if found valid, would undo faith, or at least previous perceptions of God and His nature. To entertain such emotions and doubts is to risk one's faith, one's relationship with God, and in my case, perhaps even my calling. Yet if I prefer to defend God to others, whitewashing grief and sorrow without questioning, I only wander from God as He truly is. That is an even greater peril than to honestly face the grief and sorrow. Besides that, something tells me no resolution of grief and sorrow results from such a position, only fear. I do not want to live in fear of God anymore than I want to live overwhelmed by grief and sorrow. And no church should truly want such a pastor either.

I have some doubts about preaching—how I will honestly proclaim the Gospel, the good news, of God's love—when I'm having a hard time sensing God's love for Peg in what she went through. This much I do know, I need to be honest.

At the age of 81, in a summary of gifts for which he was thankful, Lewis Smedes wrote, "every coming home to our own place and people, every new hope that sees beyond a hard present—all of them are gifts with a Person attached."[5] During my time away, I went home to my birthplace to be with "my people," members of my biological family. The gifts I received of companionship, acceptance, understanding, and distraction, to name a few, had friends and family, especially my sister, attached. I trust that coming home to my family in the faith will minister to my needs in bereavement through the people who are part of my church family.

Last week in my sermon planning, I sensed the Lord's leading to preach a series on the Holy Spirit for the next several weeks. Perhaps that will be another gift to me with the Person of the Holy Spirit attached. I will trust the Lord will minister to me in the preaching preparation in the weeks ahead as He has in the past. Perhaps the outcome will be a gift that ministers to the congregation through my person and the Person of Christ. I hope so.

It is time to once again pick up the work to which Peg and I were both called, that I am now to carry on. How I will minister to others in illness, pain, and grief, I don't know. How I will preach when I feel less passion for some of the tenets of the faith, I wonder. How I will keep up with less energy and greater responsibility, I can't see. As I said to a church friend who wondered if I would continue in ministry, I'm coming back, and we'll see where it goes from there. The fact that it will be two months from the date of Peg's death seems to signify something. Eventually I'll find out what.

---

5   Lewis B. Smedes, *My God and I: A Spiritual Memoir,* (Grand Rapids, MI: © Wm. B. Eerdmans, 2003), p. 168.

I don't have to worry about getting home or to the hospital to see how Peg is doing. That thought came to me as I was leaving the church on my first day back to work after being away for some time and brought a slight surge of relief. I was walking back across the street to the church parking lot from the post office, on my way home after picking up my mail that had been held while I was away. It was a beautiful, warm October day—the grass was still green and the temperature on the bank said 79 degrees. Maybe that's part of why that thought came to me. There were so many beautiful summer days when I would go in to the church for a few minutes, take care of some business, check for phone messages and notes on my desk, then hurry home because I didn't want be away from Peg for very long.

There were others who were willing to be with her, and we asked them to come sometimes. Still I always felt a sense of urgency to get back to her, especially as her condition became more critical. The worst experience of it was the afternoon a friend from the church came to be with her while I went to Midland to do some banking, grocery shopping, and some errands. I intended to be gone about two hours. If I wasn't home by then, I told our friend she didn't have to wait because I would be along soon.

Just about the time the two hours was up, I was headed home from the north end of the city. Rather than going south through town, the most direct route, I thought I would take the freeway around, which might be a little faster. As I approached the eastbound exit for highway 47 to Freeland and home, there were construction signs and the traffic was narrowed to one lane, moving at about 15 to 20 miles and hour. Immediately I sensed trouble and was very sorry I hadn't taken the route through town. As I approached the exit ramp, I could see the construction. The ramp was closed for resurfacing. I had no choice but to continue eastward toward Auburn at the same reduced speed because the freeway was still narrowed to one lane.

My mind was racing even though the car was crawling. I figured I would take the Auburn exit and head home down Garfield Road past the airport. It was slower driving but probably better than getting off at the exit and then back on the freeway again headed in the other direction. Besides, if the westbound exit to 47 was closed, I'd have to go back into Midland.

As I approached the Auburn exit I couldn't believe it. There were signs saying that exit was closed too! Sure enough! There was a crew also working on resurfacing there as well. As I continued on, still at reduced speed in one lane of traffic, I began to feel frantic. How many more eastbound exits were closed ahead? How far would I have to go before I could get turned around to Freeland—all the way to Bay City, more than ten miles further out of my way at that speed? At the first opportunity, I slowed and took one of those "authorized vehicles only" access roads between the east and westbound lanes. The westbound traffic was moving at freeway speed and I quickly joined it. I peered ahead intensely, hoping desperately that the westbound ramp to highway 47 would be open. It was, and with great relief I zoomed around the cloverleaf thankful I was driving Peg's little Mustang, and was off southbound to Freeland and home.

As I walked up to the front door, nearly an hour later than I intended to be, our friend was just leaving. She said Peg was sleeping—had been for awhile—and she was leaving since she thought I would be along soon. I apologized for being later than I intended and thanked her for coming. As I saw that Peg was indeed OK, I put the groceries away, began to get supper underway, and gradually my worried feelings and tenseness began to calm and my anxiety to subside.

Of course, it was useless to get so frantic about the delay. I can tell myself that now. But at the time I felt obligated to keep the schedule I'd projected. Thinking that Peg might be by herself and wondering where I was; not knowing if she needed anything; all those concerns ganged up on me to overpower my mind's ability to keep my feelings in check. That was a frequent battle, though not always this extreme, when she was at home and I was away from her during the worst of her illness. So there was a sense of relief, with a tinge of thankfulness, as I walked to the car on the way back from the post office on a beautiful summer-like day in October, that I don't have to worry. Peg is OK—better than OK, in fact. She's never been better!

Up 'til now, it has bothered me that I have had little sense of Peg's well-being in the presence of the Lord. With my intellect, I believe in Jesus' resurrection and the resurrection of the dead, but I have lacked a deeper sense of Peg's continuation since her death. Perhaps I'm finally beginning to grasp that. All the care in the world I provided didn't make her better— was powerless to make her better. But by the power of the One who raised Jesus from death, Peg is also raised from death and never happier, never more fulfilled, never more delighted than she is in the presence of the risen Jesus, her Savior and Lord. I believe that completely. At her death, God gave Peg relief from her illness and distress. On the way back from the post office, with a tinge of gratitude, perhaps He began to give me relief from that as well.

More than two months after Peg's death, there are even yet cards of condolence arriving expressing appreciation and admiration of her and

her life. One of the latest said she was "truly an inspiration to many as was evident at her funeral" where many testimonies and stories about how she influenced the lives of others were shared. A letter in another card said, "What I will always remember is how many, many lives she touched. She is an inspiration to us all." Indeed, she always made time for people and their needs. She wasn't one, however, who baked a pie or made a casserole and brought it to the door when there were troubled times in peoples lives. I do thank God for people whose gift is to minister to our practical needs in ways that provide tangible assistance, letting us know they care and God cares. Instead, Peg exercised her gift of caring by listening when people wanted to talk.

Peg was not particularly aggressive in her interactions. She would more likely make a phone call than knock on anyone's door. But mostly, people sought her out. When they did, she put her own agenda aside and listened. That might mean staying on after hours at work to get her tasks done. It might mean starting to pack to go away on the first day of vacation because someone interrupted her getting ready ahead of time. It might mean changing her plans because the time she intended to use for something was gone. Repeatedly, when her list of projects went undone, she would soothe her frustration by reminding herself that "people are more important than things." Those are her words and that was her priority.

Actually, her gift was caring *and* listening—a single gift with two dimensions working together like a pair of hands. Her physical hands worked together very well to make wonderful music at the piano. So too did her caring and listening become a blessing to so many. She listened not only with her physical ears but with her facial expression and her whole demeanor. She listened and responded with her heart, not her mouth as so many of us do. Some people can't let others finish expressing themselves before telling them how they should think or feel, or what they should do to relieve the problem or the pain. Mostly, Peg listened.

She listened with her faith, often knowing what the answers were to the life dilemma of others, or at least who they needed to turn to with the questions, but she was wise enough to know that others needed to find their own way to God. And so she might ask leading questions, questions that suggested, not questions that made others feel stupid, inferior, or put down. But mostly she listened and then she prayed.

Ironically she struggled in her prayer times feeling like she didn't listen very well to God. Part of the reason she had so much to say to God was there were so many others she wanted to talk to Him about. She always had prayer lists of people with hurts and problems. Not written lists (although she jotted a lot of reminder notes on various bits of paper for herself), but lists on the tender part of her spirit where they were easily found.

She was usually the last one to leave any activity because she had been talking to someone. It was not uncommon for her to be late getting home from practices, activities, or gatherings because she had gotten into a conversation, usually with an individual. We often joked about being the last to leave, even when we were at events at other places besides our own church. Sometimes Peg's conversations with others were about nothing of great import, which didn't matter to her, because the person was always more important than the subject matter. And sometimes the conversations were about heart-rending troubles that someone needed to unload. Oh, now and then she might be the talker, or the exchange might be reciprocal, but very often she was the active listener, which is why she touched people in significant ways.

She was a good listener at home as well, which I was reminded of on my first Sunday participating in worship after her death. Those first services were difficult without her in the congregation and the handbell choir, but not near as difficult as the quiet empty house I went home to. Usually when we got home we would talk over the events and conversations of the morning while she got lunch around. We would talk about the worship services. I would let her know how her music had gone on Sundays she was involved, who I had talked to, and things I had learned or observed that morning. She would give me an honest assessment of what I had said and did in the conduct of the service. She would point out to me things that worked well or needed improving. She would pick up on how the Spirit of God was moving in other ways than those I had noticed with only one set of perceptions, and male perceptions at that. I could talk with her about ministry, the work of the church, family, friends, even recreational interests and pursuits, and she would listen. I desperately missed her after that first service without her.

Listening was only one of her many qualities, some of which I've written about elsewhere. There are many things about her I miss but mostly I miss her presence. In truth, she was a very real person with faults and deficiencies like all of us. If it sounds like I'm suddenly turning around and contradicting in some way what I've already said, that is not at all my intent.

In *A Severe Mercy*, Sheldon Vanauken said that when he and his wife were away from each other for extended periods of time they began to idealize each other and lose a sense of each other's reality. I certainly don't intend to undo the high praise I've already given Peg and to appear unthankful to God for the blessing that she has been to me, and still is in many ways. But she was a very real person—so am I—and our marriage had periods of struggle and distress. We disagreed over many of the common marital issues including family and domestic matters. We are both first-born children, we had all the gender tendencies of most husbands and wives, and had a peculiar spin placed on it all by our different dominant nationalities and personality types.

So there were some clashes, especially in the first dozen or so years of our marriage, as well as stresses later on adjusting to the life of ministry. I don't think I'm being unfair by saying that Peg was a contributing factor to some of them, although probably not as much as I was.

In the later years of our marriage, as I said in writing about our wedding rings, most of the rough edges were worn smooth and we enjoyed a meaningful companionship and working relationship as best of friends. It's certainly not because I had become the perfect husband, but neither is it because she was the perfect wife. It was because of the work of God in our marriage as well as both of us as persons. So when I slip into idealizing her, recalling some of her imperfections does seem to minimize the distance between us, keeping her more real. That also keeps me from turning her into a goddess or ancestor on a pedestal to be worshipped. The God who was perfecting her in the likeness of Jesus, her Savior and Lord, is the only One worthy of my worship and praise. I do thank Him for Peg, for all that He was doing and has done in her and through her, but I had come to love her as the person she really was, not the idealized person, now absent.

There is one sense, however, in which she now truly is that idealized person, not made so by me or others, but by God. I believe that our personal development and character at the point of death is who we will be forever. That is why God is so interested in who and what we are becoming as persons. When we are transitioned from the reality of this world and this life by death into the reality of God's Kingdom, the realm in which God is fully and completely present forever, we are cleansed of our flaws and faults, perfected in the likeness of Christ. Yet we remain distinctly who we have become as persons. The verse printed in her memorial folder is about that. "Therefore, if anyone is in Christ, he is a new creation; the old has gone, the new has come!" (2 Corinthians 5:1).

In that sense, it is not the new Peg that I miss. It is the old Peg I lived with and loved for 37 years. I don't want to idealize her, I'll leave her final perfecting to God. She is more real to me when I remember her as she was and was becoming in this life. I do look forward to meeting her in the reality in which she now lives, seeing all that God has done in her and showing all He's done in me by then as well. We'll both have much to praise and thank Him for. But in the meantime, in this reality, I pray the Lord will help me to remember the real version, the person I had come to love, the one I have been closest to. There I find room for the God who created her and has now perfected her forever in the likeness of Jesus Christ.

"Now to Him who is able to keep you from stumbling, and to present you faultless before the presence of His glory with exceeding joy, to God our

Savior, who alone is wise, be glory and majesty, dominion and power, both now and forever. Amen," (Jude 24 – NKJV).

"And we know that in all things God works for the good of those who love him, who have been called according to his purpose," (Romans 8:28). There are probably no words that are quoted more to hurting or distressed people by well-intentioned Christians than these, "in all things God works for good..." No matter what the disaster, how great the tragedy—the bombing of the twin towers in New York, the explosion of the returning shuttle, the murder of five children by their mother, the death of thousands by cancer—name any catastrophe or disease and God works in it for good. Those who have suffered the loss of loved ones look around and wonder, what good has come out of this that compensates for the agony of those who have perished and the sorrow of us who remain.

The verse says, "we know..." God's good comes out of it. Oh, really? What good do I know has come of Peg's illness and death? I suppose many were challenged to think seriously about their own faith in God and their Christian witness. I think some were frightened into paying closer attention to their aches, pains, and health issues. But for the life of me, I can't see, so far, how any of that compensates for the losses. The church lost a talented musician, skilled administrative assistant, and dedicated servant. The Christian faith lost a vibrant advocate and a caring witness. Our family lost a vital member who was pivotal in family activities and relationships. I lost the "wife of my youth," as she is called in the Book of Proverbs, the one God's Word admonishes me to be faithful to and rejoice in. I can't say I know of any great good that has come of Peg's death.

Perhaps, then, I don't "love him (God)..." and haven't "been called according to His purpose." Maybe that's why I haven't been able to see more good in all this. I know I don't love Him as fully and completely as God must desire. In the song, *My God and I,* Austris Withal writes about walking with God in the countryside and talking with Him like a good friend. Now and then, particularly in times of outside devotions, I feel as though God and I are companions. But some of the time I feel like the tax collector "who stood at a distance. He would not even look up to heaven, but beat his breast and said, 'God, have mercy on me, a sinner,'" (Luke 18:13). Most of the time I feel more like the servant who is privileged just to be part of his master's household going about the business of serving Him while the master comes and goes attending to important things in His Kingdom. As for "called," well, I thought I was called, not simply to pastoral ministry, but to be one of the family of God through faith in Christ. Still, I can't say that I yet know what greater good God has brought out of this.

This much I will say, I believe God *can* bring good out of Peg's illness and death. If Jesus can redeem sinners from the consequences of abandoning God, who is the way to live, the ultimate truth, and the light of life, I believe He can redeem even the suffering and death of one of His creatures become His child by faith. It is the same pattern He worked in Jesus—bringing redemption through the suffering and death of one for the good of others. I believe He can do that with Peg's suffering and death. What I'm saying is I can't see that He has—certainly not for me thus far, or for anyone else—with one exception.

That one exception is Peg herself. I always figured Peg would be the one to survive me and be left to deal with my death. But God spared her this trauma of losing her life-mate. I am thankful that she has been spared what I have gone through in losing her to cancer at age 56. I do, however, think she would have handled it better than me. I think she would have gone on to become a sort of "free agent," a Christian at large in the world, traveling around doing mission work and helping out anyone who needed someone to help out for awhile, like a good friend of hers she much admired. Obviously that wasn't God's higher plan for her. Or if it was, He didn't intervene and let her illness run its course instead.

Whether she would have handled this kind of thing better than me is a pointless question. I'm just thankful she didn't have to handle it at all. That's at least one good outcome!

I came home from the church knowing I should get some exercise before making supper. It was too windy and a little chilly for biking. I thought about riding the exercise bike but knew it would be healthier to be out in the fresh air after being inside all day. Now that I am back to work and getting into the routine of ministry again, completing my first full week today, I decided to walk—the first time this fall.

As I rounded the corner onto the side street of the subdivision behind the parsonage, the chilly northwest wind hit me in the face. The big puffy fall clouds were scooting briskly along with the golden rays of early evening sun piercing through, turning their edges into glistening oranges and golds. I was thankful I had worn my winter coat.

I could see Peg walking along with me doing the same, her shoulders hunched and her neck pulled down in the upturned collar of her teal blue waist-length jacket. Her white shoes at the end of her black jeans accented every step with that characteristic little sidewise twist of her feet that gave her a distinctive walk. Her short graying blonde bangs were tossing in the wind. I could hear her say, "I'm *not* looking forward to winter! I hate the cold and when it gets dark so early."

I'd say, "Yeah, October is half gone. In just two weeks we'll be off daylight savings time and it will be dark earlier yet."

"Don't remind me!" she'd say. "Do you think we can go to Florida this winter?"

"Well, we had talked about it for this year. I don't see why not," I'd reply. (In fact, I have a note written in my pocket calendar under the heading, "Vacation Schedule" that says, "Florida – 2003/2004?")

(Peg absolutely loved our winter trips to Florida. We did them every several years, getting out of the winter cold. That was a welcome break during the lull that came between Christmas and Easter after the end-of-the-year reports, beginning-of-the-year paper work, and income tax preparation were done—she always wanted to get income tax preparation done as soon as possible in the new year. We might take in one or two attractions each trip but we didn't plan much sight-seeing, touring, or visiting. Generally, we would go to a favorite campground, Koreshan State Park, make a few day trips to the beach, enjoy the ocean, and spend the bulk of the time reading and relaxing, with a little biking thrown in to keep us active. That was her idea of a winter vacation.)

"Sounds good to me!" she'd say.

Then she'd talk about who came into the office that day, who she'd talked to on the phone, who among the ailing congregation she'd heard about that was doing better or not quite so well, and what she'd managed to accomplish (or not accomplish) in the office. I'd tell her about my progress on the sermon preparation, that I had finished the order of worship for the bulletin, and what went on at the worship committee meeting just before I came home.

Even though all those things had been a part of the day, in reality, I couldn't talk to her about any of them. I just glanced now and then to the place where a year ago she would have been walking beside me, but every glance came up empty. As I headed into the strong chilly wind, my eyes watered, tears ran down my face, and I pulled my hands a little further up into my coat sleeves.

I can't say that I particularly enjoy walking itself. I'd rather bike. But I didn't mind walking with Peg. These little half-hour constitutionals, ideally three times a week, were a part of our routine. I knew it was good for her health as well as mine. It gave us a chance to be away from distractions, to catch up on things with each other, to compare notes on church work and church matters, to make plans and solve problems, to tell stories, and laugh a little now and then besides. No wonder walking is that much less interesting now.

When I got home it was getting dim. The house was dark. There was no aroma of supper cooking and no television sitcom or game show playing in the family room. (That's the way coming home is these days.) I hung up my winter coat in the front closet next to hers, the teal blue waist length one she would have worn if we'd walked together. Then I walked down the hall into the dining area toward the kitchen. There was no chilly northwest wind blowing there but my eyes still watered and tears ran down my face.

Peg died with dignity. Her illness took it all away, but her dying gave it back. Any kind of debilitating illness and hospitalization seems fraught with indignities. There is the acceptance of medications which involves surrender to outside resources to aid recovery or relieve symptoms—a form of admission that we are not adequate within ourselves to deal with the problem. That may also involve a fear of dependence or addiction.

There are the necessary physical exams that require exposing our bodies, often to strangers and to people of the other gender. To their credit these days, medical people are very sensitive to allowing patients to use sheets or gowns exposing only the necessary body areas. One of Peg's therapists even did some examination through a sheet. Of course, he had to touch her, but at least she was not visually exposed.

Peg was always very modest in her dress and clothing styles. She did not have much liking for the hospital gowns that tied behind with the opening in the back. Unfortunately they were necessary when she had IV's so that her clothing could be changed without removing the plastic tubing. On her first hospitalization, as soon as she was able, we began walking in the halls with her IV pole. She would hold the pole with one hand and pull her gown around her with the other to keep it closed behind her. On a subsequent hospitalization, I discovered the gowns were designed with two sets of ties to overlap in the back and began tying them that way. That should have been obvious, but just wasn't evident to either of us at first. That made walking in the halls more relaxed for her. As soon as the IV was removed, she blessed the nurse who gave her pajamas to wear, and felt much more comfortable and freer in her movement.

On later hospitalizations, she was allowed to wear her own sweat pants or hospital pajama bottoms, which she greatly appreciated. That lasted until she needed assistance getting in and out of bed.

Peg's nature was such that showing pain or distress in the presence of others was demeaning to her. She was most open about those things with her closest family but even then seldom complained about pain or discomfort unless it became a problem. I became frustrated with her at times because I felt she didn't convey to medical people in particular the intensity or the extent of her symptoms and distress. I think she didn't want to arouse pity or sympathy, but the result was sometimes people who needed to know the seriousness of her condition didn't realize how serious it was. She might have suffered less had she been more expressive about her condition.

Peg also tended to think she should be able to handle things herself and when she couldn't, she felt somehow degraded. There were times she would fight back her feelings and say, "I'm such a baby!" I would try to reassure her it was OK to express her feelings and her hurt, that she was dealing with serious things, and no one thought she was being a weakling. Still, it felt like complaining to her, and she had to work at expressing it. These were some of the things that conspired to influence me to see that she had one of us with her most of the time she was hospitalized, especially as her condition declined.

I have elsewhere mentioned her struggle to keep down her food while and after she underwent radiation. I'm sure it was not only utter frustration to lose the food she had worked so hard to get down, but embarrassing to vomit while I was with her—and I wouldn't let her go through that by herself. I wanted her to know that I was in this fight with her no matter what.

Even now it surprises me that she didn't object to my presence in the bathroom. We had always conducted our bathroom functions privately, even in our present parsonage that had a separate bath off the master bedroom. As Peg's physical strength deteriorated, she allowed me to help her navigate and get settled in the bathroom, though I would usually step out of sight once she was settled 'til she needed to move again. During one of her hospitalizations in a room where the IV pole didn't fit well in the bathroom with her, I stepped back while she was indisposed and watched the door to the room to tell anyone who entered she was in the bathroom.

I mentioned elsewhere an enema we administered just outside the downstairs bathroom at home. As we were doing that, I was conscious of how much her body had deteriorated and how undignified it must have felt to be laying on the floor of the hallway, going through what she was going through. I know she must have felt very undignified although she didn't say anything—I certainly felt the indignity of it for her.

When Peg came home from the hospital while she was still undergoing radiation, we had decided to set up a bed for her downstairs. People of the church were very helpful in getting the house ready for her and very thoughtful in their preparations. One of them brought a walker and an extension for the commode and set them just inside the door from the garage into the family room. Although Peg never used them, they remained there for quite awhile where they had been placed in the family room where she spent virtually all of her time. Finally one day, she asked me, "Would you put those things somewhere so I don't have to look at them?" I moved them immediately into the garage and was sorry I had not done so at first.

When she lost her ability to walk even the shortest distances, we began using wheelchairs. We had sometimes used them when we arrived at the emergency room where they were available just inside the door and in the hospital when she needed to get around for procedures. Finally one day at home, when she was needing to go for an appointment, I mentioned to her that I was thinking about borrowing the wheelchair the church had available for people to use on Sunday mornings. I said since we had to cover some distance to get to the doctor's office, it might be helpful. I was surprised when she said she had the same thought. She must have been working through in her mind how she was going to get from the car to the office.

I do not doubt that a wheelchair is a blessing to anyone who cannot walk or walk far. My own mother is able to go places she could never go without one, especially in these days where so many places are now handicap accessible. But for someone who has been accustomed to unrestricted movement, using one means having to come to grips psychologically and emotionally with one's debilitating condition. Undoubtedly it was so for Peg.

Finally it came to the point in her last hospitalization where Peg could not get out of bed on her own to go to the bathroom. She had to have two nurses come to help her on to the portable commode which was placed next to the bed. Often the nurses would change her bed at the same time because she was sweating so profusely at that point, probably as a result of the cancer. I would step into the hall and often use the time to look after my own needs. On occasion as I passed by the partially open door, I noticed Peg sitting there, her hair flattened against the back of her head from laying down most of the time, her eyes downcast, waiting while her bed was made, or for someone to return and help her back to bed. She must have been well aware of where she was sitting and why she could not be behind the closed bathroom door where she would have preferred to be. I could sense the indignity she must have felt every time she reluctantly said she needed to use the commode.

At last it came to the point of the catheter and she didn't have even the dignity of getting out of bed to sit on the commode. Not that it mattered all that much, because her kidneys shut down and her bowel functions were nil. Gradually she became totally helpless to reposition herself, and was totally dependent on the nursing staff or us to turn her in bed. When she wanted something to drink, eventually we had to hold the glass for her to drink through a straw. When she could no longer do that, we gave her ice chips. Then all we could do was wet swabs to moisten her mouth and lips when we thought she might be feeling dry.

While she was still communicative and on the catheter, she suffered one final indignity that she evidently felt intensely. She began to feel like she was going to have a bowel movement and so we called for help. The nurse brought a bedpan—and, of course, it had to be a male nurse, the only one she had in all her hospitalizations. I don't remember her exact words but they were something to the effect of this being the final indignity. She was probably right. If there were any others, she soon wasn't able to tell us. Her illness and dying brought her to the point where she was totally dependent on others for her needs and on artificial means to sustain her bodily functions. Whatever sense of dignity there is in being an autonomous functional human being was totally gone.

Ironically, the very qualities of her nature and character that I had sometimes found frustrating were, in those very processes of her losing her physical dignity, giving her a personal dignity in the eyes of others that was not so transient. Her lack of self-assertion was overshadowed by her interest in the people who came and went from her bedside both as visitors and staff. Without prying, she learned enough about the people who cared for her to see them as individuals in their own right. She tried to avoid being a nuisance when the things they did to help didn't always go right and she needed further attention all too soon, she thought. We learned afterwards through one of the staff that nurses were pleased to come on duty and find she was one of their patients for that shift.

Her faith emanated not from a lot of words, just a few well-placed well-timed ones, and her attitude. In the last few days she lived, some of the staff were looking in on her without being called, assuring us if there was anything they could do we should not hesitate to ask. In the last few days of her life, she used very little pain medication on her own and when we had to take over to administer it, there were few signs that she needed any, even though we had been given indicators of distress to watch for. Death came quietly to her, without anguish or trauma and she quietly "went home." The way her body died may have subjected her to one indignity after another, but the way she died in her body, and death itself, gave it all back.

A Bible verse comes to mind as I write this. In its original context, it doesn't exactly fit, but let me quote it and then explain the thoughts it is inspiring in me. Matthew 23:11-12, "The greatest among you will be your servant. For whoever exalts himself will be humbled, and whoever humbles himself will be exalted." Peg typified the servant who put others ahead of self. But her illness pushed self into the foreground where she could not deny or overlook it. Yet she resisted self-assertion, even in some ways that may have been detrimental to her health care. I'm not suggesting this was appropriate, just observing at this point. As her illness gradually crowded out every functional ability, it could not defeat her spirit, a spirit grown and formed by the Spirit of Christ in her over the years. The dignity of a soul totally at peace with her Savior and Lord, Jesus Christ, and her destiny in Him, prevailed to the end. She had humbled herself in life to Him. Cancer had tried to force her to assert self in the end, but she, by the presence of Christ formed in her, refused. And the Spirit of Jesus lifted her up in the estimation of those who witnessed it happen.

So I repeat, Peg died with dignity. Her illness took it all away, but her dying gave it back. Praise be to God!

Hundreds of people were praying for Peg's recovery, yet God answered her simple prayer, "I just want to go home." That's one of the reasons I didn't begin the sermon series on prayer I was supposed to be doing this fall. Early in the spring, I had worked with our Spiritual Life Team to plan the emphasis, which came out of an open conversation I had with people who were interested in the spiritual life of our church. When I did return to ministry in October, I wasn't ready to begin the prayer series. For one thing, I was to work in advance with the Spiritual Life Team to implement the series. But more to the point, to walk back into worship and begin a series on prayer after what had happened was more than I could handle. Instead, I began a series of messages on the Holy Spirit.

Peg's illness and death left me shaken both spiritually and emotionally. It stirred many questions about prayer, and even more feelings about it, I will have to confront when I finally begin that series on prayer, probably at the beginning of the new year. But for now, I have not wanted to grapple with them. Just grappling with daily life and ministry has been enough.

I confess, I have never felt that my prayer life has been noteworthy. I am not one of those Christians we sometimes hear about who spend whole nights in prayer or who reach great crescendos of emotion and a fever pitch in prayer that storms the gates of heaven, as some describe it. My times of prayer have been usually brief and calm, seldom more than a half-hour. I spend more time talking than listening, and a good part of my silent time trying to stay focused with my mind clear of "static" from my own thoughts and distractions. I can identify with Lewis Smedes, former Christian Reformed pastor and professor of theology at Fuller Theological Seminary in Pasadena, California, who said in the last book he wrote, a spiritual memoir, "I pray a lot, but never for long stretches at a time; I am just not able to concentrate on God for more than ten minutes."

I can further identify with Smedes who went on to say, "And yet some people think that my prayers are unusually efficacious....Still when it comes down to brass tacks, my prayers do not seem to make much difference to people I pray for. When I pray that God will heal people with a terminal illness, they nevertheless die. Now and then I pray that God will let someone die....But when I pray for people with inoperable cancer, they always die. When I pray for people who are given a fighting chance, some of them get better, most of them die. And if they do get better, I have no way of knowing whether they would have gotten better had nobody prayed for them. Still I keep on praying...Mostly, though my prayers balance out between thanks for what I have and pleading for God to give poor people more to have and be thankful for."[6]

None of this is to say I have not had great confidence in prayer—not as a spiritual exercise but as means of communication with God. I have been frustrated by people who talk about "the power of prayer" and who "believe in prayer" as though it were some sort of dynamic force field we just need to access and manipulate to bring about our wishes. I am inclined to clarify that the power of prayer is the power of God. It is not just this thing we do to apply spiritual power. There is a divine Person behind it who is the source of that power and worthy of our honor and praise.

I have taken to heart the instructions of Jesus who commended secluded quiet prayer over showy exhibitionist prayer. It seems to me, God is accessible by our sincerity in prayer more than our public proficiency or bombast.

At the same time, I have believed that as more people pray with the same desire, that God is more responsive. This is where my prayer perceptions have been shaken. I know there were literally hundreds of people praying for Peg's health and recovery. Besides friends and family, our own congregation and prayer chain were praying on Sundays and privately for her. Other community churches and prayer groups were praying for her—I know because they told me. Churches we had served in the past were praying for her. Churches where our son Mike had been with his ministries were upholding her in prayer. Christians across the country and the world who had contact with Living Covenant Ministries International, Mike and Becky's independent ministry, in response to their request, were praying for her as well. When it comes to sheer numbers of people agreeing on the same thing in prayer, apparently God was not impressed or persuaded.

I believe that at any point in the progress and process of her illness, God

---

6   Lewis B. Smedes, *My God and I: A Spiritual Memoir*, (Grand Rapids, MI: © Wm. B. Eerdmans, 2003), pp. 29-30.

could have intervened and changed the direction things were headed and the outcome. If prayer is the means by which to change God's mind, it was not sufficient in her case. One part of me says He has His divine reasons that are beyond my comprehension and I should trust Him. Another part of me says, then why pray? Why talk to Him about such things if He already knows what He is going to do and won't be persuaded?

Only a few years ago, I truly believe God intervened in our circumstance to prevent Peg and I from both dying in bed by asphyxiation. What follows is the article our son, Mike, wrote for his weekly E-mail article with *Living Covenant Ministries International,* after that incident.

"The past few weeks have been a bit exhausting. It all began about a week before I headed to Wisconsin. I was invited to do a conference on the Christian Life on a Friday and Saturday night and speak in a church the following Sunday. After spending about a week in the Milwaukee area I was to head further north and make several stops in Wisconsin and northern Michigan. I was planning to take my parent's mini motor-home to sleep and cook in to minimize expenses and allow greater freedom and flexibility in travel. Our own vehicle situation was not the best as there were several major repairs that needed to be done, but with the motor-home to use, there was no urgency to get the repairs done. Becky would have decent transportation while I was gone and the other things could wait until I got home.

"My dad was concerned about a possible furnace problem with the motor-home so he bought a carbon monoxide detector to test it. There was no problem with it and I got the vehicle a few days early to have time to pack. There were several other things in life that seemed to be going wrong all through this time while I was also extremely busy trying to get my conference materials ready and prepare a message for Sunday. Then I discovered there was a problem with the motor-home's brakes. Having been a mechanic for almost 15 years, I did not think it was any big deal so I bought the parts to fix it. I apparently misdiagnosed it because the problem was still there after the repair. I began to get a little frustrated because I was to leave in two days and still did not have it ready. I finally made up my mind to take it even with the brakes not being 100%.

"Two nights before I was to leave I realized I had not checked the battery charging system for the camper part of the rig. As I was driving it down the road I flipped the switch to energize the camper's battery and charge it from the engine. That is when the fun began. The headlights went out, the engine quit, and as I coasted to a stop I could hear the battery sizzling under the hood. There was a direct short and I expected to either have the battery explode or there to be a fire at any moment. I tried to turn off the camper electrical system, but the switch had welded itself together and would not release. I jumped out to disconnect the battery but could not get the terminal free. I was in a panic and was flying through the motor-home trying to find a tool to disconnect the battery but there was none. Becky ran to a nearby house to borrow a tool while I worked feverishly to do something. By the time she returned the battery was dead, I was exhausted, my kids were scared out of their minds, and she was gasping for breath from running in the bitter cold.

"It turns out the camper battery was installed backwards. When I turned on the switch, the negative terminal of the engine was connected directly to the positive terminal of the camper. The result was a direct short and everything stopped because there was no power. I finally surrendered and decided to not take the rig but to borrow my parents car instead. I did not understand why God let me go so far down that path when I could have had one of our own cars fixed to take. I was committed to going in the way I felt Him leading me but at the last minute He closed that door. The trip itinerary was totally changed as a result.

"Would you say all that happened was bad? I wouldn't. My dad called me a few days ago. When he was done testing the motor-home for carbon monoxide he decided to put the detector in their home. Monday morning they woke up to the carbon monoxide alarm going off. It is triggered at a level 30. By the time he got to the detector the level had reached somewhere around 170. It seems the furnace in their home had failed and was dumping all the furnace exhaust directly into the house. Without that detector I am quite certain I would be going through a tremendous grieving process right now as I faced the loss of both my parents.

"We do not understand all things and we know God does not cause all things. Yet He causes all things to work together for the good of those who love Him. We are often trying to take the negatives of life and counteract them with a positive. As a result we lose our power and everything stops for us as we short out and burn up. For there to be power, the positive and the negative have to reach their goal. They cannot be connected prematurely. Through all the negatives I knew God was doing something but I did not have a clue what it might be. I had no idea that one of the things He was doing was preserving the lives of my parents. I am reminded to not eat from the tree of the knowledge of good and evil by making judgments about what might be good or bad and to walk in faith, eating from the tree of Life, trusting that He causes all things to work together for the good of those who love Him and are called according to His purpose! He is faithful! - Mike Rule"[7]

In comment on his article, republished in our church newsletter, I wrote, "I had not really thought about how potentially disastrous the situation was until I read Mike's article. Many thanks to him for letting us publish it, and for his graciousness in not mentioning that I was the one who inadvertently installed the RV battery backwards. (It *was* a dark cold night when I did it!)... And *many* thanks to God that we are still around to publish this! He truly works in mysterious ways and sometimes we are privileged enough to see that 'He causes all things to work together for the good...' - Pastor Jim"

I know there have been several faithful women of our congregation who have prayed for us consistently as their pastor and spouse. But I can't say that I thought to pray that God would prevent us from some tragic death, except when we were traveling. We always prayed before leaving on vacation or for weekends away that God would bless us with safe travel and a refreshing experience, often in the car as the last thing we did before pulling out of the driveway. And God always did grant those requests.

So in one instance, which we had no inkling to be praying about, God kept us safe. But in another instance we prayed intensely about, and rallied others to pray about, the request was denied.

Perhaps out of their need to defend God, some Christians will say, "Well, God answered our prayers for Peg's healing, just not in the way we wanted." I know what I meant when I prayed for Peg's healing and God knows what

---

7   © *Living Covenant Ministries International*, used by permission – http://livingcovenant.com/

I meant as well. When I prayed for her to be healed, I meant her physical healing, recovery, and continuation of life in this world. Granted, she is no longer subject to illness or disease, for which I can give thanks to God. But bending my request around God's greater wisdom is a distortion of what I was praying for. We tell people these days who don't know how to turn down any appeal for their involvement that it's OK to say "No!" In addition we tell children who keep trying to wear down their parents and get what they want that "No!" is a complete sentence. "No" is also an answer God can give to prayer. And God said "No" to my prayer in its fullest sense.

Prayer is indeed a mysterious thing. While Peg was at home between her hospitalizations, when it was evident things were very serious, it was not uncommon for her to be up in the night with distress or pain. I would get up with her to help her get settled and comfortable. When I went back to bed, it would always take me awhile to settle down, and I would often pray. One particular night when we were sleeping in the family room, I felt as though the Lord was putting thoughts in my mind. He was saying I needed to be not just asking but seeking in prayer.

First of all, I needed to be seeking the mind of God, not in the sense of trying to know or understand anything, but seeking contact with the mind of God much as one might seek out some great reservoir of strength or power.

Then I should be seeking awareness of God's presence—awareness that He was imminent, right there at that very moment. With awareness of God's presence, I should also be aware of His great power. All of His power was there and available through His presence. My response in all of that should be praise—given the mind, the presence, and the power of God, praise seemed like the appropriate way to respond. Even as I lay there going over these thoughts, I was aware of God there with me and I kept rehearsing what I had heard so I wouldn't forget it in the morning.

But then I felt the urge to pray for Peg. Not just from where I was across the room, but to get up and sit by her on her bed to pray. I tried to do so without disturbing her but she knew I was there. I placed my hands on her and began to pray silently. She asked me, "What are you doing?"

I said, "I'm just praying."

She said, with concern in her voice, "You're scaring me!"

I said, "I'm sorry. I just felt like I wanted to pray for you. If you don't mind, I might do this now and then."

She didn't say anything and settled down.

With my hands resting lightly on her, I waited for the same awareness to return. Soon I could sense it, the Mind of God, with knowledge and wisdom far beyond anything I could imagine or comprehend. Then I sensed God's Presence there with us in the darkened room. And with God's Presence, came all His great and mighty Power. Anything that God desired to do or accomplish He had the Mind to know and the Power to do. I was thrilled to sense God's Presence in such a profound way there with us. With my hands on Peg, I felt that God could use them to emanate His healing power throughout her body. I started to pray for her healing, but He made it clear I was not to pray with words of request. I was simply to touch her, and to sense His Mind, Presence, and Power there with us. I wanted desperately to request her healing but each time it came to my mind, I knew I needed to avoid words and let spirit prevail. Finally I realized my participation was not needed, just my willing presence. Later I would write that my part was to "Get out of the way but still be there."

That's what I did. I sat there with my hands on her mysteriously sensing God's Mind, Presence, and Power. After awhile, I don't know how long, the Presence began to wane and I began to praise God for being there, for touching Peg through me, for I felt surely that's what He was doing. Finally, I went back to bed hopeful that God had been doing something that I didn't understand that would make a difference. Though I could not sense that any healing power had been extended through me, I was encouraged that God had somehow been with us and touched her in a very special way.

Before I went to sleep, I fixed in my mind, the letters, MPPP – Mind, Presence, Power, and Praise. Then in the morning, I wrote them down and have been writing this referring to that same note.

I never told Peg about all that was going on in that experience although I did appeal to God to come to us again as He did that night. I remember it happening again while she was in the hospital as I touched her or held her hand. But I never felt as though God was touching her body with healing power. Whatever He was doing, He has not yet revealed to me.

So I am anticipating the series on prayer with mixed feelings. Time to concentrate on prayer in the Scriptures is both appealing and disconcerting. If I learn how I should have been praying for Peg in ways that would have made a difference, I will be very distressed. If after weeks of prayer emphasis it only turns out to be a review of prayer practices and platitudes we already know that leaves prayer in relation to God just as mystifying as before, I will be distressed with that too. I'm not even sure what to hope for.

One thing I do know, Peg was a woman of prayer. She didn't think so. She confessed to struggling, like so many of us, with listening to God. She had difficulty shutting off her own thought and would often express frustration. She would say she wished she could just shut up and listen. She talked to me about it on several occasions looking for suggestions but I don't think any I offered made much difference. But somewhere in the course of her daily life in the faith, she heard at least some of what God wanted to say to her, even though He may not have spoken during her quiet times. I say that because she was often convinced of something God had led her to do or wanted her to do or to work on.

She spent time every morning in prayer, except Sundays when we went to church for corporate prayer, and Mondays when we observed a private Sabbath. In addition, in the later years of our marriage, most evenings we read devotions and prayed together before the day was ended. Sometimes in her morning devotions she kept written lists and at other times she let the spirit inspire her concerns in prayer, but she always had a number of circumstances and people—family, friends, church folk, and others she'd been asked to pray for—she brought to God in prayer. On several occasions she used the church directories to guide her prayers, praying for several families each day until she went through the whole directory. Sometimes she would pray about the way she handled things and people and ask for the Lord to help her put others first.

When I was talking to her about the prayer emphasis our Spiritual Life Team was exploring, out of curiosity I asked her how she thought we could make prayer an emphasis. She quickly rattled off a list of ideas and perceptions which were so practical that I jotted them down, brought them to the meeting and shared them with the team. They were so impressed that they adopted most of them and the emphasis was built largely around her input. So perhaps when this woman of prayer prayed in her misery for her Lord to take her home, her simple prayer touched the heart of God in a way that all the rest of ours combined could not equal. It's the only thing that makes any sense to me. That's why I say, hundreds of people were praying for Peg's recovery, yet God answered her simple prayer, "I just want to go home."

Chapter 3

Holidays and Other Firsts

Today I had one of the hardest moments yet. I was looking through the accumulated messages in the Inbox of the computer's E-mail and ran across one from Peg. When I opened it, I found this card she had sent me from the office on our last anniversary, January 29, 2003.

> Happy Anniversary, Sweetheart!
>
> I hope your day goes well, and that our year holds many blessings!
>
> I thank God for you and that we can share life and have been able to work together always. I look forward to what that might look like into the future.
>
> God Bless you
>
> All my love,
>   Peg

I have expressed the disappointment of my own hopes and yearnings over her premature death. After reading her thoughts and sentiments in the card, I was overwhelmed by the disappointment of hers as well, and the emotions and grief were as intense as any I have experienced. Perhaps it was because it was not just my own disappointments I was feeling but the disappointments of one I love.

The seven months of 2003 that we had did have many blessings. But we did not have a whole year as she had hoped.

One of her hopes was fulfilled, however. She thanked God that "...we can share life and have been able to work together always." We did work together always, what there was of "always" for us, except for the three years I attended seminary. But even then, she was working to provide our income so that I could attend full time and complete my degree in three years.

Being potentially within a few years of retirement, we had talked about the future she mentioned looking forward to. There wasn't anything definite as yet but we were beginning to anticipate and to wonder what the Lord would have for us. We were considering continuing on in pastoral ministry until she would reach social security age, if we felt we both had the energy and wherewithal to continue. We also talked about retiring and doing interim ministry. We would be available for short-term service to churches where pastors needed a leave of absence for illness, sabbatical, or other reasons where churches might be without a pastor for a time. She was especially interested in Volunteers In Mission or NOMADS, both short-term mission programs to do building projects for churches or disaster relief. We would also take time to travel for pleasure and to spend periods of time just enjoying life and its blessings. I might retire and pursue writing while she would take a part-time job, at least for awhile, to stay active and supplement our income. Those were some of the possibilities and reasons she said, "I look forward to what that might look like into the future." But now there is no future for us to work together or do anything else together. That hit me hard today and I felt so bad for her, that the blessings of the partnership and companionship we shared are ended—and bad for me as well.

Perhaps it is presumptuous of me to attribute disappointment to her regarding those things that will not happen. I know that is rooted in the things of this world and she no longer resides in it. Still I wonder, was she, is she, disappointed that we didn't get to do what she was looking forward to? It seems to be a common human response when someone's dreams or aspirations go unfulfilled to feel badly for them. Even with many things on the side of completion or fulfillment, there is still a tendency to regret those that were not.

Actually, Peg was looking forward to doing more of what we had been doing for 37 years—working together in the things of the Lord and His Church—in a new and different context. Of course, we visualized short-term it would be less demanding and intense, nevertheless, allowing us to continue to serve the Lord in significant ways with the skills and experience we had been given over the years.

As I express that it occurs to me, if that is the basis for me being disappointed for her, there is not really much grounds for it. In her present existence in the presence of Jesus, she is able to know and serve Him in far more fulfilling and satisfying ways. I am remembering a passage I read recently in which Solomon prays for a discerning heart and God exceeds his request by granting him much more than he asked for, giving him wealth, honor, and long life besides. When God has our best interests at heart, we are assured He can exceed our expectations by far. God "is able to do immeasurably more than all we ask or imagine, according to his power that is at work within us...," (Ephesians 3:20).

The part that remains uncertain for me, however, is the working together. That *has* ended. And I wonder if she, too, is disappointed in that. If she is, I suppose the Lord will comfort her in it until there is no longer the separation of time and eternity between us. I guess that's what I'd like to think—that what God had given us was so blessed and special that even heaven will not be complete until the part that's here in this world is brought together with what is already there in the next.

God does seem to be rather devoted to completing what He has begun in this world and integrating it into Kingdom reality. If all of heaven rejoices over the salvation of a single soul, and if God is so responsive that He feels anger or joy over events in the earthly realm, is it not possible that the feelings of His human creatures who reside there are, in some measure, subject to what happens with us still in this world too? Peg, if that is so, I want you to know I too am very disappointed that we didn't get to do together the things you had hoped we might. And thank you for the card that means more to me today than it did when you sent it, even if the future was far different than either of us ever imagined.

"At times, dealing with the 'why' questions can be similar to running on a treadmill. Why did Payne go on that Monday trip? Why did the awful tragedy have to happen just as it seemed he was beginning to have a deeper relationship with God, his family, and more of a 'peace' in his relationships with competitors and peers?"[8] Tracey Stewart asks those "why" questions in her biography of her husband, Payne Stewart, the professional golfer who died in a plane crash in October of 1999.

---

8   Used by permission; Excerpt taken from *Payne Stewart* by Anastasia T. Stewart, © 2000, B&H Publishing Group, p. 313.

It is the "why" question that seldom gets answered. I remember preaching that in a sermon before all this happened with Peg. But I do have the answers to some "why" questions. Why am I reading the biography of Payne Stewart? Because Peg gave it to me as a gift sometime within the last year. I can't remember the occasion for sure—it might have been my birthday a year ago. It looked like a good book to read on vacation and I set it aside to read on the right occasion.

Why have I read it now? Because Peg gave it to me. When I pick up that book, it's as though she has handed it to me. She is the reason I have it and I want to honor her sentiments in giving it to me. I know why she did. I have not been an avid golfer. In fact, I haven't played golf for years. Our neighbor, Mike, who lived in the next apartment to us at seminary golfed and he offered to teach me to play. It sounded like a good idea. I needed the exercise, he was a good friend, and I enjoyed being with him. I thought it was something I could probably do with colleagues and parishioners in the future, so I took him up on his offer.

The problem with golf is it takes considerable effort and practice to be, not just good at it, but respectable at it. And if I was going to play golf, I wanted to at least do it fairly well. I discovered after awhile that there are other things I enjoy more and so I continued to play only for the social aspects of it. When we moved over seven years ago, I never got started golfing with anyone and so my golfing has languished, except on Sunday afternoons. I do find watching golf on television relaxing, especially after expending energy on Sunday mornings in preaching. It is not as high powered and compelling as some other sports on television and so I might drift off to sleep now and then. But in my wakeful moments, I got to know and appreciate many of the golfers of the Professional Golfers Association and some of the Ladies Professional Golfers Association as well. Peg was often in the family room reading the Sunday paper at the same time, and she also got to know some of the golfers.

When she happened to find the biography of Payne Stewart, whom she knew was a Christian, she thought I might like to read his life story. She was right. I'm not generally into the behind the scenes stuff about pro sports. But to read about it woven through the life story and faith journey of one of its outstanding personalities made it interesting. So thanks, Peg! It was a great gift. And there are lots of things in it that I would have shared with you, including a really neat love story about how Payne and Tracey got together.

But there is still the larger question, why this book now? I think I can answer that one too. God put it into my hands through Peg's hands for an appropriate time to minister to my need and my grief.

I am a railfan, the more common term for a railroad enthusiast. So I was parked along the railroad line between Escanaba and Rock in the Upper Peninsula of Michigan, waiting for two Wisconsin Central trains to meet and pass each other. As soon as they met and I got my pictures, I would be headed home, returning from my leave of absence to face the empty house, Peg's absence at the office, and preaching Sunday morning. As I sat in the car waiting, I started reading *Payne Stewart,* and God gave me the inspiration I needed. It wasn't something to preach in my sermon on that first Sunday back. It was something to preach to me as I faced public ministry, full of emotions and doubts.

In the first two chapters, Tracey tells how Payne won the 1999 U. S. Open. In her account of the final round, she said at the 16th hole he was facing a monstrous 25 foot putt for par, having missed the green on his second shot, and following that with a poor chip shot on to the putting surface. "Payne chewed his gum pensively as he strode on to the green. Concentration creased his brow, yet he seemed amazingly calm and composed. He leaned over, went through his normal pre-putt routine, then took a smooth, even pendulum stroke and rolled the putt in as though it were a 3-footer!" Later on, describing his performance on 16 Payne said, "I was kind of disappointed in my chip shot. It was obviously horrible. But then I got myself right back into it and said, 'OK, you gotta stand up here, read the line, and make the putt.' And I did it. It gave me a lot of belief that I still had a chance to win the golf tournament."9

I knew that's what I needed to do too. And so I wrote these words on a sticky note. "OK, you gotta stand up here, say the words, and do your job." I put them on the dash of the car so I could see them as I drove home. They went to my desk in the study until Sunday. Then I printed them in the header of my sermon document in large bold letters so every time I turned a page, they were the first thing I'd see at the top. "OK, you gotta stand up here, say the words, and do your job." With the Lord's help, like Payne, I was able to maintain my concentration and composure and make it through. God gave me the encouragement I needed through Peg's gift.

Also I have an answer to the larger question, why this book now? It has been helpful to read other's experiences of death and grief. When I was leaving for several weeks away after several weeks of dealing with aftermath following Peg's death, I looked at my book shelves where I keep my collection of books-to-read-someday, and there was *Payne Stewart.* I had forgotten about it, but for reasons already explained, I knew right away it was next when I finished the one I was reading. Even though I didn't start it 'til I was on my way back, it was timely and helpful.

9   Used by permission; Excerpt taken from *Payne Stewart* by Anastasia T. Stewart, © 2000, B&H Publishing Group, p. 4.

Tracey wrote about their good friend, Paul Azinger, another PGA golfer and his bout with cancer. Like Peg, his was first detected in the bone but originated in the lymph system. He was also told by the medical people lymphoma is a very beatable cancer. But in combination with bone cancer and the treatments involved, he found it very lethal. Azinger's battle with it as a young man in his thirties in good physical condition dramatized the seriousness of it. Since Peg's diagnosis and experience was very similar, it gave me a different feel for what she went through.

I was very interested to read Tracey's description of the sorrow and grief she experienced with Payne's death. I can't imagine what the shock must be like to be going about everyday life and then suddenly find that your partner is gone. I suppose Tracey has wondered about Payne's death experience, whereas I had the blessing of being with Peg for her passage from this world. Still the finality is hard to grasp. She too had the assurance of her partner's faith relationship with God through faith in Jesus as well as the support of the community of faith and family around her. I also believe that still having children to care for can provide self-distraction that tends to be healthy.

Peg and I were married nearly twice as long as the Stewart's and, of course, Tracey and I have different gender perspectives and experience. Still I hear her saying some things about Payne that cause me to believe we have much in common, things I have said in my writing about Peg as well. Here are just a few quoted from the words she spoke at Payne's memorial service. "I feel that I have been blessed by God, and I thank him for allowing me to share the last eighteen years of life with Payne....I realize that even after eighteen years of marriage, Payne was still the most beautiful man I'd ever seen. Not because of the way he looked on the outside anymore, but because of what he was on the inside. We shared laughter, tears, victories, and defeats. I admired your compassion for people and your talent that you were gifted with. You used it well....You will always be my soul mate and my best friend."[10]

So I at least have the answers to some of my "why" questions—why this book, why right now, why from Peg. Tracey, I'm sorry I don't have any answers for your "why" questions...but then, on second thought...!

I feel as though I am missing my therapy. My first Christmas without Peg is two weeks from today and I feel like I am stealing time to write this from other things that are pressing upon me. This is the busiest season of the church year and I have had my third funeral today in five weeks, one for a woman

10   Used by permission; Excerpt taken from *Payne Stewart* by Anastasia T. Stewart, © 2000, B&H Publishing Group, p. 309.

who died of cancer at age 49. In addition there are personal matters to attend to as well, some of them related to the holidays but others that are accruing because of pastoral busyness. So I have been yearning to delve into the many thoughts, feelings and memories that remain unexplored—an exercise that has been therapeutic for me in dealing with Peg's illness and death and my own attempt to solo since then.

Though it is hard to revisit many of the things of the past, it is harder still not too. I had time tonight to read only the first two pages of a new book written by Margaret Kim Peterson called, *Sing Me To Heaven,* in which she recounts her marriage of four years and the death of her husband. On the second page she asks, "Is the memory worth the grief?" She concludes it is saying, "It is to refuse to relinquish them (joys and sorrows) to the past, and instead to claim them for the present and carry them into the future."[11]

That's what I am missing. Grieving is on hold during this flurry of activity and I feel the want of its therapeutic effect.

Tonight I did a strange thing—I decided to wash Peg's winter robe! As I went into our bedroom's walk-in closet to get ready for bed, I stood for a moment and looked at her clothes. I know I need to deal with them...probably in the spring with some female family help. Her light blue heavy floor length winter robe was hanging there just inside the door where she always kept it handy. It was very warm and when she got up and went downstairs on cold winter mornings she used to snuggle up in it on the couch with her feet pulled up inside while she jump started the day with coffee and the Weather Channel.

When I pulled it out, just to look at, perhaps intending to picture her in it, I was shocked at how dirty it was. It needed a washing after a winter's use. In fact I'm sure she had washed it during the winter, but toward the end of the winter robe season, she wasn't mobile enough to tend to all such things and it probably went longer without a wash than it would have otherwise.

Then I noticed dirty areas on the front that looked like food stains. They might even have been stains from when she struggled with keeping her food down, although by the time she got to that point, I thought the weather was warm, and she was sleeping downstairs with sweat pants, sweat shirts, and night shirts. At any rate, they were brownish stains that she never would have tolerated had she been reasonably healthy—she kept herself and her clothes

11 © Margaret Kim Peterson, *Sing Me To Heaven,* (Ada, MI: Brazos Press, Baker Publishing Group, 2003), p. 8.

very clean. It must have gotten hung in the closet right after it got soiled and forgotten when the weather and her situation changed.

When I saw the general condition and the stains on the robe, it brought back a flood of feelings and memories of her distress and I decided I had to wash it. I told myself, of course, I wasn't washing it for her. I know she'll never wear it again. Someone probably can get some good use and warmth out of it. So I'm not so sure who I'm washing it for—maybe it really is for her or for me, as absurd as that is.

I do know what robe she's wearing now. Blue used to be her favorite color, but now it's white—white because her new robe of righteousness came out that way when she gave it a thorough cleansing in the blood of her Savior, taking away every stain picked up in this life. And He's washed away all the tear stains as well, according to Revelation. Speaking of those who have come through the trauma of this life, it says, "These are they who have come out of the great tribulation; they have washed their robes and made them white in the blood of the Lamb....And God will wipe away every tear from their eyes," (Revelation 7:14 and 17c – NIV).

I suppose if the wonderful robe of righteousness she has now received from her Savior has none of the stains of this world on it, it shouldn't matter if the one she left behind here does. But somehow it does to me. Maybe it's my way of getting rid of the stains of her illness, of cleaning up the residue of her distress, as a symbol of the fact that it is over and gone. No wonder I so appreciate that other passage from Revelation (21:1-4). "[1] Then I saw a new heaven and a new earth, for the first heaven and the first earth had passed away, and there was no longer any sea. [2] I saw the Holy City, the new Jerusalem, coming down out of heaven from God, prepared as a bride *beautifully dressed* for her husband. [3] And I heard a loud voice from the throne saying, 'Now the dwelling of God is with men, and he will live with them. They will be his people, and God himself will be with them and be their God. [4] He will wipe every tear from their eyes. There will be *no more death or mourning or crying or pain,* for the old order of things has passed away,'" (Italics added).

I brought Peg's robe into the laundry room and I will wash it with a halfway plausible reason. It will give me a more tangible sense of the conclusion of her disease as well as the restoration and purity of her new life. I couldn't be her savior taking away her illness, but I can at least wash her robe clean of its residue. And the One who is her real Savior, and mine, can handle the heavy duty cleaning for all of us of the robes that we will wear forever.

I had made a delivery to the bookstore and the owner wanted to give me a gift in return for my trouble. I followed her into another part of the store where she handed me a small book she thought I might like. It was one of those gift books with a variety of poems and sayings in it, all set in an attractive arrangement of subtle artwork and illustrations. There was a panel in it for the giver to personalize. As my eyes caught the writing it looked familiar and I realized it was Peg's. It said, "Peg Rule" with some sort of brief greeting written underneath. I was so surprised by the name, I didn't read the rest before I glanced up.

When I did, I couldn't believe what I was seeing! There was Peg, standing right there in front of me, not six feet away. She looked wonderful, perfectly healthy and well, wearing her pink button down sweater and gray skirt. She had a big smile, obviously pleased with herself for having surprised me. It took me a moment to grasp what I was seeing. It really was her! As she saw utter amazement and recognition come over me, she broke into her biggest grin. We jumped together in the biggest hug! I mean there are hugs, and then there are hugs! You know—the kind where you are absolutely engulfed in each other. It was that kind of hug! and it felt so familiar and so welcome!!!

It's not at all characteristic of me, but I was so completely overwhelmed that I think I cried out in my ecstatic joy like one of those school girls you see in the newsreels of the rock and roll days when the Beatles came on stage. I know all the breath went out of me in utter incredible joy. Peg truly was alive and well and I was seeing her. I was with her. My response was so loud, in fact, that it woke me up—I had been dreaming! I lay there for a moment with my heart pounding, a little short of breath, realizing I must have made such an actual noise, I woke myself. I was at once disgusted with myself for acting so impulsively and waking myself up so abruptly. I wanted to linger in that hug and being with Peg, even if it was a dream—of course it was a dream—but I still could have relished it for as long as possible. Even though it only lasted an instant in the dream, I can still feel it as I write this a half-hour later.

It is nearly seven months since Peg's death. Though I often wake up and realize I have been dreaming, she is seldom in my dreams in very prominent ways. Sometimes I realize she was there when I wake, and though I try to retrieve what she looked like or things she did and said, there is usually not much to hang on to. Although it was about as fast paced as a TV commercial, Peg was definitely prominent in this one! This was as vivid as any dream I've ever had, even to the physical sense of her presence.

Now that my initial reaction of mixed frustration with its brevity and excitement about its occurring at all has begun to settle, I am just grateful for the feeling of reassurance it has given. It seemed more than just a dream—almost a vision—and I receive it as a gift of the Lord. Already the way she looked is getting a little hazy on my internal viewer, blending with the last formal portrait she had done for the church directory, which sits on the entertainment center and my computer desk. But the lines of her face were much softer, the gray-blonde of her hair much more muted, and she was turned to the right instead of the left, as in her picture. If I can just retain the surroundings of book display tables, a support post to the left of her, and wooden paneling on the wall behind, maybe I'll be able to freeze the image. But even if I don't, little matter. I have seen her and experienced her in a profound, though brief, revelation, and I'm grateful. As I have said elsewhere, with my mind and in my heart I know and believe she lives in the Lord's presence and I will see her again. But emotionally, I hardly feel her continuation, and the most potent memories seem to be of her illness and suffering. Well, that's not true any longer! That dream was rather potent and highly charged.

It's just after 6:00am—there's still time to put the laptop aside, lay back down, and try to rest for awhile. I probably won't sleep, but I'll revisit the bookstore, I know. I'm sure Peg's gone and the dream is over, but it will be sort of like walking back over the ground of a significant event and letting the setting make its memory more vivid. Besides that, I want to thank God for providing it!

Something has troubled me for awhile. I have recalled and written about a variety of things during Peg's illness. But once her kidneys shut down, she declined further treatment, and we waited for death, I don't remember much significant interaction with her. Mostly I remember the physical decline she went through and the medical monitoring and attention. With death impending, did I miss moments when she struggled emotionally or physically? How could she be that close to death and I not remember confrontation with it? And why didn't we talk about the things that we expect people usually talk about at a time like that? Had I become numb, withdrawn, or just oblivious to what was going on?

On a winter trip to the Upper Peninsula, I asked Mike and Becky to tell me what they remembered about those last few days in the hospital when we knew the time was brief. Mike began by going further back during her illness. He had spent time with her on several occasions after her illness was diagnosed and becoming debilitating. He remembered her expressing frustration with God's silence. There seemed to be no word from God, no reassurance about the future. She didn't understand why this was happening to her. On one occasion in the hospital she said to Mike, "I'd rather just go home and go on with life." Well, that was Peg. She didn't have time to be sick, she seldom was, and didn't like dealing with all the medical matters. She also expressed to Mike that she found her weakness very frustrating.

As her illness progressed, she was apparently responsive to Mike when she was not to others. On Thursday, the day before she died, she said to him in a voice he could hardly hear, "I don't like it when you leave, not even for a minute." That night when it came time to settle down, Peg's brother, Frank, and I planned to sleep in her room. Mike knew he had to get some sleep, and told her he needed some rest and would be just in the next room with Becky and the kids. She seemed OK with that but he said it was hard to leave her just the same.

Becky remembered how in those last couple of days she could tell when Peg wanted something. On one occasion she figured out that she just wanted a hug. It reminded Becky of how important the presence of someone close and familiar had been to her in childbirth. She also remembered when it got to the point where Peg could no longer drink and received water only from a sponge on a stick, how she would grab hold of the sponge with her teeth and not let it go—the moisture must have been so satisfying. As they talked about it, both Mike and Becky laughed about how they had to work hard at talking her into letting it loose, but recalled how frightened they were that she might sever the sponge from the heavy paper stick and choke on it.

Becky then told how she just felt impressed to sing to Peg. What better thing could she do for one who loved music? Only a mother would think of doing that. She sang to her slowly in a soft voice—I remember her doing that and thinking what a beautiful thing to do—as she might for a child to soothe her to sleep. And she was, soothing a child of God to sleep in this world to awake in the next.

As she sang *I Am Persuaded,* Becky said Peg hadn't moved for a long time, but then she lifted her hand and held it to her face. She made some slight sounds of distress but Becky couldn't figure out what that was about and it soon passed.

Becky sang, *Be Thou My Vision,* and other familiar songs of the faith. Some of them she said she just hummed. I can just imagine how precious that was to Peg, to have Becky, whom she had come to love so very much, sing so peacefully to her.

The last thing that Mike remembers of his mom being responsive was just before she died. She lifted up her arms, even though she had hardly moved on her own for some time. Mike leaned down and gave her a hug. But something inside him said, "She wasn't reaching out to you, she was reaching out to Me!" He said he felt like she was gone after that—that the

Lord took her home with Him and all that remained with us was her dying flesh. Indeed, after that she never showed any signs of awareness.

In those last few days as the end was near, Peg was exhausted and had accepted her fate. Still, if given a choice even at that point, I'm sure she still would have said, "I'd rather just go home and go on with life." Instead, her Lord Jesus carried her to her forever home with His arms around her and her arms around Him.

The movie, *The Passion of Christ,* began its public showing the day before I wrote this, so television and all sorts of publications have been featuring articles and interviews about it with those who have opinions, informed and otherwise, as well as Mel Gibson, himself. Today, the day after I wrote what preceded, I came across a magazine article in *Christianity Today* that quoted from Gibson's companion book for the film called *The Passion*. In the book he said the movie was not intended to be a historical documentary. He said he thinks of it as contemplation intended to compel remembering in a spiritual way. And such remembering cannot be expressed with language. It can only be experienced.

Perhaps that is why I was troubled by the last several days of Peg's life. I thought they must have been marked by cognitive events as benchmarks of the ebbing away of time and her life, just as the advancement of her illness and her treatment had been. And when I couldn't recall them, I thought I had lost something. But I see more clearly now those days were delineated by a spirit that is not so easily fastened down like the timeline of her illness I compiled following her death. It wasn't like a voyage over a long narrow lake on a bright sunny day where the landmarks are clearly visible. It was more like a quiet voyage in a heavy mist where each feature along the way came into view only as it came near and then faded from sight and was gone before you knew it. And now returning to my original writing of yesterday...

So maybe I don't recall more cognitive interaction because there wasn't any. In retrospect, I think we each had our own experiences with her in those last few days that were significant in much more subtle and precious ways. However, I will allow for the fact that I was probably somewhat numb and oblivious to what was happening, given what we'd been through and what was still ahead. I didn't remember her raising her arms so soon before she died, though I must have been there. I'm grateful to Mike and Becky for telling me what they remembered. But evidently there were not the kind of things happening I feared I had missed.

As I've said elsewhere, I did tell her I loved her, that she had lived her life well, and that I was proud and privileged to share it with her. But I never reminisced with her about the joys we had shared, inquired about any last wishes, or approached matters of arrangements. Those things didn't seem as important as making her comfortable, caring for her needs, assuring her we were there with her, and not troubling her about worldly things. We would deal with those when necessary.

With other perspectives besides my own, and opportunity to work through what those last few days and hours of Peg's life with us in this world were like, I hope I will now begin to feel I didn't lose anything of value in them. In fact, I found more I didn't realize was there. I know it will be good to settle my feelings about them and find my own peace at their conclusion.

I went to Peg's gravesite with the hope of finding some sense of joy in resurrection. It seemed like the thing to do on Easter for the setting of the resurrection was a graveyard. If ever Peg's continuation would take on a greater reality for me, it seemed like this should be the day and her place of burial should be the place to find it.

It was especially appealing when I recalled that we had been there at least once before to celebrate Easter. When we served Becky's home church and were co-youth leaders with Becky's parents, the youth group conducted an Easter service there. We had a home-made tomb fabricated for an Easter play, and dramatized the resurrection with the women and the disciples discovering the empty tomb and the exciting news that Jesus is risen! With such past significance, I anticipated any significance it might have in the present.

Actually two things converged to make the trip to the cemetery something I was eager to do. I've already mentioned my desire to visit Peg's grave and secondly, I received an invitation to Easter dinner from Becky's family. I accepted their gracious invitation and left right after church.

Though Mike was in Brazil right then doing conferences and seminars, it was good to be with Becky and the grandkids as well as Becky's family, people we have been close to for many years. I greatly appreciated their thoughtful and caring invitation to celebrate the holiday with them and it was good to be around the seven grandchildren (we share two in common) who are full of life and vitality. Even though it meant over an hour's drive after a full morning of services starting with sunrise worship at 7:30[am], I accepted the invitation.

Later in the afternoon, they all were going to visit Becky's grandmother and I went on to the cemetery, which is less than a mile from Becky's family home. One of my reasons for wanting to go to the cemetery was to bring a lily, even though they weren't something that Peg was especially fond of. Her favorite flowers were red roses. In the past I had given her lilies for Easter now and then, though not in recent years. But sometimes we would have a lily or two given to us at Easter and Peg would tend them and enjoy them, though not with the same fondness she had for roses.

I think the idea of bringing a lily got started because they so strongly represent Easter and suggest to me the resurrection and new life of Jesus. I wanted to place one on Peg's grave as an expression of the new life that God has promised through faith in Jesus. So the lily wasn't as much for Peg as it was for me—a tangible expression, a sign of resurrection on her grave that she lives even now along with Jesus.

Yesterday I had to go into the city to pick up some dry cleaning and I decided I would just pick up one small plastic lily that I could either put in the flower arrangement that was already there or place somewhere on her gravesite, just to satisfy my desire. But before I left I got a phone call about a parishioner who was hospitalized, so I needed to change and get cleaned up so my appearance would be appropriate for visitation. Consequently it took me longer to get ready to go and more time to make the trip than I had planned and I forgot all about picking up a lily. When I remembered it early in the morning, I didn't know where I was going to find an artificial lily on Easter Day. Besides, I couldn't take much time after church because I was already going to be risking delaying dinner with the time it would take me to get there. I had no choice but to say, "Lord, if I'm going to bring a lily, you'll have to provide it."

When I returned to my office after the last service to put away my things and get my coat, there was a lily sitting on the floor in front of my office door. There was no note or explanation, but I gathered that someone, who had purchased one of the many flowers for sanctuary decoration, had left it for me. There had been three other varieties of flowers to chose from, but whoever left this one had chosen a lily. I said, thank you, Lord! And thank you to whoever was so generous and thoughtful.

After I left the afternoon gathering, I went to the cemetery and placed the flower on the opposite end of the gravestone from the arrangement that Becky had recently put in place of the winter arrangement that had been there since before Christmas. Then I sat under a nearby cedar tree to just spend some time in the setting. I had hoped that somehow I might feel uplifted by the flower, the day, and the memories. But all I felt was a descending sadness and the familiar sense of loss.

The wind was blowing cold out of the northwest. There were a few scattered snowflakes drifting down now and then out of the heavy gray overcast, and I was glad I thought to bring my winter jacket. The world was very silent, except for a couple of spring peepers that tried to get the entire chorus started along the nearby river's edge, but they soon gave up and fell silent again. In the distance I could hear the clip-clop of horseshoes on pavement as an Amish carriage traveled down a distant road. I remembered how Peg loved horses and always delighted to see the Amish carriages go by. In fact, one had passed the cemetery soon after I arrived, but the present sound faded slowly away and I never did see the rig.

I sat in anticipation that the Lord would provide some sign, some encouragement in response to my token placed on Peg's grave and my presence there on Easter Day. I had no idea what...just some sense of assurance that Peg was with the Lord in His presence and His glory. I had just preached twice that morning about the two confused disciples on the road to Emmaus. A fellow traveler convinced them, through interpreting the Scriptures, that the Jesus of Nazareth they knew was the Savior, the Messiah, that God had promised. Once they came to see that, in the sermon I said, "Then came the bonus. As this fellow traveler broke the bread for the evening meal, they recognized that he was Jesus, resurrected and living again." I too, hoped for a bonus.

It's not that I doubt resurrection—I preach it and I believe it. I do not go to Peg's grave feeling like she is buried there beneath the sandy soil. I know what is there is only her earthly remains and that the person she had become has gone on to be with her Savior and Lord. But I still find what I believe with my intellect is slow to filter down into my feelings in ways that reassure and comfort. That's what I had brought the lily there for on Easter Day—in the hope of finding some kind of reassurance and comfort. But all I found was the cold wind and the gray silence.

I waited for awhile thinking that maybe I was trying to make something happen and I just needed to be patient and quiet, something I find it very hard to do these days. But after awhile it seemed pointless. I had done what I came to do. I needed to head for home to get on the phone and make arrangements to meet with a family the next day to discuss the funeral service for a wife and mother, a woman in her mid-sixties, who had died unexpectedly the day before. Not only was I forfeiting a Monday day-off, but having to work with people in grief right on the heels of a stressful period of holy week services. That added to my discouragement.

As I got up to go, I was reluctant to leave the lily there, knowing that it would be unlikely to survive the cold and there was no one nearby to give it the care it needed. But I decided that the act of placing it there as a symbol of resurrection grace was more important than taking it home to grace where I live daily. And so I left it to its fate.

Still with some hesitation about leaving, I climbed the hill to the car. When I started it, the radio came on to the Public Broadcasting System station I had tuned to *A Prairie Home Companion* on my way to dinner. The radio was noisy and I couldn't make out all that was being said, but I could make out enough to tell a man was talking about how his faith in Jesus and His resurrection was helping him to deal with his son's presence in the military in Iraq. Then he went on to talk about how all the disciples were radically changed by the resurrection appearances of Jesus. I never did figure out what the program was and why it was on PBS. That radio is very noisy until it's on for awhile and once I started moving I could make out even less. But I got the message. Regardless of how I may feel through all of this, my faith is still in Jesus and His resurrection and that He will keep His promises. Whether that will ever soak into my feelings about Peg and alleviate the sorrow I cannot say. I guess there are a lot of things tied up in that and perhaps the Lord will unravel them in His good time. If not, I will pray for His provision to live in the gap between my firmly held beliefs and my disquieted feelings. But I suppose I will still hope that He will give relief to my feelings of uncertainty and a deeper sense of Peg's presence with Him.

More than eight months after Peg's death, there are still tears. I know some of them are because I have profoundly experienced the sorrow of death as the end of mortal life. Some of them are because of my own loss, not only of Peg, but of life as it had become for the two of us. But I cry with sobs and tears because of the images of her that appear on my mental viewing screen. And so I have discovered I cry for her, for myself, and for our human mortality and all it entails.

I see her in the bathroom hunched over the stool, trying to keep down the nourishing food she had fought so hard to swallow, losing the fight in tears, while I tried to reassure her it would be OK, that she wasn't being a wimp and I knew how hard it was.

I see her crumbled on the family room floor at the base of the little step down from the main floor level, a look of utter dismay on her face, and myself astounded that her strength was failing her and I failed to know it and let her fall.

I see her reclined in the passenger seat of the car, in her misery with her head turned slightly toward the window and eyes outward toward the sky, staring beyond the passing scenery, riding for the last time to the emergency room, my hand holding hers tightly as I wondered was this the last time we would ride anywhere together.

I see her in the waiting room of the hospital laboratory sitting in the wheelchair, looking gray and utterly miserable with no way to make her head comfortable, trying to endure patiently and not inconvenience anyone until she could have her blood tested to find that her blood level was extremely low.

Through the partially opened door of her hospital room, I see her hair matted against the back of her head as she sat on the commode because she was unable to walk herself to the bathroom, waiting patiently for the nurses to make her bed and lay her back down again.

I see her smooth, soft legs, and well-formed feet, beneath the hospital sheets as I gently lifted them to change their position to try to make them comfortable, rubbing them tenderly for awhile, when she could no longer move them on her own.

I see her quietly and peacefully taking her last breath, head tipped back into her soft hospital bed pillow so that her mouth could be wide open, her eyelids curved over big blue eyes that weren't quite shut, eyes I would never again see wide-open, beautifully blue, and full of vitality in the reality of this world.

But I also see her blue eyes in bed on a Monday morning on our day off, settled on her own pillow with my arm around her as we drift in and out of conversation about the day ahead, the day before, whatever might float to the surface of our minds at the moment. Sometimes those big beautiful blue eyes are looking into mine, sometimes gazing at the blank screen of the ceiling above, conveying the spirit of vitality, exuberance, and depth of soul that was Peg. And so some of my tears are because I still miss her deeply, although now and then they run down over a smile that comes over me because I remember those big beautiful blue eyes.

1686 Laurium Street. I literally wrote that address hundreds of times on the letters I sent to Peg during my two years in the Army in Japan and four months in Chicago at photography school. Now I was standing in the kitchen at 1686 Laurium Street (which is now 56437 Laurium Street since the addresses were changed to accommodate the new 911 emergency system). This was the place where Peg had lived as a little girl and grown up to become the young woman I had come to love. I could sense life and vitality had once surged through the place. She must have brought much of it as the first child of Joseph and Helen Ricca, a child full of energy and bubbly laughter. Then when two brothers, Frank and Larry, came along a few years apart, the activity and vitality increased more than three-fold in the small mining company house, as is bound to happen with five people living in close quarters along with the rivalry that develops between older sisters and younger brothers.

I didn't' need to walk over to the archway into the living room to picture

Peg standing at the foot of the stairs in her white knee-length prom dress with the green tied belt and green shoes, hair all curled, and a somewhat forced smile for the camera. I didn't even know her then, but I'd seen and admired the picture enough times for it to be clear in my memory. In fact, there were another thousand memories of my own in that house that accumulated over the years that I knew I could retrieve if I took the time to conjure them. But Mike would soon be finished securing the house and it would be time to leave. So I just looked around at the sad state of the place.

Peg's brother, Frank, was the last to live there. He had left it a few years ago to enter the priesthood in the Roman Catholic Church and had turned the property over to her. As she had begun to deal with the accumulated clutter and treasures from their years of family life, she and I were often reminded that our parents grew up in the depression era when people learned to make do with what they had. Long before recycling began out of regard for the environment, they learned to "recycle" what seemed potentially usable from worn out and broken things. Then when the depression era passed, some of their generation never reoriented their way of living with material things. That, of course, meant saving them because they "might come in handy"—that was the phrase I learned from my father.

Added to the stash were not only the "savings" from Peg's own family, but things she recognized that had come from her maternal grandparent's house when her grandmother died and her household was dismantled. In fact, Peg's father's family had lived in the same household before him and, since they were deceased before he married, he made it his family home. In addition, some of her brother Larry's things were still there, things Frank had brought home from Texas after Larry died of cancer three years previously. Besides all that, Frank had left behind some of his things when he went on to the limited accommodations of seminary. So generations of worldly goods were still in evidence under the roof of her family home.

Actually, Peg was excited to begin dealing with the property hoping to make it livable for any of the family who might need a place to go for awhile or just want to get away on vacation. In fact, she thought it might be a good retreat for friends to spend time away from home, especially people in ministry who often do not have get-away places of their own and can't afford to spend much for resorts or motels. Peg knew it needed a lot of work to bring it up to date. Her father lost his job in 1967 when the mining company closed, worked a few temporary jobs for several years, and then toughed it out until he was eligible for social security. After Peg's mother died in 1989, her dad, who was ten years older than her, lost much of his enthusiasm for life and cared little about keeping things up to date or replacing the things that wear out from daily use. After her dad died in 1992, Frank lived there

Peg in her prom dress.

for periods of time. Then when he was going to be leaving for seminary, he and Peg removed most everything of any worth or value from the premises out of concern for a break-in or vandalism and he signed the property over to us.

Peg and I had begun to invest a little time each year to sort out, clean out, clean up, and stabilize further deterioration to the structure, anticipating that the time would come when we could start to refurbish and make the house more livable. With 500 miles between our home and her family home and our need for time away to provide refreshing and respite from our ministry, we felt we could only spare limited time each year for the project. But we had begun and were making progress annually.

A year ago this month, we had planned to return to work on cleaning out the basement so that things from upstairs could be stored there temporarily while remodeling work took place in other parts of the house. In addition, our son, Mike, was going to come along and we would re-side a portion of the front of the house. Peg's brother had re-sided most of the house with a light green siding, her mother's choice of colors. Their mother had always wanted a front porch and so he didn't see any point in siding the portion the porch would cover. He nailed up chipboard as a temporary measure and painted it dark brown, intending to remove it later when that would become an inside wall. But in the meantime, their mother died, the porch never got built, and after years of outside exposure, the chipboard was flaking and deteriorating. We were concerned that water was leaking in behind it and might cause structural damage, so we intended to pull off the old chipboard and side the area to match the rest of the house. As the time for our work trip approached, Peg was called for jury duty, so Mike and I were going to do the trip together with Peg perhaps joining us in progress if her jury duty was completed early. But then her back problem began to intensify, I did not want to leave her to fend for herself, and we cancelled the trip altogether. Needless to say, she never returned to her family home again and the project was dead in the water.

I have little interest in the property, but Mike decided to keep it for the foreseeable future for a variety of reasons, many of which coincide with Peg's. So we rescheduled the project we had planned to undertake a year ago. We spent several days pulling off the old chipboard, putting up new tarpaper, and adding the missing siding. In addition, we cut out several evergreen trees, living and dead, that along with some out-of-control shrubs and a long entangling vine, had turned the area between the house and the street into a veritable jungle. With our project completed on Saturday, we had returned on Monday to gather up our tools, repack our vehicle for the return trip home, to make sure everything was secure, and to lock up.

It was while I stood there in the kitchen waiting for Mike to come down from checking the upstairs, that everything looked so depressing. I knew if Peg were still here, it would have tugged at her heart strings too as we prepared to leave it once again, still looking so abandoned and desolate inside. That's when the sense of what once had been, began to come to me in sharp contrast to the way things really are in the present.

Not only did it make the sadness of my own loss fresh and glaring, but I saw it as a gloomy statement on the transient nature of life in this world and Peg's absence from it. It seemed like a very severe way to learn that lesson.

In retrospect, I realize that every home on the 1600 block of Laurium Street teaches a similar lesson. They all began as mining company houses built to standard designs. But over time their appearances changed with additions, porches, and attached garages. Even the Ricca house had a back porch added that Peg's grandfather hauled there on one of his Solmonson Trucking vehicles from the old Calumet & Hecla Mining Company hospital when it closed. The houses were all sided with different colors and siding styles over the years as well. In addition, many had changed hands and ancestors of the original families were no longer in residence. So they are a testimony to the changes brought by the last century and the transient nature of life. Still, it was a hard thing to stand there in the kitchen surrounded by the depressing evidence of a family nearly gone (Peg's brother is the only surviving member of the immediate family, and Mike the only nephew) feeling Peg's absence.

When I heard Mike coming down the stairs, I went out and got in the car with my feelings very close to the surface. I didn't feel capable of expressing them and I imagine it was the same for Mike since neither of us said more than necessary as we drove away from 1686 Laurium Street. That's right, I forgot—it's now 56437 Laurium Street.

If only... Who of us have not thought "if only" when confronted with tragic or premature loss. I have gone over many developments in Peg's illness and death with "if only's," fully realizing they are a useless exercise that can change nothing. Still most recently I found myself expressing one that has brought some little satisfaction as I have imagined what might have been.

When Mike and I finished the project on Peg's family home and were returning to my family home were we had been staying, we had evidently both been thinking over the project and how pleased we were with the results. He said in comment on the work, "Mom would have been pleased."

I agreed. Yes she would have. The new siding and fresh paint on the front gave the house a much less depressing appearance. I thought about the fact that we had planned the same project for a year ago. Then, I have to confess, I wanted to pretend for a moment it was last year, that we were going to be able to go home and show Peg the pictures we had taken of the completed work. She would be so pleased and excited! I could just see her marveling at what a difference it made and how she would be looking forward to actually seeing how it looked in person. She would say again how she was looking forward to the house being able to be used for any and all of us to enjoy. I could get into that joy with her of seeing her family home made more livable.

So I said to Mike, "Wouldn't it be wonderful if we could just rewind this past year and replay it?"

He said, "I don't think I'd want to go through all that again."

I said, "No, I mean with a different script, where we go back home and show her the pictures of what it looks like now and we go on from there without any cancer."

He said, "I know what you mean."

From there our conversation eventually drifted back to reality and reflection on how God knows things that we don't and if we had control, how things might turn out far worse than we might ever imagine. We both agreed that God is in control, that we have to trust that things happen as they do for a reason even if we don't understand, and that the challenge to us is to accept them by faith.

Still, since we have not yet returned home as I write this, there is a part of me that would like to pretend we're going home to show Peg the progress pictures that would please her so much, and us too in the way she would respond. Tomorrow we're heading home and then there's no pretending. But that's tomorrow. There's still tonight. And I'm just not sure what thoughts I'll entertain as I settle down for sleep!

People tell me after a partner's death, getting through the firsts is significant. I have found that true. The first trip to Peg's gravesite after her burial, the first Sunday service at church without her, the first holidays like Thanksgiving and Easter, the first vacation alone, all of these and more have been a blend of memories and emotions. I knew that would be the case with Annual Conference.

Every year in May, United Methodist clergy and lay representatives of the churches of our region in Michigan meet on the campus of Adrian College to conduct denominational matters under the leadership of a bishop. It is called an Annual Conference and has to do with denominational recruitment, credentialing, ordination, and deployment of clergy, denominational ministries at the regional level, and the structures and machinery necessary to keep all of that operative. In addition, there are times of worship, learning, and fellowship. There is also a social gathering for clergy spouses and they are welcome to attend most events, although they cannot participate as voting members in official business sessions unless elected as representatives.

Since Peg was not employed, she began attending Annual Conference with me when we first started in ministry. She found the formal social time for spouses was often very enjoyable, she knew some of the lay people who came as delegates from working with them in district activities before we entered pastoral ministry, and she found the number of clergy spouses she knew was on the increase. Over the years, she became attached to a smaller circle of clergy wives who met for coffee in the college lounge. They began going on shopping excursions in the city and any other fun things they could dream up for amusement. Four of them in particular became a very close-knit group who provided listening ears, support, understanding, and a lot of laughter to help each other cope with the stresses of living in houses owned by churches, parishioners' expectations of pastors' wives, and being married to preachers. In recent years as those friendships deepened, Peg especially looked forward to attending Annual Conference.

Last year was going to be different. One of the husbands retired and this couple did not anticipate coming to Annual Conference, except for perhaps the gathering of retired clergy. But the other three wives would still get together and enjoy themselves. However, last year Peg was troubled with her back and muscle problems and was in no condition to attend. In fact, at conference time, she had just been discharged from her first hospitalization for reaction to her new pain medication. I wasn't about to leave her on her own, so I didn't attend either.

That meant that this year was my first time back to Annual Conference for two years. I realized that many of my colleagues and lay people I knew from other churches had not seen me since Peg's funeral, and others since Annual Conference two years ago. So I anticipated expressions of condolence and inquiries about my well-being, and I was right. Many asked, "How are you doing?" My standard answer has become, "OK," or "Alright."

When people ask the "How are you doing?" question, I have to confess a perverse inclination to answer, "How the heck do you think I'm doing? My wife died of cancer, for Pete's sake!" But I know they're expressing concern and opening up conversation, even though I honestly wonder myself sometimes how I'm doing. So I say, "Alright, I guess," or "OK." Sometimes I add, "It's quite an adjustment." Then I might elaborate if they seem genuinely interested in knowing more.

I knew that seeing so many of these people for the first time since Peg's death was going to be stressful, and it was. That's no one's fault—it's just a first filled with a multitude of little firsts to face.

I also knew that seeing Peg's friends would stir my feelings. They would be expressive about missing her and that would reinforce my own sense of her absence. And sure enough, the remaining two who continue to come to conference were together, we hugged, they conveyed their sorrow, and they talked about how much they enjoyed her. I couldn't say much at first but they carried the conversation, for which I was thankful, 'til I was able to participate. One of them had made pins with Peg's picture on them and they asked if I'd mind if they wore them that evening for the memorial service. I didn't mind at all and looked forward to seeing the picture.

That was the next major thing I knew I had to face—the memorial service in memory of the clergy, clergy spouses and children, and lay people in conference offices who have died during the previous year. Their names are published and spoken and a brief memorial statement is read while family and friends stand up in place and one designated person goes forward to receive a flower in memory of the one who has died. I expected it would be meaningful but not easy to handle, especially since circumstances meant none of our family were able to be present with me.

One of the most distressing things was something I didn't anticipate. Family members and friends were asked to come early and be seated up front in reserved pews. I was there in plenty of time so I witnessed many others coming through the front entrances to the chapel. In the two years, or more, since I had last seen several colleagues and spouses, I was shocked by how debilitated some had become. One in particular had aged considerably perhaps showing signs of some sort of nervous disorder that caused unsteadiness. Another's face was sunken, deeply lined, and she was hunched over walking with a cane and led by her partner. I began looking deliberately at others, not seeing such severity, but still obvious signs of advancing years and declining health for some. It actually gave me a sense of gratitude that Peg was spared of the debilitation that can accompany a protracted fight with cancer and the treatments involved. Although I do have memories of her weakened condition, emaciated body, and distressed eyes, at least she did not go on long in that condition—the Lord spared her of that—and my default images are now of her as a vital, healthy, robust woman with a winning smile and a brisk walk. I suddenly felt grateful that God spared her of the ravages of aging and prolonged illness and me the extended agony of watching it happen to her.

The service began with prayers and Scriptures that were appropriate for the occasion highlighting resurrection and hope, and celebrating the lives of those who have lived faithfully as the Lord's servants. In each instance I realized that Peg was implied and this was about her, which only made her absence more conspicuous and touching. Then we sang the opening hymn, *For All the Saints,* which celebrates all those who have passed on to become part of the great company of believers surrounding the Lord. The third verse made reference to them wearing crowns of victory.

> "O may thy soldiers, faithful true and bold,
> fight as the saints who nobly fought of old,
> and win with them the victor's crown of gold..."[12]

Suddenly I got this image of Peg, with a big smile, wearing a crown, tilted slightly over one eye—one of those gold ones with the points that have little knobs on top—and I had to smile. Peg did not like to wear hats, and there she was wearing a crown, given to her by her Lord, which she could not, would not, refuse, but would, in fact, treasure.

Actually, I think it's partly my fault that Peg didn't like to wear hats. From the time I first knew her, she seldom wore them, but on one occasion when she tried one on—I think it was in a store—I laughed, and she refused to wear one after that. Oh, she would wear a hood or chook outside in the winter, but otherwise, no hats unless it was absolutely necessary.

I tried to convince her the reason I laughed was because I had seldom seen her in a hat, it tickled me, and actually I thought she looked cute. After that, I might get her to try one on once in awhile but only for a moment. I would try my darnedest to convince her I thought she looked attractive wearing a hat—which she usually did—but she evidently thought I was working too hard at it and wasn't persuaded. So when I pictured her in the golden crown, it touched my spirit in both a light-hearted way to see her wearing it and a hopeful way considering what it meant.

The sermon for the occasion was given by a retired woman pastor who told a story about white-water rafting and being washed overboard and downstream, as the raft with the rest of the passengers got hung up on rocks and debris. They watched her being carried away and feared for her safety, but she was rescued by a guide in a canoe and brought to shore further down river. She made the story into a parable about remaining in this world and watching our loved ones carried away from us in death to a place we will one day come to as well. Her life illustration put our moments of remembrance in perspective in a reassuring way. From then on the service felt more like celebration to me. I did find my anxiety level rising when it came time to go

Peg did not like to wear hats.

forward to receive the rose in Peg's memory, but I told myself to not miss the moment and to be aware of the words being said and the friends who were standing in tribute.

As I went forward, these are the words that were read, a tribute I had composed and submitted in advance at the program committee's request.

> "The defining moment of Peg's life was when, as a young woman, she came to know Jesus, in her own words, '...not only as Savior of the world but my personal Savior and Lord.' Several years later, she graciously accepted Jim's call to pastoral ministry as her own and became a partner in the work of all the appointments he received. She pursued her deep love for youth and for music, not only while they were lay people in their home church, but during their years under appointment, serving in a variety of youth and music ministries. In addition, she utilized her office and secretarial skills informally as a volunteer in their first two appointments, and formally as administrative assistant in the church where Jim continues to serve. Despite her many gifts and talents, she is most fondly remembered and missed as a vibrant, caring, person who would listen when people wanted to talk. A Bible verse she treasured is most appropriate for this occasion and describes her, not only in this world but the next: 2 Corinthians 5:17, '...if anyone is in Christ, he is a new creation; the old has gone, the new has come!'"

Once I received the beautiful yellow rose, I only had a short way to walk from the foot of the platform back to my seat in the third row, so I really didn't see very well those who were standing, but I would guess there were 25 at least, many of whom I could name without even seeing them. I was again reminded our family is not alone in feeling her loss.

The service was completed with communion served by the retiring and the newly ordained clergy. As it concluded, I was glad not only that it was over, but that our Annual Conference includes such a service in its repertoire of events. Though Peg was never much into the agenda of the Conference, she was very much into the people who are a part of it and the Lord whose Church and service it is ultimately about. She was certainly a significant presence in each Annual Conference for me.

This Conference was very different in every respect without her and I know they will be from here on out. For one thing, the mundane is very different. In the early years, we met at the dining hall and often ate with people that we knew, renewing friendships and catching up. In later years, we started going out for meals to nearby restaurants with friends. This time, lacking a social director, I went back to eating the noon meal in the dining hall and just having a light takeout supper in my room. We always stayed in the college dorms, which were convenient on campus, though not as comfortable as a motel. Since they are double occupancy, we were each other's room mates. This year, I didn't want to face staying with a stranger and trying to adjust to someone else's habits and schedule, or imposing mine on someone else, so I reserved a motel room. I did feel somewhat guilty about it because Peg had talked about doing that several times, but I never felt it was very good economics just for sleeping and showering.

We sometimes went to Conference separately because Peg often attended a retreat that overlapped the first day. So one of us would arrange a ride to Conference with someone else and we would rendezvous there. But seldom did I ever come home from conference alone. That meant we had three hours of travel time plus usually one mealtime together to tell each other about the people we had talked with and Peg saw so many more of them coming and going than I did. I would update her on the business that took place and we would compare notes on the worship services we'd experienced together. The ride always went fast and we ran out of miles before we ran out of conversation.

Not so this time. Coming home alone was difficult. I listened to a lot of music, stopped to watch and photograph one train, and picked up some groceries before I came home. When I left Adrian, my Conference experience was over. It didn't continue through Peg's eyes and perceptions and I didn't process it by telling her my experience. It's another first—one of those "adjustments" I spoke about.

I will remember it though, this first one without her, for several reasons. I took the memorial rose to be freeze-dried. I have one of the button pictures her friend made pinned to the visor in the car—the husbands wore them for the service too and one of them thoughtfully gave me his afterward. And though I don't have an actual picture, I don't think I'll forget that image of Peg with a big smile wearing her golden crown of victory, slightly tilted over one eye. I'll remember she's gone on down the river and, somewhere around the bend, I trust she's been rescued and brought ashore. And I know this—the current of that river is carrying me in the same direction and one day I'll have a crown like Peg's, and when I do, someone will come forward when my name is read in the memorial service at the chapel at Adrian College to receive a flower.

I wasn't going to write about it since it was just another dream, but then I decided it might be more significant in relation to the larger picture than it seemed at the moment, and I think I was right. It seems to indicate that some things are changing.

I dreamed Peg and I were on a train trip. Unlike most of our train rides, we were not in a compartment, but riding coach. We were trying to get settled down and get some rest. I was laying across the seats with my head to the aisle when a boy from the other side of the train came and sat in the seat next to the window. Peg ended up across the aisle and several seats forward. She was looking back at us and I was very irritated that the boy had intruded and she was pushed out. After some sort of intervention, which may have involved the conductor but isn't entirely clear to me as is often the case with things in dreams, the boy was removed and Peg came back. I was still laying across the seat and she lay with her back up against me, as we often did when we went to sleep, and snuggled in. (It's wonderful how dreams can make seats and so many other things accommodate us!) As I often did when we settled down for the night, I put one arm under her pillow above her shoulder and the other over her body, sort of like a hug from behind. I could feel her hair softly touching my face and all seemed right with the world.

As I lay there feeling peaceful and content, I began to realize that we had been apart, that she had been gone and was back with me—not just across the aisle but gone out of my life. I had a vague sense of asking the Lord to give her back and evidently He had granted that desire. It gave me a very deep sense of joy and gratitude that we were together again and I savored it deeply.

I confess I have entertained thoughts of asking the Lord to return her—not real coherent and deliberate thoughts, but those thoughts we sometimes toy with, wondering whether we should actually think them or not. I know God could restore her. He had restored any number of people to life in Bible times, including Lazarus. I personally know people who claimed other kinds of miracles in their lives, although restoration to life doesn't seem to be one

He continues to do, at least not after extended periods of death.[13] Besides, it wouldn't be fair to put Peg through all of that, given where she is and who she's with, just to satisfy me. Returning to mortality from immortality doesn't sound like something I'd want once I'd made the transition. I know all of that sounds silly, yet such are the thoughts I've explored in coping with the loss of Peg.

In the dream, I seemed to recall approaching God with such thoughts, and apparently He had granted my request. As I felt Peg's familiar closeness against me I was so moved that I began to gently cry. But as I did, reality slowly set in and I began to realize, I was not on a train and I was not with Peg. I was actually at home in bed and actually crying slightly, which must have disturbed my sleep. My mind came to reality long before my physical senses and somehow I continued to feel close to Peg, as though she was there with me, against me and in my arms. I willed myself to not fully awake and I didn't—I was just suspended between the dawning mental realization of where I was and the physical sensation of where I'd been.

But my mind kept figuring it out and I realized the pillow was slightly against my face and my arms wrapped about the covers in such a way that I had the pleasant sensation of them actually being around her. As I continued to become fully awake, the sensation lingered and so I deliberately lay there once again enjoying the same pleasure of being close to Peg that I had enjoyed for so many years. Strangely enough, even though I was now fully awake, I knew that pleasure would continue as long as I didn't move and disturb the physical state that had come over me—and so it did. But I couldn't keep my mind from engaging with the reality of my circumstance. I began to wonder what time it was—the sun was up—how long I had slept, and a variety of other petty thoughts. I knew if I turned over to look at the clock on the other side of the bed the lingering dream sensation would be over.

Finally, mind asserted itself over matter and I turned and saw that it was 6:30am. I had slept about seven hours without waking—very good for me these days. Then I began to wonder, should I get up and write my way through this? Was there any value to reflecting further on the experience and recording another "teasing" dream? No, my first thought was to just lay there and rest for a little while before starting what I knew would be another full day. Then my second thought was to add it as another piece to this puzzle of grief and adjustment that, by itself, might not make much of a picture, but

---

13 I want to make a distinction between restoration and resurrection. Lazarus and others Jesus raised from death were restored to mortality which meant they would die again. Resurrection is to immortality which is a new state of being beyond death that is forever.

might fill in more detail of the larger landscape. On second thought, I got up.

When I sat down to write with the laptop, I did a search for the word "dream" in what I'd written previously and reread some of my earlier writing in which I mentioned beginning to dream again. I had forgotten how much of a breakthrough and how precious those first dreams were after Peg's death. Perhaps my lesser excitement about this one is an indicator of change. Not that I value this one less, but that it wasn't so colossal to dream about Peg and as traumatic to relinquish the sense of nearness. So I've added this to the larger picture in the hopes that it will, over time, help to make more visible this mosaic of grief and change.

Today was another first—the first Memorial Day without Peg. I wanted to visit Peg's grave on the day. Sunday evening Mike was teaching one of his discipleship sessions at a church near their home, so I went to hear him then stayed the night with them. In the morning we went to see the grandchildren march in the Memorial Day parade in Cass City—Rachael with her softball team and Joseph with the Boy Scouts (he carried the flag). Then we went on to the cemetery on the outskirts of Cass City for the Memorial Day service. After lunch, we visited for awhile and I went on to the cemetery where Peg is buried which is about a 15 minute drive from their home.

I parked just off the road above the cemetery, walked down the hill to Peg's grave, and stood by the gravestone for a few minutes looking things over. The flowers on the grave looked attractive. Becky had removed the winter flowers on one end of the gravestone and replaced them with the arrangement we had used last summer. On the other end she had placed a bouquet of blue roses she and Rachael had selected. The birch cross that Mike and Joseph made is still in place with a few yellow flowers that Rachael had put in the ground around it. The grass is beginning to fill in, some of it coming up from seed we had distributed in the fall and from seed Mike planted this spring.

I sat under the nearby cedar tree to just absorb the setting and the situation. The sun was shining when I arrived, although it had been raining off and on throughout the day, so everything was fresh and green. Many of the graves had attractive flowers for the occasion and little flags waved over those of military veterans in the brisk breeze blowing out of the southwest. Birds were singing in the surrounding woods. It was a very pleasant place to be—a little strange, perhaps, for people like Peg and I who had been raised in northern mining country—but a peaceful quiet setting nevertheless surrounded by undulating farmland and bordered by the wooded river valley on the north. I sat quietly appreciating the setting, if not the cause of my being there.

Besides the changing of the season since my last visit, the other biggest change was a new house built across the road from the cemetery, put up by Becky's uncle and aunt who were giving up their dairy operation to do only crop farming and building their "retirement" home on the hilltop where they could enjoy the view. It looked like it might be ready for occupancy with curtains and a lamp in the front window, although there was no garage door yet or a front lawn, and no one around.

As on my Easter visit, I sat in solitude with some anticipation about what this experience of being there on this occasion might mean. My mind wandered over a variety of thoughts that were so fleeting that I can't even recall them. I seemed unable to really focus on anything specific and I hoped the Lord might provide something to give significance to my being there. I did have some chores to tend to, and after a little while, I decided getting those done might help me settle down. I picked up the bag of grass seed Mike had sent with me and began spreading it on the thin spots. Then I raked it into the rain dampened ground. Again I spread more seed and raked that in as well. I picked up the few rocks that I had unearthed and discarded them. Next I swept away the dirt and excess seed that had accumulated on the footing around the base of the stone. Then I settled down under the tree again.

The large patch of blue sky above began to fill with heavy gray clouds rushing in from the southwest in an attempt to catch up with the mountainous cumulus clouds billowing high above in the northeast. Again I sat expectantly wanting to make the most of the time I had in this special place. Remembering that it was Memorial Day, I attempted to offer prayer of thanks to God for Peg. I am sincerely thankful for her, but somehow my heart wasn't really in the prayer and I wasn't very expressive or evidently very receptive. My being there felt like going through the motions—maybe I was trying too hard. Soon it began to rain, wetting down the new seed I had raked into the soil, and I felt as though my planting was timely and God was providing what was needed. Thunder rumbled in the distance from a storm that had passed to the southeast and I decided I would just be there and spend a little while in the shelter of the cedar tree. That was really what I came for—to see how things were looking, to provide a little care, to just be there as a way of remembering Peg, and to thank God for her on Memorial Day.

After a little while, a minivan came down the road from the west and backed into the driveway and open garage of the new house. Then another vehicle came soon after and several people were unloading things and bringing them in. I decided Becky's uncle and aunt must be moving in.

Returning my attention to the scene in front of me, I attempted to just sit and be content, and I was for awhile. Eventually the rain began to subside, then the sun poked through again, and the scene looked like it did when I had arrived earlier, except for my raked scratches in the sandy soil. I didn't really know what I had expected my visit there to accomplish other than the things already done, so there didn't seem to be any reason to stay on. I got up and headed up the hill, deciding to pay a call to the new residents across the road. Indeed, it was Becky's uncle and aunt moving in with the help of several family members. They welcomed me and invited me in to sit around their dining area table while they took a needed break, they said. All their major furniture was moved in and they were finishing up bringing down the various and sundry things they had accumulated over 37 years in the farmhouse up the road. They were doing that at the same time that their daughter was moving into the farmhouse, needing to be out of her present place by the next day.

Still they graciously took the time for conversation to bring each other up to date on life situations as well as the health and well-being of family and mutual friends, now and then acknowledging our mutual past and my reason for being there on Memorial Day. As I began to leave, they invited me on a tour of their new home, of which they are justly proud. I'm sure I kept them too long from their pressing work but they were not too hurried to visit with a friend on his first Memorial Day visit to his wife's grave.

As I got in the car, I took one last look down the hillside at Peg's grave, the shiny gray stone, the flowers, and the green grass, and then drove away. But not without a sense of the Lord's compassion in a way I never anticipated.

Chapter 4
Little Things

They say that the sense of smell is more closely linked to memory than any of the other senses, and I believe that is true. This morning when I showered I used a bottle of shampoo that came from the hospital on one of Peg's stays of a year ago. Each time she was hospitalized and given all the things she needed for personal hygiene, we brought what was left home to use up. I had found the almost full bottle of shampoo in one of the drawers in the bathroom a few days ago where she must have put it, so I took it out and put it in the shower.

As I took a handful of the shampoo and began to rub it into my hair, its distinctive odor brought me back to Peg showering in the hospital. Several times I had helped her shower with the IV pole. The nursing staff would have helped her but I was there and I didn't mind. She felt better about someone familiar being with her and like she wasn't imposing on busy people. I associated the aroma of the shampoo with that setting.

As I rubbed the shampoo into my hair I recalled that I had washed her hair a number of times, though I couldn't remember exactly where. I seemed to recall she washed her own hair in the hospital and I just helped her navigate and get in and out of the shower. At home, when she was still going upstairs, I helped her in and out of the shower and I think I washed her back for her, but I think she did her own hair. I do know when she could no longer go upstairs and was getting so weak, I did help her sponge bathe and I did wash her hair for her in the downstairs bathroom. I remembered gently working the shampoo into her hair and then running my fingers through her hair with clean water to rinse it as she sat on the commode cover and held a basin in her lap.

With my eyes closed, as I continued to rub my own head with the shampoo, I could feel the contour of her head as though I was washing her hair again. Then the aroma and the sense of touching her conspired to overwhelm me. I have discovered the shower is an excellent place for tears. No one is embarrassed or put off by them, they can flow freely accompanied by the sounds of sorrow, and they and the traces they leave are quickly washed away.

I rinsed the shampoo from my hair and lathered a second time, still trying to clarify in my mind if I had shampooed Peg's hair in the hospital, in the upstairs shower, or only the downstairs bathroom. I couldn't get a clear recollection. Finally I concluded it didn't really matter. The shampoo's aroma had brought me back to that period of time when I was so focused on caring for her and that began to dominate my thoughts. In the past I had read about people putting aside their own pursuits in order to immerse themselves in care for a loved one. I couldn't imagine what dedication and self-sacrifice it must take to do that. But now I can honestly say, it came easily in the circumstance. Though I didn't have to give up a job, retire from a career, or set aside other cherished pursuits in life to care for Peg in the brief period of her worsening illness, I think I could have done those things if necessary. There was nothing else I wanted to do. Had it gone on longer, I don't know how I would have dealt with it, but I like to think she would have continued to be my priority.

To become so immersed in another's well-being and care exposed something in me I had no idea was there. Perhaps that's because it wasn't. It wasn't there until it was needed and then God gave it through me. It is a humbling thing to think that God through us might accompany someone else through illness, distress and death—that in us the Good Shepherd might fulfill the promise that He made to walk with us through the valley of the shadow of death. Though I have been troubled by what God allowed Peg to go through if He really loved her, perhaps He loved her through it, in part, through me and others around her who cared for her and did all they could. It's not the way I had in mind for God to handle her illness, but then I hardly grasp the mind of God anyway. What I do grasp is that the sense of smell can inspire some very vivid memories the way I have heard it can.

It was the shampoo again! Each morning when I use it, I deliberately notice the aroma and it takes me back to Peg in the hospital. Though I don't find the setting very appealing, I eagerly anticipate the sense of her presence that scent rekindles. This morning, as I experienced that connection once again, I remembered how much she hated to be sick. How difficult it must have been for her to lay there in a hospital bed so many times, especially as her health deteriorated. I saw once again how her appearance began to reflect her declining health with her narrowing face and fading color. In an outburst of emotion, I cried out to the Lord, "How could you let it happen to her? How could you let her suffer and die like that?" What came back to my mind, though not exactly Scripture, which I cannot now quote verbatim, was obviously God speaking to me. "I am not the God of death and suffering. I am the God of life. I have given her life!"

Yes, if this life was all there is and God let Peg suffer and pass into oblivion, then my outcry would have no consolation. But there was consolation in what the Lord said to me. As the water of the shower washed over me, I began to feel a calming peace. I believe that's what God was doing—consoling me. Not explaining or justifying, as if He has to do either, but consoling, saying, in essence, "It is not for nothing. Her suffering and premature death is all you see. But I see her alive with me forever, never again to suffer what she did in the world where you are."

To be God and to let your creatures suffer, die, and cease to exist might be your divine prerogative, but to what end? From the human point of view, there seems no sense to it at all. If God is the God of life, and His nature is love and mercy, as the Bible claims, then it makes sense for life to be the final outcome of suffering and death. There is consolation not only in that thought but in the fact that God even bothers to offer consolation to we who encounter those things and remain alive.

However, consolation doesn't cancel the sorrow of her pain. I can still feel it with her. What it does do is add something else to experience besides the pain. Remaining acquainted with the suffering and death would seem morbid except that God wanted to "taste death"[14] —to experience it for Himself in Jesus—to see what it was like, and without a divine edge, for He refused to take even the crudest of pain numbing drugs on the cross so that He could "drink the cup"[15] to the full. I believe God also wants us to "taste"

---

14   Hebrews 2:9

15   Matthew 26:42

suffering and death so that we have some sense of the seriousness of it and the magnitude of life itself. He's willing for us to do that because He can console us about those things, suffering and death—He's been there.

Though I can still get in touch with the sorrow of Peg's suffering, I need not feel despair because God can console it with life. The "cup" I have to finish is not exactly a cup, it's a bottle—a bottle of shampoo to be exact. I could discard it and avert the risk of despair, but I doubt I will. There is anticipation of the sensory connection to Peg it brings but there is now also the prospect of consolation from the Lord. Both are worth the risk.

Death has distanced me from the created world. I'm referring to Peg's death of course. Several days after writing during a rainstorm about camping in our little recreation vehicle, I realized how distanced I feel from God's creation. To understand all of that, I have to back up to how I got close to God's creation in the first place.

I grew up in one of the little copper mining communities on the Keweenaw Peninsula of Upper Michigan. We lived in a little rural settlement of about 15 families scattered over what was once a much larger settlement. But when the mining industry declined over the years, some of the homes were torn down and others remained vacant. A handful of mines were still operating in the region when I was growing up but many others had closed, and like the homes, the mining structures were torn down or abandoned. Nature was reclaiming the land that had been logged off for timber for the mine shafts and fuel for the boilers, or cleared for buildings, poor rock piles, and railroads, and reclaiming the streams that had been dammed up for water sources for steam engines and smelting operations.

Secondary growth slowly encroached on the sands from the stamp mills and the rock piles from the mines, and cattails took over the man-made dams. It became wonderful habitat for wildlife and growing children, especially boys. Of course, that exposed me to a lot of nature's abundance in the form of pond and woodland creatures, as well as flowers in a variety of habitats. With inclinations and talent toward drawing, I began to see nature's creatures and scenery as the subject for some of my creative efforts. But then I became interested in the subjects of my artwork and began to appreciate them and to want to know more about them.

An older cousin, who had an interest in wildlife, inspired and fed my curiosity, and for a period of time I thought I might pursue a career in biology or zoology. Commercial art was also a consideration, simply because it seemed like a feasible way to make a living doing something I enjoyed.

But then I discovered photography and that was it. For a time I delved into nature photography aspiring to work for National Geographic—that was my ideal—but eventually practical considerations prevailed, I broadened my photographic vision, and I went to school for commercial and portrait photography. After Peg and I married, we bought a small town studio and I put my commercial and portrait training together, becoming a sort of general practitioner.

Peg enjoyed camping and traveling, especially to visit the scenic wonders of our beautiful country. That fit right in with my interest in nature and scenic photography. Then several years into our marriage, we both came to faith and I came to view the natural world as God's creation, which gave me a new sense of awe for something I had already learned to appreciate and another reason to photograph it. So over the years, our collection of scenic and nature slides continued to grow with pictures taken in well-known places like Florida's teeming swamps, Maine's rugged seacoast, Lake Superior's stormy waters, Wyoming's majestic mountains, California's impressive red woods, Arizona's amazing Grand Canyon, and a variety of well-known and not-so-well-known places in between. Even though the collection of little yellow Kodak slide boxes in the closet had become substantial, there were still many places on our list to visit.

On our last spring vacation together, we spent one beautiful day on the beach near Charleston, South Carolina. We sat in the warm sand, propped up against a sand dune as we ate our lunch, then read for awhile. Peg's back and legs felt better than they had for some time, which we attributed to the warm sand conformed to her body contour, and she said afterward she remembered that as the last really good day she had. She was able to walk along the shore barefoot in the sand, splashing in the salty sea water as the waves rolled in, and we felt like a couple of kids on the beach stopping to pick up shells and other ocean treasures the tide put in our path. When it came to an end, we were both thankful for that wonderful spring day when she felt so good and we felt so in touch with God's wonderful world.

But I think I speak for both of us when I say that was Peg's last real intimate experience with God's created world and the last time I felt that close to Him through His handiwork as well. When we got home, Peg's illness began to get more serious as the weather was becoming more pleasant. Ordinarily we would have been making bike excursions into the surrounding countryside on our free time, but now she wasn't able to walk without pain, let alone bike. We made a couple of trips to nearby Bay City on Saginaw Bay, just to park by the boat launch and the walking path along the river, but she couldn't do our usual half-hour walks, and couldn't even sit very long before she was ready to head home.

I have already commented on our vacation plans and how our prospect list no longer feels like mine. Coupled to that is my loss of desire to continue camping with our RV which put us so close to God's created world—something which I have explored in the last division of this writing. The loss of the one who was so much a part of these excursions into God's wonderful creation has taken the joy out of contemplating their continuation, distancing me from all of that even further. Oh, it's not that I no longer enjoy viewing God's created beauty and wonders—there were beautiful silver-lined clouds in tonight's sunset that I would have photographed if it had been convenient—but I just don't have the heart to intentionally pursue such things right now nor can I fathom finding the level of joy that we had in experiencing them together.

Last spring and summer, on my visits to Peg in the hospital or our trips back and forth to the city for medical reasons, now and then I would notice there were blossoms and green leaves and thundershowers. I saw them, but I felt like I was only a passing observer occasionally glancing out of a tiny window at the season going by, not able to get close enough to them to really appreciate them in their sensual fullness. I was preoccupied with more pressing things.

As Peg's illness advanced, I remember putting one of the folding chairs on the front porch. It got the morning sun and she could be outside for a change of scenery and some fresh air. Becky and I helped her get situated and comfortable with pillows and blankets and brought her morning smoothie to her, and whatever else she was willing to drink or eat. We did the same on occasion on the deck in back of the house later in the day. It was her favorite time of year when things were fresh and green, but even then, without knowing what was ahead, it struck me how pathetic that she could only sit there to sense the odors, the breezes, and the sun's warmth when she should have been actively enjoying her favorite season and God's gift of life in His beautiful world.

As summer progressed, I knew it was slipping away and we were missing it once again. For the last several summers we had said, as each new one approached, this summer we really needed to make sure to do outside things and enjoy the season. Since we had been at Freeland, there had been a number of summers that had slipped by us and we lamented them. In the late 90's, I spent the better part of one summer dealing with eye problems, with three eye surgeries and one extended period of rest for healing of my retina. Although Peg was seldom ill per se, she had a reaction to a medication she was given for some oral surgery that upset her digestive system and left her with a bacterial infection that took a long time to finally get diagnosed and treated. It started in the spring and went on into the summer before it was finally resolved and she was not up to her usual level of activity while that was working on her.

In the summer of 2001, her brother in Texas died, and our family traveled together there and back, spending better than a week away. That was also the spring that our congregation moved from the old building to the new and there were so many things going on as part of the transition that we hardly felt like we had time to enjoy outside things and weekend getaways.

In 2002, I took nine weeks of sabbatical to do some reading, planning, and recuperating after seven years of intense ministry with this congregation. Of course, Peg continued working in the office. But my absence from that setting meant that she picked up some of my loose ends administratively. I have to commend the great effort she made to keep me insulated and disengaged from the daily operation and circumstance of the church.

Therefore she was more stressed than usual. Besides that, she had a swollen lymph node in her neck in the spring. She was given an antibiotic for it, which gave her a mild hives reaction.[16] She then had to avoid direct sunlight and didn't feel her usual self. It didn't keep her from doing much except she didn't want to be on the roof of the garage at my family home when we helped my sister tear it down that August. She did take a three week vacation, however, so we could travel and camp together, although it took some convincing to get her to be gone that long. We were able to enjoy that summer more than most in recent years with some concentrated time together, for which I am especially glad now.

One thing we did manage to do most years was plant various annuals in a flower box and pots we hung on the privacy fence along the deck in the back. Peg also put some geraniums in a couple of crocks on the front porch because they seem to do well even without direct sun. In addition, she always looked for some hanging baskets for the front porch. Last spring we never got that done. Bless her heart, Becky took care of that and beautified both settings with flowers in the flower containers we usually used. So when Peg was able to be outside, it was in a pleasant and familiar setting. It brought a sense of normalcy to both places that said life is going on, although we didn't know that Peg's life would not last as long as those flowers she was enjoying.

Now with sole domestic responsibility, I find I spend more time in the house dealing with meals, laundry, cleaning, personal business and finances, as well as maintaining relationships with family and other people. Thankfully

---

16   In retrospect, I now believe that was a sign of the lymphoma, but when the antibiotic relieved the swelling, none of us, including her doctor, saw any need to suspect anything else. This is one of those "if only's" I have struggled with.

a good friend and neighbor just a few doors down the street often cuts the grass when it starts to look a little shaggy, which it does after only a few days with the wet and cool late spring and early summer we have had. That all adds up to spending less time outside for me increasing the feeling of being distanced from the outside world.

I had hoped to spend some of tomorrow doing some outside things and going to granddaughter, Rachael's, last regular softball game—I haven't been to one of her games yet this season. But just this afternoon I was asked to do a funeral for a relative of one of our parishioners, which I accepted. That means tomorrow, which is normally my day off (Monday), I'll be meeting with family members to discuss the service, making arrangements for other people's participation, and getting started on preparations for the funeral message. What else I do will depend on how all of that goes. June is almost gone, I still feel very much removed from the season, and once again I'm beginning to get the feeling that summer is slipping by too rapidly.

I have done one small thing, however, that I hope will connect me more closely with not only the past but God's created world. This year, when the country craft store and apple orchard just down the road, owned and operated by our associate pastor and family, added bedding plants to their wares, I collected up the flower box and other flower containers and took them in. I asked if they would plant whatever they thought would look good and do well in those settings, asking only that the pots to sit in the crocks have the usual geraniums. When I went outside the other morning, all the flower containers were sitting under the flowering crab where the sidewalk meets the driveway, looking very attractive and alive. Someone had dropped them off perhaps while I was in the shower. They are now in place and are, I suppose, my way of trying to see the life and beauty of this world, God's creation, going on even without Peg, as it will one day go on without me as well. Perhaps they will help to close the gap with the outside world of nature just a little. That's a lot to expect a few bedding plants and flowers hanging on a privacy fence and sitting on a front porch to do. But they're God's handiwork, as is all the natural world that Peg and I enjoyed together. As I come and go, I can't help but see those plants and flowers—that's why they're there—and they will need my attention to survive...

Clean socks; frozen beets; stuffing mix. These three all have one thing in common. Peg provided each of them for me. Eleven months after her death, I am still benefiting from the things she did as she cared for our domestic needs. Peg and I followed traditional roles in our home life. She did the cooking, cleaning, and laundry. I did the yard work, and the household and vehicle maintenance and repairs. She paid the bills and balanced the checkbook. I handled the budgeting and financial business.

As I work with couples in preparation for marriage, I review the wedding ceremony with them and comment on the various statements that are a part of the traditional vows. One of the statements in the United Methodist version of the ritual says, "Will you love...comfort...honor, and keep..." After commenting on the love, comfort, and honor part, I usually say that the word "keep" seems like an odd thing to promise, and, No! it isn't like going fishing where some are "keepers" and others you throw back. I tell them I think what the word "keep" means in this context is to take care of. I often say I know it isn't a good image for marriage, but it's like animals in a zoo—they are "kept"—they have everything that they need provided. In marriage, we are making a commitment to provide for each other's needs, to "keep" each other by doing our part to look after the life circumstances of the other. I go on to say it doesn't matter how you divide up the roles and responsibilities in life as long as it's mutually agreeable. But what does matter is that you carry out your part for your partner's benefit, "keeping" him or her, doing your part to look after the other's life needs.

Peg and I followed the traditional roles most of our lives, although, like many couples today, we could each cross over and handle at least some of the other's responsibilities when needed. So Peg didn't put in a full work week in our business when we operated our photo studio. During slower times, I would handle things alone. If I had appointments, she would come in to handle the phone or customers so I wouldn't be interrupted causing clients inconvenience. Then as our son, Mike, started school, we hired part time high school girls to work as receptionists after school and on Saturdays so she could be home when he got out of school. That also gave her time at home to accomplish some of her domestic tasks.

When we moved to Kentucky for me to attend seminary, she worked a full work week at the University of Kentucky as a secretary in Cooperative Extension, a job she truly loved, but she was gone nearly ten hours five days a week. Since we lived only a half-mile from the seminary and I was a full time student without employment, I took over most of the domestic chores like preparation of the evening meal, laundry, some of the cleaning, and grocery shopping. On weekends, however, she usually did the meal preparation. I think she felt like she was giving me a break and it kept her in touch with the kitchen.

Peg was never a fancy cook. Her meals were basic but always good. Her most outstanding dish was lasagna, a recipe she picked up on her own, which reflected her Italian heritage. Her national identity must have somehow seeped into the dish itself, because it was always excellent. So far, it's the meal she made that I often think about and lament not having the most. Although she wasn't really an enthusiastic cook, she truly did love to bake. Her idea of a good day at home was to spend it baking with the stereo or the TV on. I liked those days too because it meant good things to eat, very often chocolate chip cookies, and if I was lucky enough to be around when they came out of the oven, I might get warm samples with the chocolate still soft and runny.

When we returned to Michigan and our first pastorate, Peg again took over the household. I found it a challenge just to keep up with the demands of my first ministry to three rural churches of 200 members separated by 15 miles of farm land. Mike, who was a teenager at that point and a "car guy," handled much of the yard work and even much of the vehicle maintenance. Over the years, the churches did take care of repairs and major maintenance of the parsonages, although I continued to do some light and emergency repairs when necessary or because it was sometimes simpler or expedient to do them myself.

When Peg took on the full time position as secretary (really administrative assistant) at Freeland, she worked anywhere from 20 to 30 hours a week. That allowed her enough time to keep up with household responsibilities, although she always found it a challenge to get heavy cleaning and house cleaning done. Housekeeping was not something she enjoyed anyway. She struggled with it all her life, had read several books in recent years looking for techniques and inspiration, and subscribed to an E-mail homemakers' newsletter for motivation. She would always say, "Susie Homemaker I'm not!" And she was right. In the final analysis, it came down to other things being more important to her, especially people things.

I wouldn't, however, want anyone to get the wrong impression that we lived in filth. We have seen households where that was true and Peg abhorred that. We did often live in clutter, to which both of us were contributors. Her style was to eventually go through and put everything in shape, which she could do in short order, usually because there was company coming. We would both joke about it being a good thing that we had company once and awhile so we would deal with our clutter. Once Peg had it shaped up, she would then allow it to accumulate again and the cycle would begin all over again. I have continued the tradition with the dining table being the place where things are set down to deal with later, eating my meals in the family room.

Housework was a digression for Peg that interfered with the things she really enjoyed and was good at which involved people and working with office equipment for word processing and document production. Her weekly worship bulletins, monthly newsletters, meeting minutes, and other paperwork were always neat, attractive, and done well. "Good enough" wasn't good enough and she would do things over that were only "good enough" until they met her standards of excellence. She took pride in her spelling and grammar skills, which I sorely miss as a resource in my writing.

In more recent years, particularly as I began to do more of my work on the computer in the study at home, Peg would make meal preparations before going to work, and I might start them cooking at the appropriate time. I would often fix brunch on Monday, our day off, and would occasionally help her with cleaning, especially heavy cleaning when we were under pressure to get things done before company arrived, but she continued to manage our domestic life. (At least I do not have the trauma of not knowing how to handle basic domestic chores. I suggest to wedding couples that both partners learn how to handle what the other does so they can cross over, if need be. Then if one is incapacitated for a time, the other can take over without the trauma of complete disorientation. And although preparation for marriage is a happy occasion and we don't like to think about such things, I point out that if one is left on his or her own, the one who remains doesn't have the stress of learning how to deal with basic life needs and business added to the trauma of loss.)

Even though I think I am getting along OK domestically, I am repeatedly reminded of Peg's absence as I encounter things she handled or prepared. The other day, it was socks. As I opened the drawer in my dresser where I keep my socks, something was hanging over the back of the drawer into the inside part of the dresser. I pulled out the drawer to remove it and there, to my surprise, were two pair of socks neatly tucked into round balls the way that Peg used to do them. She would tuck one sock inside the other so that they were shaped like a rose hip or a blueberry. I reached in and took them out, one pair in each hand, and looked at them.

I had started out doing socks the same way when I took over the laundry in Kentucky. Then when I began doing our laundry while Peg was so sick, I naturally did the same thing. A few months ago, as I realized I now only need to accommodate myself, I began to simply dump the socks out of the laundry basket on the desk in the bedroom, which I don't use since I no longer need to go up there to work in privacy. As I need socks, I pick out one with the color I want, find its mate, and put them on. But when I was pairing socks, my work was never as neat as Peg's. Each pair always came out very round with only a slight edge around the opening where the other sock was tucked inside. I don't know that she was trying to be particular, it was just the consistency she developed from years of pairing and folding socks and underwear—something she usually did by bringing the laundry basket into the living room or family room so she could watch TV while she worked. So I'm reasonably sure Peg had done the socks I found behind the drawer because mine were sometimes elongated, had long floppy lips around the opening, and were very inconsistent. These were very well rounded and uniform in shape and she had very likely been the last one to touch them.

Still I wondered, how could they have been there so long without my discovering them. Then I remembered a while back buying heavy casual socks and having trouble getting the drawer closed when all my socks were clean. Opening and closing the drawer must have rolled them toward the back and finally they fell over the back of the drawer into the enclosed drawer space, resting there until I pulled out the drawer and found them. I stood there with them in my hands feeling a little over-awed that she was the last one to handle them and that I was still benefiting from the work she did in keeping her marriage vows, "keeping" me.

Those feelings, that I am even yet the beneficiary of things she did, are not unusual in the kitchen for I encounter them most commonly in meal preparation. Just yesterday I used up one of two stuffing mixes Peg had on the shelf. I made it in a saucepan, added peas, carrots, and cut up turkey meat I'd frozen a few weeks ago, making a main dish out of it. I still have a number of packages of frozen beets that Peg made up from beets my sister brought to us, grown in her garden. Most of the frozen food Peg prepared I have used but there are still cans of tomato sauce, tomato paste, fruit, and other ingredients she kept on hand for her meal recipes. Perhaps I will add some of her recipes to my menu as time goes on, although my main meals now are very basic usually consisting of rice, pasta, or potatoes, vegetables, and a serving of meat or fish, with a couple of soup and salad meals each week. So at this rate, I will have the canned goods she purchased for awhile yet.

While there are plenty to choose from, taking any of those items off the shelf and using them up seems just fine, even kind of neat, knowing that Peg provided them. There's one package of stuffing mix left. I don't think I'll be stuffing a turkey, and there's enough left over from the one I just made for another meal. So that will probably be around awhile. The beets have a little more significance because she prepared those herself. I will eat them but I'm not as crazy about beets as Peg was, so they'll last awhile. The big issue right now is those socks. I must admit, the thought of undoing those socks and wearing them feels a little traumatic. All I can determine is that somehow, as I contemplate using the last of the things she touched, handled, and prepared I am severing my connections with her in this world. I can't fathom that I'm saying such a thing, much less feeling that way, but so much of what I've experienced in this last year hasn't made good rational sense. And I can tell myself I should "know better" but that doesn't make it "feel better."

So I set the socks aside telling myself I wanted to keep them intact until I had time to explore my thoughts and feelings about them, and I have. Now I have to face undoing them, the work of Peg's hands, and wearing them, after which they will blend in with all the other socks and lose the uniqueness that came from her. They're only socks, that's all they will be once I put them on and they join the rest of the laundry, but right now they seem to be so much more. So that's what socks, beets, and stuffing mix have in common—they are tangible evidence that Peg "kept" me and her vow to "Love...comfort... honor, and keep...." It has been terribly hard to lose her, hard to lose her daily love, comfort, honor and keeping. I do believe I have relinquished her, the person she had become, into the Lord's hands—that's done. Still I have to continue relinquishing these little evidences of her, one meal and one change of socks at a time, and that's not all done. But then, what's the rush?

It was a year ago today that Peg had her last radiation treatment. As we drove home from the hospital, I remember how I tried to bring a sense of celebration to it being over, hoping to give her a sense of progress. But she was so exhausted, she was just glad to get it done and to get home and sleep. Her physical misery overshadowed any possibility of elation. So my sense of optimism for her was nullified by the fact that she felt so badly. I couldn't celebrate with her and I couldn't celebrate for her. That anniversary from a year ago today brings back that last period of almost three weeks she spent at home between hospitalizations—a time during which her health and condition continued to decline.

Like today, as the anniversary of various events in Peg's illness come, I try to remember them, which is just a matter of looking at the "Peg's Illness Timeline" document I put together after she died. Remembering isn't pleasant in most instances and I'm not sure why it seems important, still it does satisfy something in me—perhaps the need to *not* forget.

I can identify with the World War II veterans who recently returned to France to commemorate the 60th anniversary of the Normandy Invasion and remember that fateful event. As they walked over what once were battlefields, observing where life and death encounters took place, remembering their own fears and suffering and the suffering and tragic deaths of close friends, I could identify. I too am walking through the battlefield of a year ago where Peg fought—we fought—with cancer, remembering her struggle, suffering, and tragic death. War is certainly a horror on a whole different scale than any I have experienced. Still I know what it is like to remember desperate actions, dreadful feelings, and the horrors of a fateful struggle in which a close friend suffers and loses life.

I suppose the redeeming factor for the survivors of Normandy is knowing how it came out in the end and the satisfaction of just having been there and having a part, no matter how big or small, in the monumental invasion that set in motion the eventual end of global conflict—they made a difference. All made a difference in the eventual outcome of the conflict and some made a difference in the immediate outcome of the action around them. As I remember the anniversary of each event in Peg's struggle, I too remember what we had to do, the feelings, and the trauma of Peg's illness progressing. And I too remember the outcome. As we went through it, it was an ebb and flow of dread and hope with treatments and relief from pain and distress and the onset of new dilemmas and uncertainty. I tried to make a difference in the outcome of the conflict, but nothing I could do made victory possible. But I think I did make a difference in actions around us in which we were engaged on a daily basis.

Although I don't remember specific instances when she said so, I know Peg was appreciative and thanked me. "Thank you for taking such good care of me" are her words I know I heard often enough that they linger in my mind. I had forgotten them until this writing. She was the only one who ever commended my care for her that I can recall. And I have to confess, it would have been affirming to hear that I did take good care of her, not to feed my ego, just simply to assure me that I did, if in fact I did, to ward off regret.

Regrets seem to be common in the aftermath of a partner's death and like most others, I have some. They are mostly preceded by the words, "why" and "should have." Why didn't I say "I love you" more often? Why didn't I take Peg to more concerts and places she liked to go? Why didn't I take her on an overseas trip somewhere? Should I have been more assertive about seeking medical attention when she started having trouble and more aggressive about finding answers when we weren't getting any? Should I have encouraged her to seek medical attention elsewhere? Should I have...Why didn't I... I have attempted to work my way through some of those questions rationally, though they still have some emotional kick a year later.

One of my biggest regrets came several months after Peg's death when I read a booklet written for those who are facing terminal illness. I wanted to try to grasp what it was like from her side. The booklet said, "You grieve your illness and the limitations it brings, your family and loved ones you will leave behind, and your hopes and your dreams for the future. As you approach death, coming to terms with the losses you will face is a difficult but necessary process."[17] Peg was troubled by her decreasing mobility and strength. She said to me, with obvious grief in her eyes and her voice as she touched my face, "I'm worried about you." There were still things she wanted to do, most of all to see her grandchildren grow up. In retrospect, I know Peg experienced many of the things she hoped for, but at the time I never thought about her losses as grief in facing death. I only thought about keeping her free of pain and getting her well, until it came down to the last few days. Then when it was evident she was going to die, I was so stunned, I hardly thought to help her grieve.

Months later, after reading the booklet, I began to feel maybe I wasn't as much help to her as I thought. And so I teeter precariously between feelings that I looked after her physical and medical needs but was oblivious to her emotional and spiritual needs. So as I go through Peg's illness again, once removed by a year this time, it is mostly with sorrow over what I know the outcome was in the end and with some regrets: that things didn't turn out differently; that I wasn't more sensitive to Peg's inner experience of illness and dying; that I didn't take her physical distress more seriously early on; I should have...why didn't I...?

Raymond Mitsch and Lynn Brookside, in their book, *Grieving the Loss of Someone You Love,* say, "It is nearly inevitable that we will go through intense self-examination following the death of someone we love....We all have regrets."[18] I know I do and remembering freshens them in the present and runs the risk of creating new ones. But I suspect once the first year has passed, the dates will not be so prominent each succeeding year. And perhaps the Lord will help me to feel that I need not regret my care of Peg—if we lost the war we won some battles just the same.

In my ministry, for a long time, even before Peg's illness, the Lord led me to pray not only for those who have a serious illness but for those, usually family members, who are going through it with them. I began to observe that the one whose body has the disease or ailment suffers the physical symptoms and distress, but those around them, especially family care-givers, also suffer from the illness. They may not feel the physical pain but they suffer everything from sympathetic pain to helplessness to anxiety to hopelessness, grieving with and for the one who is afflicted. Their lives are altered by the changes that affect the other, which is as it should be when people are in relationships. I do not know all that people deal with in the long-term chronic illness of

---

17 *Journey's End: Characteristics of the Dying Process* published by Excel Printing/Publishing Services, Overland Park, Kansas, © 2002.

18 Raymond R. Mitsch and Lynn Brookside, *Grieving the Loss of Someone You Love,* (Ventura, CA: Regal Books, 1993) p. 97.

a loved one, except I have seen enough to know their lives can be radically altered and changed forever too. But I do know when death comes, the one who died is set free of that illness and the survivors are left in an aftermath of grief with an assortment of doubts, shattered dreams, sorrow, and/or regrets.

I am asking the Lord to help me be more attuned to the regrets of surviving care-givers. Whether they are people I know well or hardly at all, which is often the case when I am called for a funeral, they may need to hear that the care they provided and what they have done hasn't gone unnoticed in the world or by God. God doesn't want us shackled by regrets. Where there is genuinely something to regret, it can be forgiven, which is another matter entirely. But where there are regrets resulting from the usual maze of "I should have's...and why didn't I's...?" I see they can be bridled and tamed if not completely overcome.

In their attempt to minimize regrets, Mitsch and Brookside close their meditation on "Forgiving Yourself" with 2 Corinthians 7:10 and I will close with it as well from the version called *The Message.* "Distress that drives us to God does that. It turns us around. It gets us back in the way of salvation. We never regret that kind of pain. But those who let distress drive them away from God are full of regrets, end up on a deathbed of regrets." No one who remains in this world should be separated from God and afflicted by regrets as a lingering contagion from a loved one's pain and terminal illness. One victim is more than sufficient! Lord, remind me of that in all the anniversaries of these next weeks.

Others who have lost a life partner tell me it's the little things that get you—and they're right. By mid-afternoon I finished my preparations for tomorrow's Sunday service so I decided to go into the city to run some errands and do some shopping. As I was coming home, I thought about picking up something to eat, rather than have to fix something after unpacking and putting away groceries and other items. But I'd had my big meal at noon and decided it wouldn't take long to put together a light supper. There were some things that should be eaten anyway. As I thought about it I realized I was tired, it was already into the evening, and besides it was Saturday. So I decided to stop at a sub-sandwich shop and pick up something I would enjoy and wouldn't make at home.

As I was coming out of the shop with my sandwich, it hit me. This was exactly what we would have done on a Saturday if Peg was with me. We'd have picked up sandwiches, hamburgers, or a pizza, what we called a "fun meal," to take home to eat while we watched a movie on tape together. We often did that in similar circumstance. We would haul in the groceries and other things we'd purchased. Peg would put away anything that needed to be refrigerated or frozen and we'd have supper. Then she'd take a break from the movie to put the other things away after we ate and we'd settle down later to finish the film. It was no big deal, just something we did together now and then as a conclusion to a mutual shopping trip.

Picking up a sub-sandwich for supper tonight was no big deal either but it certainly stirred up my emotions in a big way as I got back in the car and headed home. Others are right. There are so many little things that come out of nowhere to rub the raw spots of sorrow and solitude. A friend whose husband died more than ten years ago said finding his hat hanging in the garage got to her years after he was gone.

I have decided it's sort of like turning on the faucet, and not because the tears may flow, though they surely can. You get a nice strong flow of water from the faucet but it's nothing compared to the big reservoir of water that is stored up at the water company. The little stream coming out of the pipes in the house taps into something much larger beyond.

A little sandwich tapped into the reservoir of feelings of being alone and missing the companionship of shopping, running errands, watching movies, and eating a Saturday night "fun" supper with my life partner. All of that never seemed like a very big deal when we did those things, but it sure is now. And it's no use to wonder about what it will be next because it will be just some little thing I'll not see until it turns on the bigger things.

This past week has been the hardest personally and professionally that I can remember in recent years. Throughout the week several people came unannounced to me as the church's pastor needing assistance materially and otherwise. A couple of parishioners needed urgent medical attention and one was hospitalized for surgery. A teenage boy who had been battling leukemia for seven years had relapsed in the spring and died a week ago today. Both Peg and I had gotten very close to his family over the years so there were not only issues for me to deal with professionally, but personally as well. The grief I shared with this family over their loss also stirred up sorrow for all of us over Peg and her death. Then the day after the boy's death, a retired couple of the church were in a car accident and the husband was tragically killed while the wife survived without major injury. The funerals on succeeding days both filled the church and involved more than minimal arrangements and preparation.

All this was on the heels of the deaths in the two preceding weeks of two older long-time church members who both left surviving spouses. So this meant that in three weeks I had ministered with four families and conducted four funerals, not just for people loosely connected with the church, but with people most of whom I knew well, and some very well. In fact, in the last five months, I have conducted ten funerals, which are more than I have conducted in all but one year since I've been in ministry.

At the same time personal matters have been on my mind. My son, Mike, was traveling in Australia doing seminars and retreats. That's always a concern, not only because of the air travel, but the exhausting schedule and the fact that he is entirely on his own—no partner and no sponsoring agency or institution. In addition, my mother's health continues to gradually decline with osteoporosis, congestive heart failure, kidney failure, and now some ensuing mental confusion. She lives more than 450 highway miles away (nine hours of driving time) with my sister who lives at home with her but needs to work as well as provide for her care. Thankfully Mom is still able to look after her own needs during the workday, with some visiting assistants and now minimal Hospice care. But my sister is finding our mother's needs impinging more and more on her available time, energy, and wherewithal.

I am supposed to begin a couple weeks of vacation tomorrow, most of which I have intended to spend with family. But now there's a complication. To really put the frosting on the cake, I came down with what seems to be a cold or sinus infection and laryngitis. It started out like seasonal allergies for late summer but seems to have settled in my sinuses and throat. Thankfully, the Sunday in the middle of all this I had planned as a song service and we sang the congregations favorite hymns, so I didn't have a sermon to prepare or preach. In addition, I was to be away this Sunday so didn't have a sermon to prepare this week either. But by the first funeral, I had to push to speak and by the second funeral, I had less than half a voice. Thankfully our sound technician is good on the mixing board and did wonders with what I had. But I'm concerned about bringing sickness into the household up north and my traveling is on hold 'til I see how things go with this respiratory thing.

I've experienced periods before when things seemed to accrue together at certain points in time, although not usually to this extreme. And I'm sure there are colleagues who could "one-up" my situation. It's not my intent to "cry the blues."[19] The only point in mentioning it now is that today is one year to the day (Friday) of Peg's death. For awhile, as I anticipated its coming, I wondered how I would deal with this day, never thinking that I would come upon it so abruptly at the end of such a week, exhausted and not feeling very well.

Last evening (Thursday), Becky and the grandchildren and a mutual friend came and brought supper. We all enjoyed one of Becky's wonderful meals and a visit. Then they went to begin their family vacation time at a nearby resort motel where Mike was to join them when he flew in today.

I went to wait with them at the airport this morning and to see Mike come in about 10:00am. Although I had remembered the time of Peg's death was 9:00am, when the time came around, I was getting ready to leave for the airport and it escaped me. Later on about 10:30, while we were waiting for Mike to track down his lost luggage, I realized the hour had come and gone and I had missed it. I thought I might feel intense remorse over it but I didn't. Oh, I regretted I hadn't remembered to take even a minute to pray and I thought about that exact anniversary being gone forever, but it seemed OK. It was still the day, if not the hour.

It was later in the day that the stronger mix of feelings came. They say good things come in threes and that was true today—in this case, three cards. One came yesterday in the form of a card which I reread today that said, "With Caring Thoughts" requesting "May the Lord bless you with the strength you need as you deal with the many situations." It was from very good friends who were aware of much I was dealing with and the coincidental timing of things. Though it never mentioned Peg's death directly, I understood what was meant.

The other two good things were cards that came today. One was from neighbors who sent "A Prayer For You In Time of Need" and were "... thinking of you at this time." Again, I knew the need they were thinking of, and though they didn't know all the other needs, I knew the One who hears prayers heard theirs in the fullest sense. The other card today was from a very caring couple in the church who have been supportive and thoughtful right from the beginning and especially so throughout this whole ordeal. "We especially want you to know we are keeping you in our hearts and prayers on the anniversary of Peg's death. We all miss her so much. Love..." I appreciated

---

19 The day after writing this I read Acts 20:13-38 as part of my morning devotions. In this passage Paul is on his way to Jerusalem, not expecting to see many of the believers ever again in this world. He recounts the hardships he went through in his ministry and challenges them to be diligent in their work for Jesus Christ. Lest I should start to feel sorry for myself, the Lord reminded me of the nature of the work and life to which those who serve Him are called.

their willingness to actually mention Peg and her death—the only people who have directly done so to me on this day.

It amazes me how sentiments can sometimes evoke tearful and heart-wrenching responses, and yet satisfy something deep within. It must be the reason people like sad movies or stories—but then when you think about it, every completed biography ends with departure from this life.

I received all the cards not just as greetings or sentiments like those that come at Christmas or birthdays but as wonderful gifts. And, yes, I know last night's dinner was a "gift card" too—a real gift of thoughtfulness, labor, love and presence—their way of saying what friends, neighbors, and people of the church each said in their own way, "We know, we remember, and we care." Again I am blessed by God and touched by those He works through.

It was my intent today to reread "Appendix A: Illness and Death," that I wrote last fall. I wanted to remember all that led up to that Friday a year ago. As I did, it vigorously stirred the mix of feelings. And so it served the primary purpose it was written for. It took me back into the tangled journey with medical people, friends, church friends, neighbors, family, and even strangers, through a mixture of uncertainty, shock, dread, hope, frustration, doubt, gratitude, resignation, and sadness that were ours until Peg finally left for home "…and she was gone at 9:00am." Rereading that part was intensely overwhelming, even a year later.

When I started writing "Part I – Aftermath," I thought aftermath would last until I returned to ministry after my leave of absence. Then I would begin dealing with individuation. But it became obvious, much of what I continued to encounter was not just part of becoming an individual again. It was still aftermath, things I had to deal with and face because of her death. Then I remembered people talking about "the first year" and going through things the first time and began to think once the first year is over the aftermath of Peg's death will begin to minimize. But I now believe aftermath has no last page with "the end" as a conclusion. Though I expect it will diminish, which I am finding true, I do not think it will go away, for if it did, it seems like it would detract from the blessings Peg and I had and what I continue to have because of her. Counselors learn that the things from the past that exert power and influence on people in the present do so because they have significance and meaning. So it seems to me dealing with aftermath, as long as it isn't debilitating, is a sign of the significance of the past—for me, a sign of the blessings, joy, and satisfaction Peg and I found in each other and our marriage.

Except for observing the exact time of Peg's death, I was able to carry out most of my intentions for this day, although I feel that the circumstances may have somewhat diminished my ability to enter into them. Maybe it was the Lord's way of distracting me from more maudlin introspection. I did have time to reflect and remember and explore the day's significance. And again today, as on other occasions meaningful to me, blessings came in ways I wouldn't have expected. All the more to the glory of God "...who is able to do immeasurably more than all we ask or imagine, according to his power that is at work within us, to him be glory in the church and in Christ Jesus throughout all generations, for ever and ever! Amen," – Ephesians 3:20-21.

Friday was Peg's death-day, the day of the week a year ago she died; today was the anniversary of her eternal birthday, August 8, 2003. I am indebted to Harold Ivan Smith for the "eternal birthday" idea. In his book, *Once In a Lifetime: Reflections upon the Death of a Father,* he says about his dad, "I think his day of birth is no longer as important as his date of death. For in eternity, his date of death becomes his eternal birthday. And boy, do they celebrate!"[20]

I didn't feel like celebrating Peg's "death-day." As I said previously, I wanted to remember that day looking back over all the trauma we went through leading up to it. But Smith's observations about "eternal birthday" had a forward look and such hope and anticipation attached to it, I wanted that too.

Originally I scheduled my summer vacation for the middle two weeks of August. I would conduct the church service on the 8th and then begin my time away. But as I worked with the planning for the services up to my vacation, I realized I would be scheduled to preach on the date of Peg's death, and I decided I didn't want either the distraction or the occupation. (I hadn't yet thought about the distinction between the day of death [Friday] and the date of death [Sunday]). So I added the 8th to my already scheduled time to be away. I didn't know what I would do with the day, but I didn't want to be conducting worship and preaching. I asked myself if that was avoidance of something but I decided it was actually confronting things when it would have been easy to escape into the familiar routine.

As it turned out, the Lord's provision was in it. A newly certified lay speaker in the church came forward and said she felt she needed to volunteer

---

20   Harold Ivan Smith, *Once In a Lifetime: Reflections Upon the Death of a Father,* (Originally published by Thomas Nelson, Nashville, TN, 1989; © acquired by Augsburg Fortress Publishers: Minneapolis, MN), pp. 92-93.

.to conduct worship whenever there was occasion—no rush, just whenever... I said, boy do I have an opportunity for you! and we worked together to help her prepare for the day. Indeed it was providential for me because of my exhaustion at that point and illness besides, as mentioned earlier.

But what to do with the day? With all that had happened up to then, I wasn't prepared to leave to spend time on my own somewhere and now there were concerns about visiting family if my illness was contagious. In conversation with my sister the previous evening, I had at least decided if things didn't seem very improved I would go to a walk-in clinic and find out what I had and whether it was contagious or not. Then I would know whether I could begin to turn the wheels to head north. When I got up this morning, my right eye was filled with matter but not as bloodshot and the left one seemed pretty good. I still had some congestion and a tickle in my throat but that seemed a little better. I equivocated. It seemed to be clearing up but I still didn't know exactly what it was. A church friend had mentioned the day before that his wife had pink-eye and I had been to a meeting awhile back that she attended. I knew that was highly contagious. If that's what I had, I was definitely risking infecting others, so I decided to get it checked out.

I really wanted to participate in worship somewhere, however, so I decided to join Rev. Robert Schuller's congregation on television. (I had been one of his parishioners in the past when I was confined following back surgery and later on, eye surgery.) Rev. Schuller began the service with the familiar words from Psalm 118:24, "This is the day the LORD has made; let us rejoice and be glad in it." That sounded to me like appropriate celebration for an eternal birthday and my spirit was lifted and hopeful.

Then the choir sang an anthem with *The Prayer of St. Francis* as the lyrics, and the words "It is in dying that we are born to eternal life" were timely. Happy eternal birthday, Peg! Surely this was going to be a special day.

After getting cleaned up and having breakfast, I headed for the walk-in clinic in Midland. The route I took was the way Peg and I often went together to the hospital and traveling it for medical purposes felt very familiar. But I noticed that it didn't have the stigma today that it sometimes did, even recently. I took that as a sign that perhaps something was changing for me.

The diagnosis at the clinic affirmed my decision to go there. Yes, the physician's assistant said, I had a sinus infection, inflamed lining in my throat, and pink-eye. She gave me a prescription for eye drops and an antibiotic and sent me on my way telling me definitely not to visit my mother for at least three days.

As I stopped at the drug store, I concluded this wasn't really my idea of celebration, but I figured I'd be home by noon and things would take a different direction then. This was the same store where I had often waited for Peg's prescriptions. I realized that when the clerk asked me had I gotten prescriptions from them before. I said, "Yes," but she couldn't find my name in their system. Then I figured out it was Peg's prescriptions I had filled there.

While I wandered the aisles of assorted merchandise waiting for my order, a singer's voice on the radio caught my attention. In fact, I could sing most of the song's words and the countermelody. Suddenly it dawned on me. This was the song that Peg and I were learning and going to sing at the request of a church friend for his wedding early last summer! Part of me said, "Oh, not now! not today!" but something else said, "Listen!"

What I heard was Bryan Adams' *I'll Always Be Right There.* I recalled how important it had been to be there for Peg as best I could to see her through, as she would have been for me, as the wedding vows say, "...in sickness and in health...until death do us part."

Peg and I sang that song many times together in practice—I can easily see us standing in the sanctuary with Peg at the keyboard—and we were all set to sing it for the wedding. I know time alters perceptions, but we did sound pretty good together with the electric piano sound we'd chosen for accompaniment. But we never sang it publicly for anyone. That Friday night, Peg ended up in emergency and that Saturday morning, the day of the wedding, we got the diagnosis that she had cancer.

I tried to find something in the words of the song to restore some sense of celebration to trump the all too familiar sense of grief as I stood there in the aisle in front of shelves of merchandise I couldn't even see with vision blurred by more than pink-eye. The song celebrated two people being exclusively together forever. But we weren't together! Well not right now. But wait a minute—the song was wrong. It wouldn't be only Peg and me. We would be together in the Lord's presence forever eventually. Actually we'd already begun sharing life in Him. This time of parting was only an interruption of that and only for a while.

The rest of the lyrics rang true, however. The longer we were together, the more we cared, and for as much of life as we had together, we were there for each other. Well, I wasn't always there for Peg, I know, but that improved in recent years, and she certainly was there for me all through our marriage. Still these things from the past caused me to leave the store feeling like the spirit of Friday had cast a shadow over Sunday.

At home I had lunch, got squared away with my medications, and relaxed in front of the TV for awhile. But I was beginning to feel the day was slipping away and I still didn't really know how to celebrate an eternal birthday. If they were celebrating Peg's eternal birthday in heaven, they were keeping it pretty much to themselves. Finally I pushed the "off" button on the remote and asked the Lord how I could celebrate.

At one point I had thought about driving to Peg's grave but that seemed more focused on mortality. I remember celebrating her worldly birthday last August by looking through pictures. Even though that had been a good thing to do, that also seemed very worldly and too backward looking for today. This needed to be forward looking and hopeful. But what I knew and believed about the future seemed very general and this needed to be specific to Peg.

Then I remembered starting a new book that morning in the clinic waiting room. I had read the table of contents and most of the introduction. Since God often speaks to me in the books I read, that's what I would do next. I skipped ahead to chapter six, "Crucifixion and Resurrection" of John Polkinghorne's, *The Faith of a Physicist.* God gave me several passages for the occasion.

"the resurrection is not only the vindication of Jesus. It is also the vindication of God: that he did not abandon the one man who truly trusted himself to him....If Good Friday testifies to the reality of the power of evil, Easter Day shows that the last word lies with God."[21] In the backward look from Friday, Peg's death-day, there were blessings of the Lord, but there was plenty of evil to recall too—the pain, the suffering, the despair, the dread, the doubt, and most of all, the illness. Peg, herself, had seen that.

One night Peg was propped up on the bed in the family room with pillows stacked behind to make her as comfortable as possible. This was after her third hospitalization and diagnosis while she was going through radiation. I sat on the edge of the bed and we talked. I said to her, "If your cancer were sitting here looking at you on the edge of the bed like I am, what would you say to it?" She looked me straight in the eye with a penetrating stare and said with great intensity, "I'd tell it, go to hell!!!"

It might not be the most rational theology, but that is indeed, where I believe it has gone—not because Peg said so, but because the Lord has so promised![22] The devil and all his angels of disease could destroy her mortal body but could not destroy the person she had become in that body. All that destroys human life and the human soul with both repulsive ruin and

---

21   © John Polkinghorne, *The Faith of a Physicist,* (Princeton, NJ: Fortress Press, Princeton University Press, 1994), p. 121.

22   Based on a synthesis of Matthew 25:41; Revelation 6:7; 20:14; 21:4.

enticing appeal is part of an old order of this world superceded by a new order not yet fully come. Well, it has come for Peg—I believe that because I believe it came for Jesus.

It's not that God needs to vindicate Himself to us, explaining or justifying anything, but Jesus' resurrection does make it clear that Jesus' evident defeat is not defeat at all; it is victory over sin and mortality. When we look at Good Friday in light of Easter we can say, so that's what God was up to! This is the vindication Polkinghorne is referring to. In the promise of resurrection and immortality applied to Peg, I can trust that God did not abandon her to her cancer. He did not defeat it in the old order of this life, though that was our desperate hope and prayer. But the resurrection of Jesus and His promises offer assurance that her disease is superceded in the new heaven and new earth that will come in its fullness and completeness at Christ's return.

The problem, of course, in all of this is the backward look from Friday has been sensually experienced with all of the hurts and distresses already reviewed, and those that linger for me still. The forward look from Sunday is not accessed with the same faculties. There are no vivid visual images, no raw emotions, no cognitive facts to be reviewed, and no timeline to consult. It can't be relived the way the past can. Peg's eternal birth can only be imagined, anticipated, and revealed as God so chooses, by faith, in light of Jesus' resurrection and promises.

"[4] These earthly bodies make us groan and sigh, but we wouldn't like to think of dying and having no bodies at all. We want to slip into our new bodies so that these dying bodies will, as it were, be swallowed up by everlasting life. [5] This is what God has prepared for us, and as a guarantee he has given us his Holy Spirit. [6] Now we look forward with confidence to our heavenly bodies, realizing that every moment we spend in these earthly bodies is time spent away from our eternal home in heaven with Jesus. [7] We know these things are true by believing, not by seeing," (2 Corinithians 5:4-7 – TLB). The only offset we have to the grief of losing someone close to us in death is the Holy Spirit, the one revealed in other passages of Scripture as The Comforter, given as a guarantee, according to verse five. Indeed, the Holy Spirit has a monumental task in the death of a spouse—to comfort the experiential trauma we have been through in losing a flesh and blood partner, one given to us by God with His blessing. Belief has to stand up to all of this and exceed its impact on our lives and hearts in order to overcome grief—no small task!

Continuing with the resurrection of Jesus as vindication, Mr. Polkinghorne says, "Finally, the resurrection of Jesus is the vindication of the hopes of humanity. We shall all die with our lives to a greater or lesser extent incomplete, unfulfilled, unhealed. Yet there is profound and widespread human intuition that in the end all will be well."[23] I agree we human beings have an intuitive sense that we exist for something more than we find in mortal life. Certainly we are able to dream, plan, and undertake more than we can ever accomplish in a lifetime. (As I entertain thoughts of retirement, this is a good reality check for me to help determine what I can consider as realistic to pursue, God willing, and what dreams, plans, and undertakings are best left undone.)

This helps to put Peg's unrealized dreams and hopes into perspective. As with all of us, dreams and hopes were always part of her life. As some were fulfilled or superceded by changing values and priorities, others arose to take their place. It's part of the way we are made always with the ability to hope and dream. But to see Peg's hopes and dreams lost and gone forever left me with a sense that we were both cheated.

Mr. Polkinghorne's statements put that in perspective pointing out that this life always leaves something in us unfulfilled. As death approached, Peg's ultimate hope was her heavenly home. It was not just a desire to be released from illness and suffering, it was a hope to find her ultimate place and purpose beyond this life. It was the one hope that remained. "I just want to go home!" and that hope was fulfilled. That is what her eternal birthday is all about!

Though the Lord had provided helpful insights and encouragement in the reading and reflection, at that point, I still didn't feel I had really celebrated Peg's eternal birthday. Soon there was a knock at the door. It was a neighbor who is also a parishioner who has been most helpful and caring throughout this ordeal. I invited him in and we sat in the living room and talked. He had been away on vacation so we caught up on his travels and developments since he'd been gone. But his visit was not just an afterthought. He knew what day it was—he'd been close to Peg as well—and he wanted to say that he still missed her too. I was deeply grateful for his willingness to express his own sentiments and not avoid the subject (and later told him so). Then I went on to tell him a little about what the day had been like for me, being especially pleased to tell him about the "eternal birthday" discovery.

After he left, I called Mike and Becky to let them know about my diagnosis and that all of them who had been to visit on Thursday had been exposed to pinkeye. Since Mike and Becky were out on a date, I talked with a mutual friend who was staying with the grandkids. So I had occasion to tell her about the "eternal birthday" as well.

Then I called my sister to let her know my diagnosis and delay in coming. She was the third to hear about the "eternal birthday."

By now, the day was about at an end. I still didn't really feel that I had

---

23 © John Polkinghorne, *The Faith of a Physicist,* (Princeton, NJ: Fortress Press, Princeton University Press, 1994), p. 121.

"celebrated" in the usual sense. But God had given me a point of reference in the "eternal birthday" that had turned my focus forward. He had taken me through some exploration of resurrection and given me the realization that Peg's unfulfilled dreams were not unique but a part of the human experience. I had come to see the difference in kind between the things that had caused my sorrow and grief and the only thing that could bring relief. There were no specific countermeasures or compensations but only the basics of dependence on the Holy Spirit as the Comforter.

In retrospect, I realize that celebration is not solitary by nature. It is usually done in company with others. In that respect, I had "celebrated" Peg's eternal birthday with three different people and we had all been blessed by it.

In the Christian tradition, every Sunday is a mini-Easter, a commemoration and celebration of our Lord's resurrection. So there's one last blessing I'm sure the Holy Spirit provided with a smile. The first anniversary of Peg's death-day and eternal birthday fell on Friday and Sunday, following the pattern of Jesus' death on Good Friday and His resurrection to new life on Easter Sunday. That could only happen in a leap year when the days and date would advance with two days between, instead of one. Now, that says something about God's provision and celebration. Happy eternal birthday, Peg!

Today I had an auditory reminder that considerable time has elapsed since Peg's absence. I opened the passenger door on the car to place some things on the seat to use while traveling. I've concluded I might as well set things there I want handy while I'm riding since anyone seldom rides there anymore and there's no one to hand them to me from harder to reach places. When I closed the door it squeaked. I opened and closed it several times to be sure that's what it was and it definitely makes noise. I'm sure it's from corrosion of parts from disuse. Aftermath continues!

PART II
INDIVIDUATION

In *Part I: Aftermath*, I related thoughts, feelings, and experiences that came about following the death of one so very close to me. These were very much the direct consequences or results of losing her. *Part II: Individuation*, also includes thoughts, feelings, and experiences that occurred over that same period of time, but these are filtered out and gathered under this heading because they began to establish me as an individual in my own right, separate and distinct from who I had become with Peg. The following begins a few weeks after her death.

Chapter 5

Discovering the Void

I have come to identify another phase in all of this that I call individuation, becoming an individual again, a person distinct from who I was as "one flesh" with Peg. Like C. S. Lewis, I do not want to regress to who I was before I was married to my wife, but to be who I have become with her and because of her, retaining what God has done in me through her. Part of that individuation seems to be conserving. By that I mean conserving the past and the life we shared together. Sheldon Vanauken spent much of the year after his wife, Davy's death, doing what he called an "Illumination of the Past," writing letters to her as he retrieved memories from the journals they kept and from conversations with friends. I have looked through pictures and gathered together tape recordings of Peg's music as she played for worship services and other occasions. I suspect that originates in a fear that, even though I have lost her, I do not want to lose who she was, what she contributed to life, and what we experienced together.

Among the things Peg contributed to my life were vitality and exuberance, things that attracted me to her in the first place. She was always high energy and active, very interested in people, especially after she came to a faith relationship with God through Jesus Christ. Oh, she enjoyed time away from people as well; in fact she needed that to reenergize. In that sense she was truly an introvert. Together our life was a rhythm of activity with and for people and retreat for rest and revitalization. I will miss the vitality that she brought to my life. These are some of the things about her I want to conserve.

If one side of individuation is conserving, the other side seems to be expansion, letting who I am and my desires expand into the void. As a marriage partner, love and consideration put a spin on my needs and my desires to accommodate Peg's needs and desires. In fact, chief among my desires as her husband needed to be aspiring to bring about what was best for her and our marriage, though I certainly did not always perfectly achieve that. Still, that's the ideal.

The Apostle Paul said he thought it best if everyone was single as he was in order to be fully devoted to Christ because some time and energy went into pleasing one's partner that could have been spent pleasing God. Certainly pleasing God needs to be first and foremost. Yet I think what Paul didn't take into account is that love of one's partner in marriage pleases God, the Creator and Designer of male and female and the marriage relationship. When it does not preempt relationship with Him, God receives it as reverence for Himself. God used Paul's own words to express that very thing when he instructed us to "Submit to one another out of reverence for Christ....Wives, submit to your husbands as to the Lord....Husbands, love your wives, just as Christ loved the church and gave himself up for her..." (Ephesians 5:21, 22 and 25).

The point is, my identity as a husband was strongly influenced by Peg and our marriage and vice versa. Now I must discover a present identity influenced by her and God through her, but no longer subject to her as an active partner in marriage. To do things now Peg liked to do, as I did with her when she was living in order to please her, no longer makes sense. God does not expect it, neither does she, and neither should I. If I want to continue to do them out of some sense of satisfaction in the present, that is fine. But I do not need to do them out of love or some sense of duty to our marriage or her. That is at least part of what I need to be testing—letting go without losing. I think I will have to venture into some of the things we used to do and some of the things I might like to do to find all that out. Being almost 60 years old and thinking about retirement, it sounds risky and challenging at a point in life where I was looking forward to comfort and refuge in what we already had together.

Peg went home to be with the Lord, on Friday, August 8th. Today, I am home as well. I have come back to the home where I grew up. I'm sleeping across the hall from what used to be my bedroom, which has now been converted into an upstairs shower room. The room I am now in is used as a guest bedroom. I slept in it for awhile when my great uncle Bill lived with us. He was my grandmother's brother, a widower, and lived with us for several years. Then my sister came along, we needed more space, and he needed a quieter setting. In the rearrangement that followed his moving out, I went to his room.

I came here to begin what I consider the individuating phase of my adjustment to life without Peg and today is the first day. In truth, it has not seemed that much different so far. I had a leisurely start to the day by sleeping 'til almost 9:00am, checking the weather on TV, showering, and reading some more of *A Severe Mercy* until time for lunch. But even though nothing really feels different, last evening's prelude to the day was reassuring.

My sister, Nancy, and mother came to spend some time with me, vacation time that my sister had scheduled quite awhile ago before things got so serious with Peg. With her experience with medical records from her hospital employment, Nancy was a tremendous help in the aftermath of dealing with the medical bills. She also helped me to catch up on several months of checkbook balancing, something Peg had always done before, not to mention all of the domestic chores she did during her visit, which didn't turn out to be much of a vacation for her.

I decided to return home with Mom and Nancy for a few weeks just to get out of the parsonage setting, to have some time for reading and reflection, and to work on redefining my life and myself. Thus when we headed north on Sunday, I considered the aftermath phase to be ending and an individuating phase beginning. Of course, I know that things in life don't neatly compartmentalize that way and that there are still some things to be finalized as a result of Peg's death. Still, it seems helpful to regard this as a distinct change of orientation.

It is about 450 miles from Freeland to Calumet, the last 250 miles of it over two lane highways. From early afternoon on we had driven through rain. As we rounded Keweenaw Bay, the southern boundary of the region known as "The Copper Country" where both Peg and I grew up, the evening sun began to poke through. The rain clouds were retreating across the bay to the east against a dark slate-gray background of distant clouds we had earlier passed beneath. Toward each end of the nearer low-hanging layers of dissipating rain-clouds, now vividly colored by the setting sun behind us in the west, there was a slice of rainbow. But even the slices were broken by missing pieces of cloud or hidden by other cloud fragments passing in front. The vibrant blues and teals of the clearing sky and water were accented by the whites and golds of cloud remnants illuminated in the spotlight of the late evening sun. Gradually, the colors began to deepen and a curtain of gray began to creep upward from the water as the shadow of the peninsula's backbone began to block out the sinking sun.

As I looked at those fragmented rainbows against the darkness of the distant storm, I thought about the hopes that I had for Peg's healing and recovery. Like that fragmented rainbow, they were never made complete. I still do not see any promises of God connected and completed even though that storm is past. But I trust the light of God will provide some sense of promise against the stormy darkness.

I don't know how God will keep me mindful of all that Peg went through, and I with her, for I do not want to forget it, and yet I know I cannot live in that or even in the better memories of the past. If anyone can accomplish a weaving of such variegated thoughts, feelings, and memories into a tapestry that is worth anything in the future, only He can. I want to suppose that He will. I am taking the beautiful scene across Keweenaw Bay as a prelude for such a point of departure in this place where both Peg and I lived before we met. (The cover photo is the scene as I photographed it that evening.)

It was an MG that did it to Sheldon Vanauken. In *A Severe Mercy,* he came out of class and saw that car looking so forlorn and void, that he hardly got off campus before breaking into tears. He said he had to see everything that way at least once. That car was that strongly associated with his wife, Davy, and the void left by her death after 15 years of marriage.

I have that same sadness about going biking without Peg. Sunday when it came time to pack up to head north, I went to the shed and took only my bicycle out, leaving hers behind. In the garage, I took down only my helmet and accessories, leaving her bike bag on the shelf, removing from it the little rear view mirror she always wore attached to her glasses to watch for traffic from behind. I took the bike lock and cable we used to secure our bikes together when we needed to leave them. It was an emotional struggle to pack only my biking equipment and not hers.

Though I would be traveling with my mother and sister, we would be in separate vehicles, and the reason for the empty seat to my right would be painfully evident. We rarely ever made the trip back "home" solo. Once when we lived in Kentucky for me to attend seminary, Peg flew north ahead of us to be there for some special occasion, and Mike and I drove up later on to join her. After some time apart, we met at our friends' house for a wedding in the town we had lived in before leaving the Upper Peninsula. Then we went on to visit family at Calumet. As soon as feasible, I arranged for a day away for just the two of us, touring the beautiful Keweenaw scenery, swimming in Lake Superior at my aunt and uncle's camp, supper at the Keweenaw

Mountain Lodge, and a romantic excursion home along the lake shore drive. We stopped at places where we used to go before we were married to watch sunsets over the lake and the lake freighters rounding Keweenaw Point, while listening to popular music of the day on the car radio.

I imagine I will visit some of those places before I head back to Freeland, and I imagine I will feel the void. Not only objects but places evoke that emptiness.

"walking with God has been for me inseparable from walking with Doris."[24] That is what theologian and Christian writer Lewis Smedes said about the affect that his wife has had upon his faith and relationship with God. I can say the same, "Walking with God has been for me inseparable from walking with Peg."

Not long after we were married and living in Chicago where I was going to photography school and we both were working at the Woolworth's store on North Michigan Avenue, we began attending a neighborhood church. Although Peg had been raised in the Catholic Church, she was discontent and we were married in the Methodist Church, the church of my heritage. So it was that denomination we sought out. One morning communion was served. We were to receive it seated in the pews. When the elements came to me, I passed them on to Peg without communing. As we walked home from church, Peg found a way to bring up the subject. I said I didn't take communion because I wasn't even sure there was a God. She didn't react or panic but she told me later that she was astounded. She always believed in God and now she discovered she was married to someone who didn't. We had never gone to church before we were married or even talked about religion. She kept her shaken reaction to herself.

When we moved back to the Upper Peninsula to own and operate a photography studio in Negaunee, Peg was pregnant and we were preparing to become parents. Children have a way of stirring deeper things within us. For one thing, we both knew that we would need to have our child baptized and so we needed a church affiliation. (Beneath my expressed un-faith apparently there was a sense of some sort of spiritual responsibility.) Very conveniently, the local Methodist Church was across the street from our studio and apartment on the corner of the block. We began attending. The pastor stopped in to get acquainted and by the time our son, Mike, was born, we had become frequent attendees, if we weren't away on the weekend visiting family.

---

24 Lewis B. Smedes, *My God and I: A Spiritual Memoir,* (Grand Rapids, MI: © Wm. B. Eerdmans, 2003), p. 80.

Within a few years, we both were moved by Billy Graham's appeal through his television ministry to make a decision for Christ. Although we came to personal faith in Jesus on different occasions, without talking to each other about it, eventually we began to open up. When a friend, Lois, whom we had gotten to know at church began talking openly about her faith, I saw an excitement and conviction in her I didn't have, and began to talk about my new found faith as well. So did Peg. From then on, our life in the faith and increasing involvement in the church was common conversation.

Before long, the United Methodist Youth Fellowship needed leaders. Peg really loved teens and was excited about the possibility of working with them. I wasn't so sure, but her excitement was contagious. Although we both felt ill-equipped, we became convinced that if it was something God was calling us to do, He would give us what we needed to do it. God was faithful and we had a good experience working with the youth for several years.

Then I began to sense a call to full-time ministry, although I couldn't believe God would call me. Finally, the urge became so strong that I began to be overwhelmed by distressing feelings whenever the subject of serving the Lord came up in worship or sermons. Peg and I were going away for a weekend to Green Bay, Wisconsin. It was fall and dark outside as we rode south. In the safety of the darkness, I screwed up my courage and broached the subject of full-time ministry. Peg was way ahead of me and responded eagerly. She would do whatever was necessary and was willing to go wherever the Lord might take us in His service. Obviously God had been calling and preparing her as well.

So she took on a heavier load at the studio, doing some of the things I had done previously, to keep our business going while I worked and went to college to complete four years of a bachelor's degree. Then we moved to Kentucky for me to complete seminary and she worked full-time at the University of Kentucky as a secretary in the Agricultural Department. She loved the job, the seminary and college town of Wilmore with its spiritual opportunities, and Kentucky with its white fences, horse farms, and warmer climate. In fact, she wondered if we might transfer to the Kentucky Conference of the United Methodist Church. Had I agreed, she would have been thrilled to stay.

Back in Michigan, she became a stay-at-home mom and church volunteer taking on youth work once again and doing typing and paper work for me that left me free to do other ministry tasks. She was always handy to consult and to talk through ministry and faith issues whenever I felt the need. She was very astute about people matters and well grounded in the faith through teaching Bible studies to youth, seminars she had attended, and her own Bible reading and study. Above all, she was a good listener.

In my second appointment which involved serving as pastor of one church as well as director of a cooperative parish of seven churches with a staff of three other clergy, a home missionary, and a part time secretary, Peg took on an even bigger role as listener and encourager. She also became active in music ministries, eventually serving as the church's organist, and we once again became leaders with the youth. The isolated location of that appointment meant spending a lot of time in the car driving to make hospital calls and attend denominational meetings. She was usually free to go with me, so that meant a lot of time to talk through faith and ministry matters.

The basic pattern of our relationship continued in my third appointment, the single church we were serving when Peg died, where I am continuing in ministry. We no longer worked directly with youth, feeling that our energy for that kind of ministry was diminishing and it was time to focus on other things. That decision was hard for Peg but she poured herself into music ministries in the new situation and pioneered a revived secretarial position, hired by the church, something the church had not had during business hours for a period of time. In fact, she developed it into an administrative assistant position, doing much more than simple secretarial-receptionist work. We worked very closely which set me free to concentrate on ministry and church development. That paid great dividends to me and the church as we entered a building program for an entirely new structure, which was completed three years before Peg's death.

I can understand the inclination that people experience following the death of a life-partner to "cut and run," to get away from the familiar that is laden with reminders of the one who is gone. I have done that to a degree in this "individuating" time away from the church and parsonage. It would be easy in my circumstance to ask the bishop for a new appointment, to move to a new town, a new church, and ministry with new people. But I would still carry with me the faith that God formed in Peg and me together, as well as my approach to ministry that is team-based. Whether I go or stay, my ministry needs to be reformulated. I think it best be done in familiar settings with familiar people.

So I need to further adapt Lewis Smedes' statement, adding the underlined words. "Walking with God <u>and serving Him</u> has been for me inseparable from walking with Peg." The time for my official period of bereavement and retreat is drawing to a close. Soon I will begin to ease (I hope "ease" is possible) my way back into ministry.

I believe that the original call to ministry I heard was "our" call, because Peg heard it and God prepared her for it too. I did the formal studies, received the degrees, acquired the credentials, and was named in the appointments, but we served throughout those 21 years as partners in that call. She had her own areas of service that did not overlap mine, but our ministries intersected and were linked in a holistic ministry as we called on each other for help, wisdom, and encouragement. Peg has finished her labors and I am sure has heard the Lord commend her, "Well done, good and faithful servant!...Come and share your master's happiness!" (Matthew 25:21). Indeed, all that she did, she did well with excellence, with even the least significant things as unto the Lord.

Why God chose not to preserve the team a little longer, I do not understand. But I do not believe Peg's death removes me from the field of labor. I have not yet heard the summons to the Master's day of reckoning. I believe I am to continue in my call though I do not expect it will be the same—I know it cannot be. A solo is always different than a duet.

If God has a different direction for me, I have not yet discerned it. If He does, I trust He will make that clear. Meanwhile, I do believe that the One who has called me is faithful and will supply what I need to do what He has called me to do, just as He did when Peg and I worked with youth and went on to this work, full-time pastoral ministry. But I *sure* don't see why God chose to break up the team!

Being single is causing me to struggle with my vocabulary. Early on in our marriage, Peg and I changed our possessive pronouns from singular to plural. When we acquired a car, it was *our* car. When we acquired a photography business, it was *our* photo studio. When we bought a house, it was *our* house. When we started a checking and savings account, it was *our* money. When Mike came along, he was *our* son. In fact, we had to work at communicating to some close to us that these things were *ours* together, not Jim's car or Peg's house, and we wanted them to regard them that way.

Oh, there were some things we considered our individual property. My model trains have always been my trains. Peg's keyboard was her instrument. And the Ford Mustang we bought was her car.

Peg liked Mustangs, especially the older ones. Back in the '80's, she had a 1964½ Mustang our son, Mike, found that needed complete restoration. He was going to do the work, so Peg bought the car. But life as a young adult got very absorbing for Mike and he wasn't able to make progress on the project. I began doing some work to it but didn't have the skill or inclination to do the extensive work necessary to make it road worthy. So after awhile, Peg sold the car without ever driving it except in the driveway. At least she made some money on the sale.

When we needed a second vehicle in the late '90's, we found a 1989 Mustang. She thought that body style was OK, liking it better than the second generation of Mustangs and better than the newer ones. It wasn't blue, which was her favorite color, it was dark red. But it was a stick shift, which was a requirement on her part, in decent shape, and it was a Mustang so we bought it. To correct a grave oversight on the part of the Ford designers, I bought a pair of Mustang emblems as a gift for her, and put them on the side of the car, like they used to be on the original Mustangs. It became our runaround vehicle saving our primary one from added short run mileage. It was registered in her name, we regarded it as "her" car, and she enjoyed shifting gears and driving her little Mustang back and forth to work or to her other activities.

For practical reasons, I doubt that I will keep it. It's getting older and beginning to show its age. (I was keeping my eye out for another comparable Mustang for her in better condition with lower mileage.) I doubt that I need two vehicles just for general transportation, so at some point in the future, I will probably sell it. Besides that, Mustangs were her thing and when I look for another vehicle, it probably won't be a Mustang. In the meantime, it will be Peg's Mustang as long as I keep it, even though I've now transferred the title to my name.

I suspect there will be some things that will always remain "hers." Things that were her personal possessions that I retain I imagine will always be Peg's, like the reading light she used in bed and for traveling that I've now begun to take with me when I'm away from home. As I pack it up and put it in my suitcase, I think of her and consider it hers.

Other things I am feeling more awkward about. Previously when I talked about Mike, Becky, and their children, I referred to them as "our" son, "our" daughter-in-law, "our" grandchildren. I am still doing the same. In one sense, they will, of course, always be "ours,' but somehow it now seems awkward in talking to others to use the plural possessive when I am now single. Even though the minivan has always been "ours," it now seems like I should call it "my" minivan. Yet when I refer to it I trip over the selection of the pronoun.

I suppose I will have to work my way through the assortment of things we shared and work at settling on labels for each one—what will always be Peg's/hers, what will remain ours, and what will be mine. I think the struggle is that the word "mine" has such a possessive ring to it and we had worked at sharing, being in partnership. We modeled with our material things the partnership that we wanted the non-material things in our marriage to assume. So now when I refer to something we co-owned as "mine" and not "ours," technically I suppose, I'm not being possessive and denying Peg's co-ownership. I am identifying the one to whom it belongs in this world.

Still, when she made a substantial contribution to the choices, productivity and yield of our life together, it somehow seems I'm ignoring that with the word "mine." Besides that, "my" and "mine" reminded me I am now a sole proprietor, no longer a partner, sharing the stuff of life with another. Only when the word "mine" has a different ring to it in regard to some things, will I be able to say it without it rubbing a tender spot.

I was riding out to Mike and Becky's and to visit Peg's grave for the first time when a song I had not heard for years revealed to me something I didn't know I was feeling. I had brought along some old tapes to listen to—tapes that we had accumulated over the years. I was going to check them out to see if they were worth keeping. The song was on one of them.

Peg and I had made three cassette tapes of old 78rpm records that came from her grandmother's house, and this was *Tape #1*. She remembered listening to many of those records when she was a girl spending time with her grandparents. They ranged from old John McCormick songs, to Frank Sinatra hits, with everything in between including Bing Crosby's *White Christmas*, Gene Autry's *Rudolph the Red-Nosed Reindeer*, Les Paul and Mary Ford's *Tennessee Waltz*, and a whole lot more. We played with features on our stereo amplifier and made them sound as good as we could, minimizing the scratches and clicks, figuring that even with their flaws, we would enjoy the nostalgia of listening to them in the future. It was many years since I had heard them.

The first song, *Oh How I Miss You Tonight* by tenor, Charles Hart, caught me off guard.

"The days are so long, seems everything's wrong,
for now I'm alone and blue.
I still love you, dear, I wish you were here.
Come back and forgive me, please do.

"Oh, how I miss you tonight, miss you when lights are low.
Oh, how I need you tonight, more than you'll ever know.
I may be seen for awhile, hiding each tear with a smile.
But my heart won't stop aching, please keep it from breaking.
Oh, pal, how I miss you tonight."[25]

25 *Oh, How I Miss You Tonight* sung by Charles Hart, 365-D (140503), Columbia Records.

I wasn't ready for that! Little matter that the vocalist was singing in a style from decades ago, with instrumentation just as dated, through the rushing sound of a worn record accompanied by the clicking of a scratch on every rpm. Peg and I had made those tapes together, the records were connected with her past, and the first verse expressed my sentiments exactly. And the chorus!—Oh, how I missed her, especially when it was time to settle in at the end of the day. And even though I'd never called her that, she was indeed my "pal," my dear companion, and the term really got to me. Though the sun was shining brightly, the road got a little blurry for awhile.

The songs that followed were mostly love songs about lovers and their blue feelings over being jilted or wronged, sung by Perry Como and Bing Crosby—a nice assortment of stuff popular in the forties, I would guess. Next was Kitty O'Connor, the Girl Baritone. She sang an old tune called, *If I Can't Have You.* It was another older number from the same era as John McCormick. Then came side two of her record. Kitty sang of her lover who seemed to be so perfect but turned out to be unfaithful. Then in lament came the title line, *I'm So Disappointed in You.*

That was it! That's what I was feeling. In consoling me, a number of people had told me, "It's OK to be angry with God!" I knew that. I had shared the same thought with a number of people in pastoral counseling sessions when they were struggling with some hurt or distress they felt was unjust or unfair.

I had learned it was OK to be angry with God, even before I went to seminary. At a youth retreat when Peg and I were counselors, the host pastor had told us how, when their daughter had cancer and was seriously ill, his wife had gone into the church sanctuary and had it out with God. She had voiced her anger and told God what she thought of Him, and God didn't strike her down with a lightning bolt. In fact, we were told God could handle our anger just fine and it might even do us good to let it out.

But I wasn't angry with God, at least not at that point, nor am I yet, after nearly three months since Peg's death. I knew what it was to be angry. I discovered after moving to my present appointment that I had been angry in my previous situation. It wasn't a hot intense anger that flared up against anyone. But I was angry because the demands of my responsibilities, as I understood them, were impossible to meet. I was over-extended trying to keep up with multi-layered responsibilities of the denomination and the seven-church cooperative parish. There was very little built in support from denominational structure and greater responsibility for funding salaries for personnel was gradually being shifted from denominational sources to the local level. I felt I had responsibility without authority to bring about the necessary and expected results. After ten years, I was burned out and requested to be moved to a new situation. After awhile in my new setting, I discovered that I had been angry in a very internal unhealthy way.

So I know what anger is and I wasn't feeling anger following Peg's death. But that old song had identified what I was feeling. It was disappointment. I was extremely disappointed that God had not prevented Peg from getting such a dreaded disease in the first place, and in the second place, for not intervening and healing her of the disease if she had to have it, especially since I knew He could.

Unlike the first song, *Oh, How I Miss You Tonight,* I didn't feel like the verse and chorus of the second song paralleled my sentiments exactly. I could identify with believing in someone and then being disappointed. But I have never felt deceived by God.

The basis of my disappointment is not in that I deserved something better than to lose my wife, but that if anyone was one of God's favorites, surely it was Peg, just as John was a favorite of Jesus. Yet He didn't spare her of grave illness, didn't prolong her life in this world, and didn't choose to grant her earthly hopes and dreams. Evidently the ministry we were carrying on and the potential we still had together as a diversified team, His team, didn't matter. He let it come to an end while she was only 56. That is a great disappointment to me. I believed we had the energy and wherewithal for several years of active full-time service ahead of us and perhaps interim ministry for some years beyond that. Then there was our hope for me to do some writing, something she really wanted me to pursue, which she would have been a tremendous asset for. Besides that, we had looked forward to a less hectic time of enjoying God and appreciating His good creation together in retirement. I'm not angry about any of those things being derailed for me—in fact some of them could still happen. I am disappointed that Peg will not be a part of those things, if they come to pass, or anything else in this world. Mostly, I am disappointed because it seems to me the relationship we had with God wasn't what I believed it to be. A whole array of things that I thought mattered to God evidently weren't as significant as I had presumed. That has been a troubling disappointment.

I am not the first to be disappointed with God. Philip Yancey wrote a book with that very title, *Disappointment With God.* I had forgotten that until I identified my own disappointment. I went to my library at the office to find my copy with all my under linings and markings, which is the way I read books of my own. It was nowhere to be found. I had evidently loaned it out and it had not been returned so I borrowed Mike and Becky's copy.

As I browsed through Mr. Yancey's book, I remembered how he had introduced his theme and then quickly moved into the story of a young theology student who suffered severe disappointment with God. Ironically his struggles all came to a head while he was writing a book on Job. In a conversation with Mr. Yancey, he said, "So many times God had let me down....God came through for Job after all his pain. He didn't come through for me."[26] Though we may hope that a follow-up on the story reverses this young man's position before the end of the book, there is no such happy ending, and the last time he appeared in the book he was not only disappointed but angry with God.

Should we think that disappointment with God is a modern phenomenon, Mr. Yancey sites examples of Old Testament Bible personalities who were disappointed with God. He starts with Abraham, who receives promises from God that his descendents will fill the land and be as numerous as the stars in the sky. But his wife is childless and has no child until they are well past the normal child bearing years and Abraham dies with only one son surviving him. He continues with Joseph. "If anyone had a valid reason to be disappointed with God, it was Joseph, whose valiant stabs at goodness brought him nothing but trouble."[27] Then there is Moses in the wilderness for 40 years, never entering the Promised Land. The list goes on with one disappointment after another. I am not unique in my experience.

As I am dealing with my disappointment, the Lord is helping me to see that disappointment has two sources. One source is the character or behavior of the one who is perceived as the source of disappointment. The other source is the expectation or belief of the one disappointed.

To disappoint someone is considered a very inconsiderate thing and the assumption always seems to be that the one who is disappointed with someone else is always justified in that disappointment. We rely on someone for some perceived need or necessity and they fail us. So the source of our disappointment is in the one who is seen as its cause. If children experience some sort of disappointment in their childhood that affects them as adults, their parents are at fault, and they go to great lengths to never disappoint their own children in that fashion.

Truth is that sometimes our expectations of others are for perceived

---

26   Philip Yancey, *Disappointment With God,* (Grand Rapids, MI: Zondervan Publishing, 1992), pp. 31 and 34.

27   Philip Yancey, *Disappointment With God,* (Grand Rapids, MI: Zondervan Publishing, 1992), pp. 65-67.

needs or necessities which they have no obligation to meet or cannot even deliver. With our parents, they sometimes disappointed us for our own good knowing that what we wanted or thought we needed was not in our best interests then, or maybe ever. So disappointment can arise out of our own unrealistic or false expectations.

Concerning my disappointment with God, it seems theologically impossible to make a case for our Heavenly Father being a negligent or unconcerned Parent. Although my feelings may contend to the contrary, I am constrained, however, from such a conclusion by Scripture. As Job received the brunt of Satan's afflictions and reeled under their distress, we are told, "In all this, Job did not sin by charging God with wrongdoing...In all this, Job did not sin in what he said," (Job 1:22 and 2:10c).[28] That doesn't mean the struggle was any less real for Job—certainly he agonized in his condition and struggled with his relationship with God—but he did not cross the line of fixing in his mind that God was unjust and making that his final position. I think he was getting close but backed down when God intervened and came on the scene. Then Job recognized there were things about life and God he could not know or understand. Likewise, I have to admit the same.

So that leaves only one other source of my disappointment that has been somewhat discomfiting to consider—my disappointment with God may be rooted in me. If my disappointment is rooted in my own expectations, I have had to ask myself, what was I expecting? Well, I believed that God sustained us as co-partners in carrying out His work and I was assuming He would continue to do so. He had made us a functional team. Why would He prematurely break up the set? I expected that Peg would be the one who would have to deal with my health issues as we aged as she had done 'til now. She was in better all-around health than me, and I expected that would continue. Why should God want it otherwise? Then when she did have health issues to deal with, I expected God would bring her through. I know He has the power and wisdom to do so. Besides, she had such faith in Him.

I guess I expected, or at least hoped, that we would have some retirement years together to pursue some of our dreams to travel and her desires to do mission projects in other parts of the country. Certainly God wouldn't be opposed to that. And I have to admit I may have been presuming God

28 I find it noteworthy that Satan did not take Job's wife from him. She doesn't seem to be much of a spiritual comfort even though she may have cared for his physical ailments, so perhaps Satan saw no need to remove her. Or he may have known that he dare not ask to separate what God had joined together. Job did have more children when God restored him and blessed the latter part of his life. Since only one wife is mentioned in the book, I think it is safe to assume these children were by Job's original wife and she was not taken from him.

would grant that in compensation for years of service we had given in three demanding appointments spanning a quarter of a century. She had made the sacrifices involved in being a clergy spouse without complaint or regret and I thought God would bless her with earthly fulfillment as a sign of His approval. I figured I was along for the ride on the coat tails of her favored status with the Lord. I guess I had forgotten that "...there is no favoritism with him" (Ephesians 6:9), that "...He causes his sun to rise on the evil and the good, and sends rain on the righteous and the unrighteous," (Matthew 5:45).

But not only does He distribute His blessings without partiality, He doesn't prevent His favored ones from suffering or sorrow either. Since Peg's death, I have become aware of many other people of faith who have died what I would call premature deaths including prominent Christians like Larry Burkett of Crown Financial Services, Payne Stewart of the Professional Golfers Association, and Nancy Lightfoot, a missionary to Africa for the United Methodist Church, who died in an auto accident. In addition, I am aware of many other less prominent people who have died prematurely of illness, disease, or accident, even since Peg's death, and some of them much younger than her. Why did I expect that we would be an exception? Truth is I didn't. I just never worked through the possibility that it would be a reality. If I died prematurely, I never anticipated disappointment. I'd be with the Lord. But I hadn't worked through the possibility of it happening to Peg. Nevertheless it did, and disappointment was my response. I had no preventive measures against it because I didn't know I would need any. But now I *do* need to deal with it and by the grace of God I will.

I have explored disappointment in the Scriptures and, despite Philip Yancey's discovery of it in many biblical situations, I find disappointment with God as an explicit Biblical expression conspicuously absent. Those who are specifically spoken of as disappointed are so because they have trusted in human alliances (Jeremiah 2:36b-37); they have relied on their own plans (Proverbs 15:22); they have put their hope in their own strength (Job 41:9). Instead, the Scriptures claim that those who look back at what God has done in the past will see that God has not disappointed His people (Psalms 22:3-5); those who trust in the Lord's promises are not disappointed (Isaiah 49:22-23); those who believe in Jesus will not be disappointed (Romans 9:30-33). Disappointment that arises from the character or behavior of the One who is the object of my disappointment is not specifically supported biblically.

As I lay my disappointed expectations up against the things that God promises not to disappoint, I can see that my expectations have been all very much of this world and God has been dealing with higher and greater things.

In all honesty, I don't expect those feelings of disappointment are going to suddenly go away because I've worked this through to this point. I'm still very much alive in this world and attached to it. So the next time I see an Amtrak train and realize Peg and I will never make anymore of those wonderful trips together, I'm going to feel a little sad (I do right now just thinking about it). As the grandkids continue to learn piano and have their recitals and other occasions to perform, I'll be proud of them but feel a little regret that Peg isn't there to enjoy them and offer encouragement. Even today as I selected songs for Sunday's worship service without Peg's musical input on hymn tunes, I missed that part of the team.

But even as I write that, I sense the Lord reminding me that I can be grateful for the travels we did enjoy and give thanks for the piano knowledge and interest in music Peg did convey to the grandchildren. Still it's OK if I feel some sadness or regret on those occasions in this world because when I pass from this reality into the reality of God's Kingdom, Peg will be there too, in the wonderful and complete reality of Jesus' presence where there will be nothing lacking for "....he who believes in Him will not be disappointed," (Romans 9:33 - NASB). "...those who hope in me will not be disappointed," (Isaiah 49:23).

So then, do I still feel disappointed? Well, yes! But at least I know it's only about things in this world that arise out of my own desires and short-term hopes. God's promises in the preceding Scripture passages are all future tense, that "...I *will* not be disappointed..." in His presence beyond this life. I do believe and hope in that—in Him—and trust it will be so. May He help me in the meantime.

She could not possibly be dead. That's what Sheldon Vanauken wrote in one of his letters to his wife, Davy, after her death. He told her it had to be only an act they were putting on which they would later laugh off. I often have similar thoughts concerning Peg. I do know this is not a bad dream I am having, that morning will come and I will wake up—it's too real for that—but I do catch myself thinking surely there is some mistake, that Peg will come home from wherever she has been.

No, I need to correct that. I don't find myself thinking that. With my rational mind I know Peg is dead. I was with her when she died, exactly three months to the date of this writing. I was there at her burial. I have been to her grave several times. Rather, it is a feeling that comes to me that this can't be real. None of us became hysterical when Peg died, as I have heard people sometimes do when someone close to them dies. There weren't any protests of "No! No!" No expressions of anger or denial at that moment, just a mixture of sadness over losing her, tinged with appreciation that her death was peaceful. But in these recurring feelings of the impossibility of her being gone, now something in me protests "No! No! It can't be real!!!" Then my emotions flare for a few moments as I grapple with that reality and eventually I settle into whatever I was about when the protest came over me.

I am not always sure what brings it on. Usually it happens when I am alone and going about the mundane things of life. Less commonly it may be seeing something that was hers such as her shoes in the closet, realizing she will never wear them again, or her travel bag for toiletries that is still on the counter in the bathroom. Some might think I should dispose of such reminders and reduce the risks. In fact, I have begun to use up and give away some of the contents of her travel bag along with the toiletries that were hers we brought home from the hospital. I know her clothes, her books, her music, all of her personal belongings will need to be dealt with eventually but I can hardly fathom that now. Perhaps in the spring when the world has come through the season of death and darkness into fresh life I will be ready for that. But there is another significance to all these things that seems important right now.

The things that were hers provide some familiarity which is very welcome. It is worth the risk of leaving the very things that can potentially stir reminders of her incredible absence in place because of the familiarity that they also provide. To remove them would make them conspicuous in their absence and only emphasize the loss and finality.

I have faced finality before. I remember how final it felt when we sold our photo studio and house, surrendered the keys, and moved to Kentucky for me to begin attending seminary in preparation for ministry. I felt like a phase of our lives was over. I remember how final it felt when we left our first appointment, three little rural churches and the wonderful people we had gotten to know and love, and headed north 300 miles to a new situation and people we didn't know. Many of the same feelings returned when it came time to leave those people ten years later. There was a feeling of finality in each instance—a knowing that we would never again return to that circumstance.

Yet there is something about the finality of death that is harder to accept. For one thing, there is no excitement about the unknown and sense of adventure of the new to counter the loss. There is only this incredible void. I was about 15 when my grandfather died of a bowel obstruction—I have since concluded it must have been an abdominal tumor. We lived in the same household, my grandparents and my mother and dad. I saw him taken to the hospital, carried down from upstairs where he was bedridden, on a wooden dining room chair because his abdomen hurt badly and having his legs pulled up provided some relief. I remember him groaning quietly in pain and my grandmother all flustered going with him crying out, "Oh, Tom! Tom!" He never came home again and that was the last time I saw him alive. The house was different after that although his absence became a part of the way it was from then on.

Perhaps that is why the finality of Peg's death seems so incredible. Her absence will be the way it is from now on, and I don't want to believe it. Surely it can't be so. And yet it is, isn't it!?

My son, Mike, and I poured the cement base for the headstone where Peg is buried, and I will be too, at the little country cemetery in Evergreen Township of Sanilac County. I built the form and together we dug the cavity for it, laid in gravel for a footing, mixed the cement and poured it. While Mike was gone on an errand, and I was waiting for him to return, I worked to level the sand and gravel that had been mounded up on the grave. As the metal rake clinked and scraped over the assorted stones I was extracting from the sand, I couldn't believe what I was doing—raking the earth over the place where Peg's body is buried.

Every now and then something will cause me to feel this is so incredible, it can't be real. I have never had difficulty accepting anything like I have accepting Peg's death and absence.

I first met Peg when I was home on leave from the Army before going to Japan for two years. We very quickly developed an attachment to each other and it was hard to go when I went overseas after only two weeks together. I remember looking out of the window of the Greyhound bus as I headed south to Chicago through the night, watching the star that had become our star. I was already deeply missing her bubbly vitality, soft blonde hair, and unique scent that was hers alone.

Although I couldn't imagine not seeing her again for two years, I knew there was the future ahead of us. She had high school to finish. I had a military obligation to complete. Somehow I would just have to get through it. At least we would be able to carry on our relationship with letters and anticipate getting back together. Eventually I was able to resign myself to it and the deep sadness was soothed with hope.

There were other occasions after we were married when we left behind people we had come to love and care about. When we sold our photo studio and moved to Kentucky for me to attend seminary it was difficult to leave our church family and friends but I didn't regret the adventure. Whenever we moved to serve a new appointment, there were difficult things about each change but we discovered that the Lord has His people everywhere. I have said, however, the trouble is they're not the same ones. Yet I have accepted the changes, even though initially it has sometimes been with considerable resignation.

Never before has anything been so incredible to accept as Peg's illness and death. Even resignation is illusive. Perhaps it will come and eventually soothe the deep sadness as a prelude to hope as it did the last time Peg and I were worlds apart.

On my last Sunday away, I attended church with my mother and sister at First United Methodist Church in Escanaba, where we spent the weekend visiting friends. When the pastor began reading the text from Job, I knew he was going to be preaching to me. He did. God ministered to me through him but not with soothing comfort or answers. Instead he disturbed me with his text for the morning and left me with yet another question—a question of integrity and acceptance God evidently wants me to face. "His (Job's) wife said to him, 'Are you still holding on to your integrity? Curse God and die!' He replied, 'You are talking like a foolish woman. Shall we accept good from God, and not trouble?'" (Job 2:9-10) [29]

---

29 Published as an article in the *Connection,* the newsletter of the Freeland United Methodist Church, November edition, 2003, under the title, *A Question of Integrity and Acceptance.*

Chapter 6

Holidays Again

Yes! I would read from an old standby today, *The Upper Room.* I have been using other devotional material recently, but when I saw the current issue of *The Upper Room Daily Devotional Guide* there with the other things I keep next to my recliner, I decided to use it. After all, its Thanksgiving Day and reading a devotional specific for the holiday rather than the material I have been using that is not geared to the calendar sounded appropriate.

As I got into Viola Ruelke Gommer's *"Thanksgiving Tradition,"* as she called it, I knew the Lord had directed me to it. She tells how it is their family tradition before they sit down for their holiday meal to name those not able to be with them for the occasion, or anyone who has touched their lives. In addition, she writes, "Our tradition also encourages us to name those who have touched our lives but are now in the presence of the Lord. Often there are tears of thanksgiving for what these people have added to our journeys through life. Each one has been a gift of grace from God. Gratitude fills our hearts. Who has had an impact on your life? Why not begin today to offer thanks to God for that person? To speak the name at this season's celebration gives witness to another's life of faith, which is God's gift to you."[30] Peg! Who else would I name right now, although there are many others I could name. Exploring ways she impacted my life and thanking God for her suddenly appealed to me as a good way to spend some of this holiday.

I have to confess, I seldom thought about the impact that she had on

---

30   First published in *The Upper Room: Daily Devotional Guide*, November/December, 2003, © 2003 Viola Ruelke Gommer.

my life prior to her death. It's not that I didn't recognize and appreciate the blessing she was, but I just didn't think about the impact, the influence, that she had on me. First of all, I am thankful for the moral influence she was. There was never any tendency on her part to pursue activities or involvements that were morally degrading or harmful. Her biggest "vice," and I'm stretching the term to use it in this regard, was love stories. She was loyal to certain television soap operas for many years—an interest that she shared with her mother. After her mother's death, she continued to watch two of them in particular and, if there was nothing of great importance going on, daily life was arranged so that she could be around the television while they were on.

Within the last ten years or so, although she never admitted it to me directly (I was unwise and unkind enough to be vocal about my opinion of soap operas from time to time) I observed she began to wean herself away from them. Even before she began working the secretarial position at Freeland, she had given up on them. I do believe it was something she and the Lord had confronted together. I don't know the inside story because by then the Lord had given me enough wisdom to back off, convincing me it was between the two of them, and she never confided in me about it—something I didn't deserve anyway after my previous performance.

I am sure what drove her interest in soap operas was her fascination with love stories. She thoroughly enjoyed romance novels. More than 75 percent of her reading was love stories. Oh, they weren't the only things that she read—she always had a Christian book or two going that she read a portion of each day during her quiet time. But novels were almost all of her recreational reading. That was our final activity of the day, the way that both of us relaxed for sleep. My form of escape from the stresses and problems of life and ministry has been to read mostly non-fiction about history, nostalgia, railroads, maritime, and nature, with occasional fiction on those subjects mixed in. Peg's escape was romance.

Our reading was often the topic of conversation. Over dinner in a restaurant, one of us might ask, "What are you reading these days?" It was an unnecessary question because we usually knew—we could see each others books plainly since we were laying next to each other in bed. Actually what we were saying was, tell me about the books you've been reading, and we did. So we benefited from not only our own reading but each other's as well.

Peg's favorite authors for light reading were Emilie Loring, Grace Livingston Hill, and Elizabeth Ogilvie. Those authors' books were always written with good moral taste—just "a good love story" Peg would say. Ogilvie evidently went through a period in which she dabbled in somewhat occultish themes, and Peg didn't enjoy those novels as much as her others. What she did like was the New England flavor and coastal Maine setting for many of the stories. In fact, that fueled her interest in visiting Maine, which we did twice. She absolutely loved it and wanted to go back again. The stories enhanced her visits and the visits enhanced the stories to the extent that she started collecting Elizabeth Ogilvie's books. Even though she'd read many of them before, she was reading them again. Every once and awhile, when we wandered off in different directions at used book stores or library book sales, she'd seek me out and, with great pleasure, show me an Elizabeth Ogilvie book she'd not read before. Though it might only cost fifty-cents or a dollar, she considered it a great and valuable find.

She also enjoyed Taylor Caldwell, George MacDonald, and another author she had more recently discovered whose work had much of the moral tone of Hill's and Ogilvie's, Agnes Sligh Turnbull. When we would leave on vacations, she always had a collection of novels she hoped would last 'til she got home.

Consequently, she tended to counter my less romantic view of life and relationships. I'm not referring here to matters of intimacy between two people so much as to what brings two people together in the first place. In that she was truly a romantic. She believed that we were meant for each other. We attended the same high school though we weren't acquainted then. When I was a senior, she was a sophomore, and I don't remember her from school, but she did know who I was. She remembered seeing me in conjunction with some yearbook function—I was editor in my senior year—and she said her stomach did a flip. Once we got together, she remembered that, and it didn't surprise her we ended up together.

In later years as we talked about such things, I said I didn't believe that any two people were necessarily destined to be together, that two people who were attracted to each other could, with God's help, develop a love relationship. She was never totally convinced, believing it started before the two even knew each other. The romantic part was the events and attractions that moved the two people toward each other, sometimes despite themselves. The greater the resistance, the stronger the counter currents to overcome it, then the higher the romance, making it mysterious and, for lack of a better word, "romantic." Her all time favorite romantic movie illustrates that, *Somewhere In Time.*

Even before her death, I had begun to weaken, and since then, I am even less certain of my previous pragmatic opinion. If God determines even a few significant occurrences in our lives, is it not possible He might have something as significant as a particular life partner in mind for us? Peg definitely had a romantic impact on me and it wouldn't surprise me if, as I'm writing this, the Lord is letting her look over my shoulder and she's just grinning.

This much I do know, her reading was a way of escape that mirrored the moral fiber of her life. (I think the increasing immorality of the soap operas began to bother her and influenced her forsaking them.) Her interest in reading and her moral standards reinforced my own.

Consequently, I never felt any anxiety about her devotion to our marriage, for which I am grateful. If we were apart, or involved with different activities and people of the other gender, I never worried about her fidelity. That wasn't just a naïve assumption. At different times, both of us dealt with attractions to other people that could have threatened our relationship. Through the Lord's provision, doors were opened for us to talk about those things with each other. Neither of us panicked or over-reacted, recognizing there were things beyond our individual control, and coming, I think, to the realization that we had to trust God and each other for the future of our relationship. I think we learned some important things about each other in the process, perhaps the most important being we were in our marriage for the long haul but couldn't take each other for granted either. I am grateful that Peg was a woman of profound moral integrity and never gave any cause for me to be suspicious, jealous, or defensive in our relationship. I am grateful to God for the moral character He fostered in her and the impact of that upon me.

Peg took seriously the biblical mandate for a wife to respect her husband. Peg was an excellent musician, knowing music technically very well, and she was very accomplished as a pianist, and later became a competent organist, though she never considered that her instrument. I was self-taught on the guitar, knowing enough chords to accompany myself for singing. When the folk music era came along, we sang folk music for fun. Later we began to sing in church. Then we began leading group singing with me on the guitar and her as song leader. As that continued, my lack of musical knowledge frustrated her. I know my musical timing on the guitar was unpredictable. She could see if I was following the printed music instead of "feeling" my way through it, her part would be easier. So she wanted to teach me to read music and to further my musical knowledge, but I was resistant, just wanting the enjoyment of it without getting studious. For awhile, she was very impatient with me about it and it wasn't fun for either of us. Then I had some health problems complicated by nervous exhaustion and anxiety, and I began to decline singing publicly to avoid the stress and tension.

Once I got out of the swing of it, we did very little, then my guitar began to deteriorate, and I finally sold it. In the last several years, we have been part of a very musically gifted church. Peg was in her element and loved it. But she did want us to do some singing together again. She liked to sing with the guitar so she was free of accompanying to concentrate on singing, but she would play the piano for us since I no longer had a guitar. I found she was much more relaxed and patient in teaching me new music. I believe she truly enjoyed singing together and had come to accept what it took for us to do that. I think she had come to respect and value what we had as opposed to what she aspired for us to have. That was the only area in our life together in which I can say there was ever a struggle over respect.

I am also grateful that Peg was never manipulative. Oh, she could be assertive and vocal about her desires. She was half Italian, from her father's side, and a quarter each Norwegian and Finnish from her mother's side. I have said she was Scandinavian on the outside, in appearance, and Italian on the inside, referring to her temperament and passion. But she never tried to make me or anyone else feel sorry for her or used guilt to her advantage. Someone she was close to related to her and others that way and she determined she would never do that, and she didn't.

In my comments at her funeral service, I expressed gratitude for being the one who was privileged to live most intimately with her. "Just like all couples, we had some bumps and we had some bends in the road of our marriage. But I believe that Peg would agree with me wholeheartedly that Christ is the one who brought us through. And through 37 years of marriage, we had a really neat relationship as co-workers, as partners in ministry, as companions, and, well, best friends. So I thank God for what He did in her life and for what He has done in my life through her, for the privilege of being the one to share intimate earthly life with her. Praise God!"

I am thankful for the spiritual influence of Peg. Basic to her faith was a total commitment to Jesus as her Savior and Lord. Her spirituality started and ended with Him. She was frustrated by the tendency in some church circles to avoid Jesus and to make God generic and impersonal in worship, Bible study, literature, and other areas of the Christian life. For several years in her office in the old church, she had a quote printed out and taped to the wall, which may have originated with Mother Teresa, which said, "You will never know Jesus is all you need until Jesus is all you've got. Then when Jesus is all you've got, you will know Jesus is all you need." She kept Him conspicuously central in her life privately, and lived out of that relationship with Him publicly.

I have already reflected on her faith throughout her illness and in the face of death. That was only an application in a time of crisis of the faith she lived on a daily basis. Though she was completely dedicated to Christ, she was less dedicated to the institutional church than I am. If we were vacationing or traveling, especially if we were camping, on Sundays, she would sometimes ask if we might just have our own "church" instead of finding a church service to attend. Since I was aware that some of my interest was driven by a desire to see what other churches and clergy were doing, sometimes I agreed. If we were traveling, the one who wasn't driving would read Scripture passages and we would share what those stirred in us, we would pray, sometimes we'd sing, remembering that Jesus said where two or three were gathered in His name, He was there. We would sometimes do the same in a motel room or at a campsite.

Prayer was always important to Peg. Usually before we left home to travel, we would take a moment in the vehicle before we pulled out of the driveway to pray about our venture. If I didn't initiate it, she would remind me. She was usually willing to be the one to voice a prayer if I asked. She was often the one to initiate prayer at activities she was a part of. There was never any doubt that the Spirit of Christ lived in her and influenced her will and her choices. The spiritual bond of faith we shared in Jesus is perhaps the deepest bond we shared because it influenced every other facet of life. I miss that intensely but I am also aware it is the very bond that continues beyond the severing of all others such as the physical, emotional, and practical bonds we shared for life in this world. Though that spiritual bond is altered, it still exists and will be renewed when I follow her beyond this life. I am grateful that Peg was a woman of faith, for the impact she had on me spiritually, and, to use a biblical turn of phrase, that we were equally yoked in marriage.

I am grateful that Peg had a sense of humor. She was not one to tell jokes especially, or one to pull practical jokes. For the latter I am *especially* grateful! But she enjoyed laughter, tended to see the humor in situations, and was tolerant of my attempts to be witty and took my "pun"ishment. I acquired an appreciation of verbal humor that uses the play of words and puns to provoke laughter—the kind of humor that causes us to groan when we get it or see the secondary meaning. She was always gracious when some of my puns didn't work very well or I tried to push them too far.

She had an excellent memory for jokes, and though she wasn't one of those people who always has a new one, she could usually recall one or two if invited, and could tell them well. One of her favorites for many years was one her dad told her that I believe he picked up from a Johnny Carson show, from an old actor who used to do bit parts in the movies, who was on the show as a guest. It seems there was a fellow who went ice fishing. After he had been fishing for some time without any success, he noticed that a young boy not far from him was pulling out fish, one after the other. After he watched for awhile, he finally couldn't stand it any longer and walked over to where the boy was fishing. As the young fellow pulled out another fish, he asked, "Say, I've been here as long as you have and I haven't caught a thing. I hope you don't mind me asking, but what's your secret?" The boy looked up at the other fisherman, kind of mumbled something, and went on with his fishing. "I'm sorry," the fisherman apologized, "I didn't get what you said?" Again the boy mumbled something and went on fishing. "I'm sorry," the fisherman replied again, "I still didn't get what you said!" The boy put his hand up to his mouth, spit a big wad of something into it, and said in very plain and clear language, "Keep your worms warm!"

There are some who would be surprised to learn that Peg's sense of humor sometimes had what I'll call an "irreverent" streak in it. Her sense of humor was influenced by her dad, who liked hunting stories, western and cowboy humor, and somewhat seedy jokes. He would have a new one for her every now and then and she was on the alert for stories she thought he'd like. If she heard one, she'd say, "I've got to tell Dad that one." Their stories were often somewhat undignified, but never sexual in nature. (She would tell me one of those now and then if she heard one she thought was genuinely funny.)

She liked comedy movies, especially older films that were not morally offensive, like Doris Day's movies, W. C. Fields, and the Marx Brothers. She particularly enjoyed musical comedies like *The Music Man, My Fair Lady,* and *The Sound of Music.*

Last Christmas things were so hectic and we were so exhausted by the holiday that we compared notes several days before and found neither of us had done our shopping for each other yet. So we decided to give each other certificates we could redeem after the holidays. One certificate I gave her was for a shopping trip to pick out a movie she would like from a video store. We found a copy of *Flower Drum Song* and she was in a quandary—it was more than $20 and she couldn't see spending that kind of money for a video. Since she hadn't seen it for years, and really had been wanting to see it again, she gave in only when I convinced her I would have bought it for her if I were shopping alone before Christmas, that it was something she would really enjoy and would probably watch more than once. She did enjoy it and I was so glad at the time I convinced her, and even more so now. There were so few things she ever really wanted, and even though it was just a small thing, I'm glad I was able to give it.

Perhaps her all-time favorite film was the western comedy, *Cat Ballou,* starring Lee Marvin and Jane Fonda. We have a copy and she watched it numerous times—now and then together—but she would also watch it by herself when I was away for seminars or conferences. When Lee Marvin, in a drunken stupor, stumbles into the wake for Frankie Ballou, is reprimanded for his disrespect and asked, "Can't you see what's going on here?" then looks at the candles burning near the coffin and bursts into singing, "Happy birthday to you!" she could never stifle her laughter. She always found it hilarious when it came to the scene where Lee Marvin, waiting to rescue Cat Ballou from the gallows, is mounted on his horse and both are leaning against a building with Lee Marvin half asleep, and the horse is standing with its head down and legs crossed. That scene just tickled her dad no end and her as well.

She also enjoyed many of the situation comedies from the golden era of television comedy prior to the moral downturn that began with *All in the Family.* She especially enjoyed *The Beverly Hillbillies, Dick VanDyke, The Honeymooners,* and *Gomer Pyle.* I was not much into television in the early years of our marriage, but as my energy has begun to decline, as it became possible to control what we watched with video recording, and as we found things we could both enjoy watching together, it became something we could share. I am grateful that we could laugh together and for the sense of humor that Peg brought not only to our amusements but to all of life.

I am grateful that Peg was a good money-manager and very responsible financially. She was always very wise in her spending. So much so, that she made some things difficult for herself. When we first started in ministry, our only income came through with my name on the paycheck. Before that, she had either been employed on her own or been a partner in the work that produced our income. So she began to have difficulty spending money for herself. If there was something she could use or wanted, she was reluctant to buy. It took awhile to figure it out, but she felt like she was no longer contributing financially even though she was a partner in ministry. We talked about the fact that I had not been earning a wage while going to seminary. Still I felt free to spend some personal money. I felt that no matter whose name was on the check, it was our family income. After that we began budgeting personal money for both of us to spend in whatever ways we chose. Seldom did she spend all that was budgeted for her personal use, but it did loosen up her willingness to spend for herself.

She was a careful shopper, using coupons, watching the sales, buying generic or house brands if there was no difference in quality, using ingredients in the kitchen rather than prepared foods, and economizing wherever possible. In recent years as life became more complex for us, she began to see the sense of spending some money in reasonable ways to save time, but without extravagance or waste.

She saw it all as part of her Christian responsibility to be a good manager of what God had entrusted to us materially (it's called stewardship in the Bible). She was very dedicated to recycling believing not only that she was doing what God wanted her to do with material things but that she was extending the availability of materials for her grandchildren and their children yet unborn.

Inevitably, when it was time to dress for a holiday worship service or a special occasion, I could count on her standing at the closet and saying, "I've got to go shopping for some new clothes!" Yet when we would walk through Sears in the mall or past the clothing department in some other store, she might spot something she liked but refuse to pay the price, especially if it wasn't on sale. I do have to admit, I have seen her pick out things from the racks she did like, but not find it in her size or color. It seemed clothes shopping was always a frustration to her given her popular size, conservative taste, and frugal approach.

Though she scrutinized very carefully what she spent on herself, I don't ever recall her being critical of anything I spent money on. She might sometimes question purchases I proposed, but it was seldom over the money issue. More commonly her question was did we really need it or was there a lesser model? She was, however, willing to spend money for good quality items if she thought they were legitimate needs. Right from the beginning in our marriage, we learned to make major purchases together, which I'm sure also helped to reduce any potential financial tension.

She had a number of ministries and causes that she felt very strongly about supporting. In recent years, following a stewardship emphasis at church, she endeavored to cut back on some when she learned that it is more effective to support a few ministries with larger contributions than a larger number with small gifts. She was also a proponent of switching over some of our Christian giving to support the ministry that our son, Mike and his wife, Becky have begun, *Living Covenant Ministries International.* I am grateful that money was never an issue in our relationship, that God always supplied what we needed, and that Peg was a responsible partner and co-manager of what God has entrusted to us.

There are many other things about her that I am grateful for, including her congenial companionship, her acceptance and love of my family, and many more. But it is time to bring this expression of gratitude to a close and go on to Thanksgiving dinner with one of the several families who graciously invited me to join them. Perhaps when I return I will close this with a prayer of gratitude to God for Viola Ruelke Gommer and her reminder to make this a day to say "thank you" for one who isn't with me today in her physical presence but is very much with me in the impact she has had upon my life, for Peg.

Thanksgiving Prayer as the Day Ends

Dear Lord, you are often called Divine Providence and Comforter, and You have been both, and more, to me today. You have provided me with people who have expressed their care through invitations to celebrate Thanksgiving with them in their homes around their tables with the food they have prepared and You've provided. You have inspired phone calls from friends and family expressing their care.

You began this day by calling me to not feel forsaken in the present, but to appreciate my blessings of the past that continue in the present, and there are many. But the one You have placed in the spotlight today I am truly grateful to celebrate, and that is Peg.

As I reviewed the impact Peg had upon my life, I have come to a deeper sense of appreciation of her many qualities of character and personality in a way that is somewhat different than before. My only regret is that I was not as appreciative to her while I enjoyed those very things. But then death did stop the merry-go-round and gave me a look at many things that I did not see while life was revolving rapidly day to day, week to week, and year to year. Since I cannot directly ask her to forgive me for not telling her about all the ways she's affected my life, I pray that You will forgive me, and if You do such things, that You will tell her my sentiments.

I am grateful for the impact she had upon me and upon our marriage, both in the positive things she contributed and the negative things she avoided through her moral character, her tolerant disposition, and her loving heart and spirit. Though Jesus said in your Kingdom no one is bonded to anyone else in an exclusive relationship of marriage, except that we all will be bonded to Him like a bride to a bridegroom, I will be grateful if Peg and I can know each other and sense a connectedness in You that reflects what You began in us in this world.

With so much said about holidays being hard for those experiencing grief, I am grateful for a day in which I felt less the loss and more the gain from "One who isn't with us today." That is the thanks I give to You as this day of giving thanks comes to its end.

Amen!

I stood on the rugged coastline of the Pacific Ocean in California and said, "I am here, right now, at this very moment!" I was trying to absorb the fact that after years of looking forward to being on the rugged California coast, I was finally there. I knew it was a very special experience and it would not last, so I impressed it upon myself by realizing where I was and saying, "I am here, right now, at this very moment!"

Our being there on the California coast enjoying the ocean's beauty was the realization of something we wanted very much to do. For our 30th anniversary, we had taken a train trip around the country, traveling from Chicago to New Orleans to Los Angeles to San Francisco to Seattle and back to Chicago, laying over in several cities for several days. It was a wonderful experience and we both enjoyed it thoroughly. As we traveled on Amtrak up the California coast from Los Angeles to San Francisco, we were so impressed by the beauty of the Pacific coast that we determined to come back there some day and explore what we had observed through the train window.

We put it on our list of things to do some day, and several years later we did it, with my sister Nancy as a traveling companion. We took the train to Los Angeles, rented a car, and took about a week to drive up the coast to San Francisco where we took the train back home again. It was a wonderful place and we were fascinated by the seacoast with its unique atmosphere and features. There was so much to appreciate and absorb that I tried to maximize the whole experience. That is why I wanted to firmly fix in my recollection being there in that place we had looked forward to, because I knew the moment would not last. I can still distinctly remember the wonder of that dream coming true, standing there with the ocean rolling in against the rugged rocky coast, the salt spray and the sea air blowing in my face and saying those words, "I am here, right now, at this very moment!"

God brought those words back to me in my time of prayer this evening. I heard them, though I didn't make much of it. I was ready to settle down for bed. But the Lord impressed upon me He wanted me to write about it the way I had been writing down my own thoughts and feelings. Though I wasn't deliberately voicing it or even formulating it consciously in prayer, I guess I had been arguing in spirit with the Lord about His joining Peg and I together, then tearing us apart. Once again, it was feeling unfair.

I did have to admit to God I knew that one of us would eventually precede the other in death. That is a given. My argument was that it was premature, that there should have been more time for us to be together in this life. Then the Lord reminded me of the California trip and my words. He impressed upon me that my situation is something like being there on the edge of the ocean. Our marriage in this world was not a permanent address, it was an excursion into something that was only for a time. I acknowledged that in the wedding vows when I said, "Until we are parted by death." I assumed that meant until we both reached old age—but that wasn't anywhere in the fine print or even between the lines. So all along I was living on the edge of something very precious without stopping to say, as I had on the coast of California, "I am here, right now, at this very moment!"

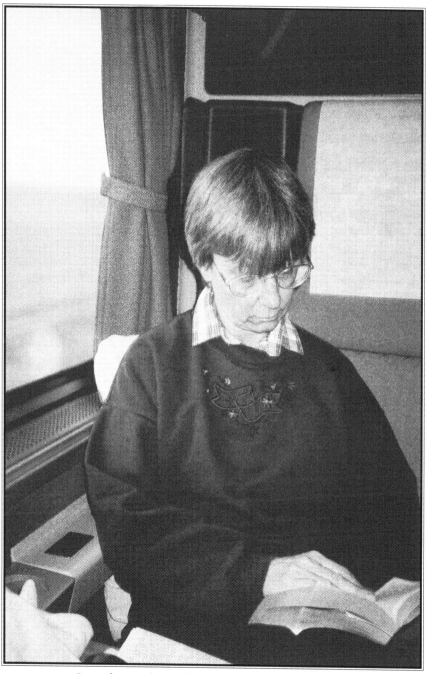

Somewhere in the Southwest on Amtrak with a good book.

I am still standing on the edge of life in this world—we all are even though we seldom comprehend it—just as I stood on the edge of the vast Pacific Ocean. The main difference is that trip west was something I desired intensely to do, whereas I do not desire to be where I am right now, not since the view and atmosphere has radically changed. Yet I sense the Lord is saying to me, "You are here, right now, at this very moment! Notice and appreciate where you are. It will not last forever either." Just as we eventually got back on the train and headed back home, so I will one day head "home" to be with the Lord. Eventually this life and all it contained, happy times and distresses as well, will be even farther removed than I am now from that California coastline. So I need to do as I did there on the edge of the ocean and make the most of where I am because "I am here, right now, at this very moment!" but it's not forever.

Lord, I guess I need to sleep on that.

Everyone said the holidays would be the hardest, but I didn't find it so, at least not in the ways I was led to expect. That is in part due to the attentiveness of family and friends as well as the pace of life with personal and church-related activity over the holidays. The kindness and inclusiveness of friends has been touching and helpful. Many have extended invitations, checked on my welfare and state of mind, and remembered me with thoughtful expressions of love and care.

Mike and family gave up their Christmas Eve and Christmas morning at their own home, as well as the Christmas weekend, to be here. I surmise that was out of concern for me, but I also hope out of their own need to be in the setting where Peg's things and presence are still in evidence. Here in our home, we connected as family, which included Peg's brother, Francis (Frank), who came to visit for a few days as well. Truly Peg is our common earthly bond, although I rejoice that we have a greater bond in Jesus Christ as Savior and Lord, who entered the human family and whose birth is what the whole holiday thing is about anyway. I trust that was good for all of us.

What has been hardest is the let-down, the return to solitude, and anticipation of routine. It is a little like the adjustment I went through after the funeral when everyone went home, although I didn't go back to ministry right away on that occasion. Today was only the second day of the new year, but I felt it profoundly. Along with it came the realization that I must get back to working through grief and tasting again the bitterness of sorrow and loss. Yet I wouldn't have it any other way—in fact being distracted from them has created difficulty all its own. Grieving is sorrowful, but not grieving generates a kind of anxiety and sorrow too. I have lost something—someone—of great value and now it is as though something else of great value, the thoughts, feelings, recollections, and memories, are slipping by and being lost like great waves and swells on a vast ocean disappearing in the wake of life.

As the new year gets under way, things will be returning to normalcy which means I will be resuming the usual schedule of weekly meetings that were suspended to make way for holiday preparations and events. I don't anticipate with great eagerness resuming the usual, but I do anticipate more eagerly resuming reflection and writing, something I have yearned to do for several weeks now. I know the conversations I had with others during the holidays about all that happened during Peg's illness and death and my adjustments since, especially with Mike and Becky, have been helpful. Even so, I have missed the writing time.

Before I resumed this journal, I read through the brief notes I have jotted down that capture idea fragments I want to explore and develop more deeply in writing. In the past, if I didn't come to available time with something fresh to write about, I would read over the notes, find inspiration in them, and set off in a direction. Tonight they felt cold and distant. That in itself is grievous, the feeling that I may be losing impetus to garner all I can from this unwelcome experience. I also sense that the additional holiday services and preparations have exhausted some of my energy and capacity to recall and write. Again, I am reminded if this is of the Lord, I must rely entirely upon Him to provide for both content and execution. Even as I say that, I find myself reminded to be reliant on His Spirit—that what I have written thus far has been given as a gift—why would it be any different in the new year?

I have heard it said that we must complete our grief work. If indeed it is being at sea, as I alluded to above, due to seasonal winds and currents, I have been on a slightly different course for awhile—not off course, just tacking around the islands of the holidays to make progress. Now that I am once more on the open ocean and the prevailing breezes are again blowing, I trust the Navigator will readjust the course and we will be sailing in the direction He has charted. I don't even know the precise destination of this voyage—though some who've made this journey before me point out some of the ports of call along the way—but by the feel of the air and rhythm of the swell, I will be able to tell when we are making progress as we did before. It is good to be able to look back and see where I have come and to look ahead knowing this is all going somewhere. At least when I can still look back and see where we've come from, I know we're not going in circles. The island holidays blocked the view for awhile. But so far the Navigator has been willing to help me identify the fading shore and there's some reassurance in that. When I come to the place where all I can see is horizon all around, then

He knows I've got to rely entirely upon Him. All I can do is hope He'll make me ready!

I have just come home after morning worship and preaching two services but this morning was so phenomenal that I have to sort it out right away. I preached on Jesus in the Garden of Gethsemane and His experience of prayer right before His arrest. The sermon emphasized Jesus praying "My Father, if it is possible, may this cup be taken from me. Yet not as I will, but as you will." After taking us through the Garden experience with Him, I made six observations on praying for the will of God. The fifth one was "Praying for God's will brings us to accept the unfolding of events as God's response to our prayers."

In my sermon preparation, I had decided I would talk about praying for Peg's healing and recovery as an illustration of that fifth observation. I planned to say in the sermon, when her kidneys shut down and nothing would induce them to begin functioning again, I could see she was not going to recover. If God had wanted to miraculously spare her, there were plenty of opportunities that had already passed by that would have been miraculous. I would follow that by saying, "God could have sent ten thousand angels on a miraculous rescue mission when Jesus was breathing His last on the cross. But He didn't because He had already made His will known and the circumstances were playing that out." Likewise, God's will was made known to us for Peg in her circumstances.

I knew it would not be easy to get into all that, but with the Lord's help, I would do it. I had several days until Sunday to be prepared to handle it. Saturday morning, between preparations for Sunday, which included practice preaching the sermon, I did a few little things around the house. As I was tidying up, I picked up Peg's devotional books and a couple of small notebooks she kept with them. Last Christmas, I had given her a new notebook that was bound like a book with an attractive cloth cover to use as a journal. I opened it to find it empty. She had never quite gotten to using it. The other notebook on top was a small spiral bound 4x5 "Fatbook" with a plastic cover, blue of course, from a dollar store. I had given it to her from my stash of supplies when she was looking for something to write devotional notes in—thus the idea of giving her the more attractive book as a gift.

I was curious to see how much she had written in the "Fatbook" so I opened it to find she had only used about fifteen or so pages. As I did, it fell open to a page and the words she had printed at the top caught my attention—they were printed for emphasis—the rest of the page was written. I started reading.

BACK UP -
THOUGHTS FROM THE HOSPITAL
TRUST!
Job 2:
rhythm &

I know You are in control & my life is in Your hands...I sing that all the time. New awareness of what that means.
Surrendering my will to Your will, knowing You only want what's best for me...You mean it for <u>good</u>
How can I trust & fear at the same time -
The thing you're thinking about is the thing that owns you - let <u>Jesus</u> keep your mind fixed on <u>Jesus</u> not the circumstance!

Even as I was reading what Peg had written, I knew that I would have to add that as introduction to what I intended to say about her in the sermon for Sunday. Her notebook had been sitting there for months, in fact I had moved it around before, but I knew God had led me to put my hands on it with it falling open to that page at that precise time for that reason. It would be hard enough to just talk about accepting "the unfolding of events as God's response to our prayers." Now I was supposed to read her words on accepting God's will besides? My immediate response was "No!" That was more than I wanted to handle.

After my initial response, I went back to that thought to explore it. It seemed to me if I floundered emotionally in the preaching, it would make me the center of attention, detracting from everything else the sermon stood to accomplish, let alone what it would put me through. I put the notebook back and walked away from it satisfied that it wasn't a good idea.

But before long, I was back to it, rereading what Peg had written. It was compelling. And who better for the congregation to hear from on the subject of praying for God's will? After all, most of them knew her, many of them knew her very well, and what she had to say was significant to them too. I took her writings to the sermon material to see how it might fit in. I had to relent and allow that it added strength and impact to the message. After all, it was Peg's prayer for God's will patterned after Jesus' prayer for God's will, which was exactly what the sermon was dealing with. What better way to convey acceptance of unfolding events than for one who is dying a tragic death to say, as her Lord had taught her, "My life is in your hands..." I am "...surrendering my will to your will, knowing You only want what's best for me..." OK, I would take it with me Sunday morning reserving the option to not include it when the time came if I was so inclined.

While I was trying to maintain an optional attitude toward it, I knew what God's desire was, and so I resorted to an additional recourse—prayer. (It never occurred to me I was doing exactly what Jesus did in the Garden when He was troubled by the way events were headed regarding His own fate. He prayed—a risky thing to do when we know there is a chance that what we want is vastly different from what God might want.) I e-mailed our son, Mike, and daughter-in-law, Becky. I wrote out Peg's words and sent them, told them the situation and asked them to pray for me to have what I needed for the preaching. They, in turn, passed my request along to their prayer team. In a phone conversation that evening with my sister, I told her the same story and asked her to pray as well. If I couldn't avoid this I knew I would have to do it by the Lord's provision.

God honored our prayers. I could tell that many in the congregation were moved during the message, particularly regarding Peg. After both services, a number of people responded with comments, affirmation, and observations of their own. Peg never preached a message in a worship service at Freeland, though she had occasionally spoken words of praise or testimony during the sharing time and introduced music with her own faith experiences or comments. But this morning, she ministered to the congregation in word and example.

However, what made the whole experience phenomenal for me was something else Peg said only to me, unexpectedly, while I was in the middle of preaching about her writing and her experience.

In the second service, reading her statement out of her notebook was a little harder the second time. I felt myself faltering as I moved into my statement about our prayers not being answered as we desired and her kidneys not resuming function. As I did, I moved her notebook out of the way to see my sermon notes, and for the second time it opened providentially. As I moved it, I caught a quick flash of what she had written on the last page on which she had made entry. Though I only saw it briefly, what I saw was very clear and distinct with words and writing I'd recognize anywhere. In fact, it was something she'd written to me many times before. In large letters that covered the whole page she had written, "I Love You!" I immediately took them as her words to me, followed by realization they were God's words to me as well! I continued the sermon with my mind only half engaged with what I was saying, trying to absorb the dual message from Peg and the Lord, wondering if this was something I needed to insert impromptu into the sermon. No! this was for me, and I kept it to myself. It was meant for me in the moment and I took it as affirmation and encouragement in answer to prayer, a sort of "well done" from God who was further illustrating the good of His will, not mine, being done.

As I concluded the sermon and we sang the closing song, I kept going back to those surprising and profoundly compelling words, "I Love You!" Who were they written for? Peg had often said them and written them to me, and I knew they were intended for me this morning, but these were in her devotional book and they were probably originally intended for God. Were they her last written words? I was at the same time moved and mystified by them.

I fought to keep my attention on the close of the service and my emotions in line as I concluded the sermon. The song I had selected earlier in the week for closing the service, *I Stand Amazed in the Presence of Jesus the Nazarene*, now described me. Every time we sang the words of the chorus, "How marvelous! How wonderful is my Savior's love for me," I could see Peg's "I Love You!" flash card. Though I couldn't maintain enough voice to sing all the lines of the song, especially the chorus, I had enough for the benediction to conclude the service. I continued to contain my eager desire to explore the context of those closing words in Peg's notebook as I greeted people leaving the sanctuary. I compelled myself to do my usual after-worship routine putting things away, gathering up my sermon materials, and tending to other miscellaneous after-worship tasks.

When I got home I disciplined myself to first change my clothes, took Peg's notebook out of my briefcase, and got comfortable in my chair in the family room. Once again I read those precious words, "I Love You!," Peg's words to God, given back to me from her and the Lord, months after she wrote them. I backed up into her notes to find out what preceded them.

"Good morning, Lord. Thank you for sending your loving arms to hold me first when I asked to know You are here! You must speak volumes to me, & I am so oblivious. Thank you for opening my spiritual eyes this morning. Please keep me from closing them, or rushing off to do <u>my</u> thing, instead of listening for what You want to do each day. Thank you for the reminder that You will <u>never</u> leave me nor forsake me! I'm so ashamed that I let myself get so far from You—and yet You've been right here within me all the time. Forgive me for giving You token attention. Help me to give You primary focus, cuz I can't do it—only You can move this stubborn heart of mine.

I

Love

You !

Thank you that You love me so much. I really am excited about what else You want to tell me. Please just give me the grace to deal with the pain for as long as You choose to leave it."

That last line came to the bottom of the page and then on the reverse side she wrote the message filling the page, which may have been the last words she ever wrote...

Coming to me as it did, when it did, and from whom it did, that's a pretty phenomenal message!!!

I was in Wal-Mart writing a check at 5:00pm when it hit me. Today was our anniversary—it would have been our 38th! My immediate response was, how could I have gotten this far into the day without remembering it? I remember thinking last week I would be on vacation spending time with family at my family home on January 29th, the date of our anniversary, and wondering how it would go. I suppose I should be pleased that not remembering the day didn't hurt anyone's feelings—certainly not Peg's. But it did mine. It hurt to think that after all these years of learning to remember anniversaries and birthdays, I forgot the day of our anniversary on the first occasion to remember it without her.

This all started on Sunday the 25th. After church, I traveled with Mike and his family to visit Becky's aunt, wife of her mother's brother, who just recently lost her husband to a longer battle with cancer at age 60. (He was only 12 days older than I am.) After an overnight stay, we came on to Calumet to spend a week in snow country for the children to enjoy winter recreation. I knew it was Thursday when I got up in the morning because of several things I needed to do at this point in the week. But the date totally escaped me until writing the check in Wal-Mart.

It isn't that I didn't think about Peg during the day. As we shopped at a variety of places, I thought about other occasions when all of us had been there to visit family and made the rounds of favorite shopping places together. At one of the resale shops, I remembered how she enjoyed shopping there and, on one occasion, had found a Green Bay Packers jacket that she fell in love with and bought.

Even though I thought of her throughout the day, it being our anniversary escaped me. I suppose there's some consolation in the fact that the first time I saw the date on the day, I recognized what it meant. I am, after all, on vacation and have not been paying attention to the days. I remember questioning yesterday what day of the week it was and about how rapidly the time is going.

Still, it troubled me that most of the day passed before I realized what day it was and I had to force myself to concentrate on the check-writing and the transaction with the clerk. I determined to not confront the feelings that were wanting to surface until later. But now that supper is finished, I have excused myself, retreated to the solitude of the guest bedroom in order to reflect and make this writing become my anniversary observance.

How we observed our anniversary had changed over the years. We started out giving each other anniversary gifts and cards, and having something special for an anniversary meal together. Eventually we started going out on an anniversary date, usually for supper, on the day if at all possible. Then as the years went by, we decided we didn't have the heart to do more shopping for each other after the Christmas season, and we would sometimes decide on some special thing we might buy to enjoy together. Eventually we backed off of that because they were usually things we would buy anyway and it seemed pointless, especially to me, to label them anniversary gifts. Besides that, we were both struggling with the material stuff that we seemed to be accumulating.

Even though we altered the gift giving, we continued to give each other cards on the day. And we almost always went out for dinner on our anniversary or as soon as possible thereafter, usually to some place a little more up-scale than we did regularly. Sometimes, when we took a mid-winter vacation, we would postpone our celebration 'til then, go out for dinner at some special place wherever we happened to be, and call that our anniversary celebration. That way we remembered our anniversary on the day and still did something special with each other to commemorate our marriage, without the pressure of that being bound to the specific day. I think that was pleasing to both of us. Besides that, beginning with our 25th anniversary, we would do something special for those years that ended in zeros or fives. For our 25th anniversary, we took an Amtrak trip around the country from Chicago to New Orleans to Los Angeles to Seattle and back to Chicago with stop-overs of a few days at New Orleans, San Francisco, and Seattle, a twelve day trip in all. In 1996, we went to Florida with our motorhome for our 30th, and right at the moment I don't recall what we did in 2001 for our 35th.

I don't know what we would have done for our 40th but there were several possibilities. Years ago, we realized there were all these places in the world we wanted to see and we weren't visiting many of them. Following the advice of someone we heard in a seminar, we worked out a list of places by mutual agreement, and began projecting in which years we might make those trips. The idea was that by working out a plan we would accomplish more of those trips than we would if we only said to each other we'd like to go here or there some day. And it was true. We made trips to Maine, Florida, the Grand Canyon, California, and other less extensive trips that we would most likely not have made had we not been intentional in calendaring them. I always kept the projected itinerary penciled into the back of my pocket Daily Suggester, Peg wrote it in one of her pocket calendars as well, and when we took regular vacations, we would review and sometimes revise the plan as desired or necessary. We both marveled at how close to our projections the actual travels turned out. Each year, when I discarded my old Daily Suggester and started carrying a new one, along with all the other pertinent information I transferred from the old to the new, I would write in the projected itinerary which I called "Vacation Schedule." Here is the plan as it last read in my 2003 booklet:

Florida – 2003/2004
Denver – summer 2004
Amtrak to Maryland and Washington DC – Spring 2005

Route 66
California north from San Francisco
Bike across the Upper Peninsula
Scranton and northern Pennsylvania
Nova Scotia
Texas

Peg really wanted to go back to Florida again, so that was top priority. In fact, if things had remained status quo for us, we would be making final plans and preparations right now to leave in February. But traveling to Denver and the Rocky Mountains to see steam narrow gauge tourist railroads there was my interest, and because that needed to be a summer vacation, we were going to do two in 2004. We both loved Amtrak trips but had never been East of Chicago on the train, so that trip included places in the East we wanted to see. The others without projected dates we would get calendared while we were on future trips—we always came home with an updated itinerary when we made a trip—but I figured it would be Texas in 2006. Peg wanted to make a return visit to her younger brother's grave in the National Cemetery at San Antonio—he was a Viet Nam veteran who died in 2000 of cancer linked to agent orange.

Here it is, the middle of the 2003/2004 winter, and I am far from Florida. In fact, family circumstances took me the opposite direction instead. So I have asked myself, will I continue to travel alone following the itinerary we had planned together? My inclination thus far is to say, probably not. As I've already mentioned, many of them were places Peg wanted to visit. When we went somewhere that was of primary interest to her, I would work in some things that I wanted to see and do in that region and along the way. Likewise, she would do the same when a trip was something I had suggested. There were a few things one of us was interested in that the other was not, but that didn't matter because there were more than enough options we could both consent to or both felt equally as excited about. So I may consider doing some things that were on our list by virtue of my desires and others that were not on our list at all.

I suppose that is representative of the way life needs to go for me in general. It doesn't make sense to do things because Peg wanted to do them, as if that would some how or other fulfill her desires vicariously. Doing things because she wanted to do them and we never did, in order to satisfy any feelings for not doing them with her, doesn't seem healthy either. It seems I will simply have to learn to accept such things as lost dreams. I will have to examine my own needs for recreation, travel, and time away and work out suitable solutions for myself. That seems to be part of the adjustment required in going from being a twosome to a solitary individual. That's why I am here right now in the Upper Peninsula, because Mike and Becky offered me the opportunity to come north with them. It afforded an opportunity to see family here when I would be unlikely to venture into mid-winter in snow country on my own, a respite from the work of ministry after a busy holiday season and beginning of a new church year, as well as a time to enjoy being with Mike and family for an extended period. And perhaps spending the first anniversary after Peg's death alone wouldn't have been the best either, although undoubtedly I would have remembered it before it was almost over.

But I did remember it once I took out the checkbook to write the date. And I feel this reminiscing is a form of celebration, a way of remembering the special lady the Lord gave to me for 37 years, which would have been 38 today. I haven't done anything today I would construe as celebration. But then, as I have pointed out, we often didn't celebrate on the day. So perhaps I will find some way yet to do that in the days ahead in keeping with what had become for us common practice.

That seems like a good way to end this writing and this day, thanking God for 37 years of marriage to a wonderful woman, and asking, "Oh Lord, God, Creator of man and woman in your image, giver of life and health, and giver of new life beyond death in this world, You are the One who joins male and female so deeply in marriage. You have reserved to Yourself what You have instructed no one on this earth to do in separating husband and wife. Thank You that You joined Peg and me so deeply in marriage, even though the pain of that severing has been so hard to bear. Thank You for the times of celebration that You provided in our anniversaries of the past and for all the blessings that were ours to celebrate and remember. I pray that You would now give me a suitable way to remember the past, to appreciate what lingers, and celebrate in the future, to your honor and glory and to the credit of the wonderful wife of my youth, Peg, whom I still love very deeply and miss very, very much today. And thank You for the special anniversary blessing of not letting this day go by without bringing it to mind as our anniversary. Though it's not been easy, I wouldn't want it any other way. Amen!"

How is it possible to be surrounded by people and feel alone, especially when they're mostly young people who are full of life and vitality? But tonight I did. I went to the Valentine's Party for the youth at church that was the kick-off for a fledgling youth ministry. But then being around youth always makes Peg's absence obvious to me.

She loved working with youth. It all started when we were lay people and new Christians first becoming involved in the local United Methodist Church. The United Methodist Youth Fellowship was an established group that needed adult counselors in order to continue, and we were asked. Peg was excited about it and convinced me we could do it even though I was skeptical. She'd had experience working with Campfire Girls when her mother was a group leader and thoroughly enjoyed it. Since she really wanted to do it, I consented because she could handle the leadership and all I would have to do is provide a male presence. But of course, eventually I got drawn into the leadership and interaction with the youth, doing lessons, designing and conducting activities, and chaperoning youth events and outings. It was one of the things the Lord used to introduce me to ministry with people.

After that, once I completed my education for ministry and we began serving churches, we served as youth counselors in all of them except this last appointment. We had decided that it was time to step back from youth work when we moved into the new setting. We felt we both needed a break from the demands of youth ministry. We had been active in it for about 16 years of the previous 26 with seven of those years intervening for me to complete my bachelor's degree and theological seminary. Since youth work requires so much energy, time, and emotional wherewithal, given the kinds of stresses so many youth are dealing with these days because of their family situations, we thought it might be time to retire. It was a hard choice for Peg because she loved working with teens so much, but she felt in our new setting there were other endeavors where the Lord was directing her focus.

Every once and awhile she would lament not working with youth and as our present church struggled with trying to get youth ministry off the ground, would be tempted to get involved again. We would end up reviewing our reasons for not pursuing it here and then she would be reminded of the rationale for discontinuing our involvement. It still troubled her to think that there was the potential for a youth program, knowing the blessings that such things can be to young people and the fruit such things can yield in their lives, but she would eventually work her way through it, coming to grips with our original decision.

I went to the youth gathering tonight to lend my support and to observe the event without any particular responsibility. If Peg were here, we might have both attended. With other adults to provide leadership, she probably would have been content to just observe and be supportive, but would have thoroughly enjoyed it, I know. I couldn't help thinking about that as I visited with some of the young people, ate lunch with youth and adults, and watched the adult leaders interacting with the youth.

During the singing time, I remembered how involved she was with music and the youth. She helped to get a tape lending library started with one youth group, selecting contemporary Christian music that she thought would appeal to them, that they would listen to—and they did. She was always on the alert for concerts or music events that she could take them to and she would do whatever it took to get them there. We both saw so many young people influenced by Christian music and many who made faith decisions when appeals for commitment or life challenging decisions were presented at youth events. She loved music and youth and God worked through her to bring them together in life changing ways.

God touched me tonight as the musicians led us in singing one song in particular, *You Are My All In All.* As we got into the song, I was glad I was sitting behind the group and the lights were dimmed so we could read the words projected on the wall. In fact, I felt a strong inclination to just leave for awhile but decided I've not walked out of anything thus far for such reasons and I ought not to start now. It was the same song that had touched me in the hospital the night before Peg died. The youth group Mike and Becky had taken on a mission trip came and sang softly and sweetly, with guitar accompaniment, to her in her hospital room. Their voices blended so beautifully in soothing melody singing, *Jesus, Lamb of God,* (I heard that same sweetness again tonight in the singing). As the youth left the hospital room, I thanked them for coming and told them Peg must have thought that she was already hearing the voices of the angels singing. I know I did. They graciously came to her funeral service and sang that song again in celebration of her life and praise to God. All of that came back to me in the darkened fellowship hall as the voices of the music leaders and the youth blended once more in that beautiful song.

I don't know how much I will be around the new youth ministry. I do intend to be supportive in whatever ways I can—it's far too significant to neglect. But I do know that whenever I am connected with it, Peg's absence will be apparent to me. It's just one of those things I will live with. There's too much of our shared past and ministry connected with ministry to youth to ever forget it or to want to. Maybe I wasn't feeling alone around all of those people after all, just lonesome for the one who it seems belonged there with me.

Chapter 7

Vulnerable with Scars

After this week, my assessment of what happened some years ago with a man in one of my churches, whose wife died suddenly, is more certain. One evening this past week, I met with the church's visioning team to receive the results of a church-wide survey and to go over how to interpret the information. As we did so, opinions about the church's schedule of multiple worship services were in evidence. Some in the church have wanted that particular issue addressed since we entered the new building four years ago. It does need to be considered for a variety of reasons, but since any changes in that regard could effect participation and the present growth we are experiencing, I am reluctant to see us make any changes without adequately examining all the factors involved. Nevertheless, I keep hearing of discontent with two services, and of a desire to return to one service now that we are in a larger facility.

The visioning team working with the survey, of which I function as leader, was formed not long after we moved into our new building. So it seemed wise not to push us into over-drive and we were taking our time, attempting to be thorough, in the components of our visioning work. Besides, there was no deadline and nothing immediate hinging on results of the team's work, except that as the church began to recuperate from the flurry of activity of the new building project, a greater sense of direction would be needed. So we would take our time, expose ourselves to a variety of input, and listen for what we believed the Spirit of God would want us to hear.

But then the worship schedule began to become an issue. The survey was one logical step in the approach to dealing with it to give the church's decision-making body a cross section of the congregation's point of view. Formulating the survey to address the broader concerns of the visioning team, as well as the worship schedule, took more time than anticipated and seemed, to some, only to delay getting at the issue they where anxious to address. When that lagged behind their expectations, the level of static around the matter increased.

Though the work was taking longer than some liked, we expected to have the survey completed last spring and the results in the hands of the visioning team for decision making and recommendations to the church's board in time to influence the schedule for last fall. Even though the survey was ready for distribution by late spring, with Peg's illness concurrently and death in the summer, the work of the visioning team ground to a halt.

While I was away from ministry in the early fall, the survey was circulated, and when I came back to active ministry, as soon as I was able to do so, I called the team back together and we began exploring how to tabulate and utilize the information. One of our parishioners designed a very comprehensive computer program to put it into useable form and we are now ready to begin interpreting the wonderful array of input we have received. That's what we were doing in the meeting, distributing the tabulated results, learning how to work with them, and informally chatting about what we were seeing there.

As the discussion continued, we commented on opinions and perspectives we saw in the survey—no one was advocating taking any action—it was just incidental discussion. But as the conversation continued at some length about the worship schedule, I found myself becoming very disturbed. Finally, I began to express my point of view, becoming very adamant that we would make no changes in our schedule until we had a variety of informed input to make a decision that was in the best interests of the church. I was not about to put at risk the increasing number of young families who are becoming involved in the church without knowing if there is any connection between their attendance and the present arrangement of worship services and Church School. I am sure my voice and demeanor conveyed my agitation and conviction. With some emotion, I went on to say I had come back to ministry not sure that I could continue and I was still finding that out. I knew I was not yet up to speed. I still wasn't sure if I could get back to my previous level of function and I felt like I was being pushed.

As I talked, I was surprised by the emotional pressure I felt inside. I knew I was beginning to loose rational control. It didn't make any sense to expound these things to people whom I happened to know, for the most part, we're not personally troubled by the worship schedule and were only responding to what they were seeing in the survey for the first time. Yet I felt compelled to express my frustration, and as I did, I felt it rising within me, asserting itself more forcefully. When I sensed what was happening, I was able to wind out and then to let the topic go, after assuring everyone I wasn't agitated with any of them, but because of the impatience I was encountering on the issue.

Later, as I thought about my reaction, I remembered a man in one of the churches I served who, though generally was very mild mannered and congenial, became very upset in a board meeting. When a decision was made requiring expenditures to be handled in a particular fashion, he felt it was a reflection upon him and the way he was conducting the business of the committee he chaired. He confronted the maker of the motion about his intent, defended himself very strongly, and wandered off into other matters that upset him that seemed to have little to do with the matter at hand. I later commended the board for the way they had all handled his flare-up and the maker of the motion for not responding in kind. They had graciously let him blow off steam. In fact, the man who made the motion tried outside of the meeting to make contact and establish good relations, but to no avail. I followed up with private visits and conversations. We all felt very deeply for him. He had lost his wife of many years suddenly in death and we knew he was devastated. I always thought that his reaction in the meeting was fueled by pent up emotions and stress that caught him off guard and overwhelmed him, which he couldn't stop. I now believe that even more.

The experience this past week is not my first experience like that since Peg's death. There was another meeting a few months ago, in which I found my emotions rising. Although I was expressive about my point of view, I wasn't as animated and I didn't feel the flare inside then to the degree I did recently. I don't even recall at the moment what the issue was, although I suspect it was related to matters of church attendance and growth, but I knew my inner response was out of proportion to it.

So do I feel like a bomb waiting to explode against someone or something? No, I don't think so. I have always had a long fuse, but there is a charge at the end of it, if it burns long enough. I'm not worried about that. But at the same time I know my tolerance is reduced in some ways. Perhaps what underlies this isn't the issue so much as it is the feeling that my energies and wherewithal are absorbed in trying to deal with grief, sorrow, individuation, and the basic functions of day-to-day and Sunday-to-Sunday ministry, while some are only concerned about issues I see as peripheral in light of what I have been dealing with.

The man whose wife died several years ago we eventually lost to the church. He gave up his leadership position immediately, came only to worship, then came sporadically, finally not at all, and eventually dropped out of our membership and found another church. I don't think it was because he wasn't reassured, forgiven, and accepted. I think it was because he embarrassed himself, couldn't face the people he had been so vulnerable in front of, and maybe didn't understand himself why he acted as he did. It was just easier to avoid all of us than to confront his vulnerability.

I just looked up the word "vulnerable" to see if that was what I really meant to say in the context. Synonyms are: weak; defenseless; helpless; exposed; at risk; in a weak position. Maybe that is what disturbed him about his reaction. It was an expression of his helplessness exposing himself to us in ways that unsettled him and he couldn't understand. We understood, I think, but he didn't and he was embarrassed and couldn't risk it again. Maybe those in the meeting the other night understood too. One did tell me afterwards he could not imagine what it's like to go through such a thing, meaning Peg's death. Should this happen again, when those feelings rise inside, perhaps the Lord will help me remember how defenseless, helpless, weak, and exposed I am, and I'll not be afraid to be vulnerable. That may not prevent it from happening again, but if it does, it's OK—I won't have to find another church too!

As I was traveling home on a misty March afternoon, the fog was rising from the melting snow in the tunnel of barren trees that line M-127. I was returning from the church I had served previously and officiating at the funeral of a former parishioner who had died after six years of incapacity following a stroke. Since I had known him when he was a healthy and active man in the church and community, at his widow's request, his present pastor graciously welcomed my participation.

As we stood together in front of his open casket, I said to his wife, "It's hard to believe that just seven months ago we did just the reverse." She had come to stand with me and comfort me in front of Peg's open casket. We had all four known each other well and shared ten years of life's journey together. Later in the funeral sermon, I found myself tying together the loss of her husband with the loss of Peg, things I experienced, and things that ministered to me, in the hope that they would minister to her and others. I always attempt to make funeral sermons personal, celebrating and commemorating the life of the one who has died, but this was perhaps the most personal one I've ever preached because it included the two intersecting losses.

With an evening funeral, I had stayed overnight with a former parishioner who continues as a good friend. Then after visiting for part of the morning with another friend I haven't seen for awhile who has been struggling with health problems, I began to travel the four and one half hours home, much of it down the desolate and sparsely traveled freeways of northern Lower Michigan. I listened to tapes—at first tapes to challenge and inform my faith and theology, then music to rest my mind and lift my spirit. But then the Lord began to apply what I was hearing to me personally.

I was listening to *Scripture Memory Songs: God's Grace.* The lyrics for the song, *I Will Restore,* were from two passages of Scripture, slightly adapted for singing and sung repeatedly, as is often the case in contemporary praise music. The passages were Jeremiah 30:17a – "But I will restore you to health and heal your wounds," and Song of Songs 2:11-12a – "(11) See! The winter is past; the rains are over and gone. (12) Flowers appear on the earth; the season of singing has come..."

As I drove past the melting snow and the barren trees, in the grayness of the day, I could sense that spring was impending. I had preached a message of hope sandwiched between faith and love—1 Corinthians 13:14, "And now these three remain: faith, hope, and love. But the greatest of these is love." I was assured by former parishioners, who also knew and loved Peg, that including her in my message was meaningful to them. In return I said that it was also helpful to me. I am sure that message of hope influenced me as well.

The musical message of Scripture began to give me a sense that the intensity of my wounds of grief and my ailing soul may yet find some relief. Whereas I believe I have been clinging desperately to the memories of the last months and days of Peg's life involving her illness and death out of a desire to maximize every possible meaning and significance, I now am beginning to get a glimmer of it being OK if my scope is broadened—that God has more for me if I can accept that. I'm not yet sure that I can or want to, but if God does have more, I at least need to be open to that. I don't yet see, however, how that's possible for me without losing something of the precious seasons that preceded. But if the barren trees, surrounded by melting snow, will soon be surrounded by spring flowers, followed by green buds and opening leaves—and they will because I've seen it before—then I need to allow that God can turn my season of grief and sorrow to something fresh as well.

The conundrum in all of this, as I've already said, is that I don't want to lose all that was precious from the past in the 37 years of life I shared with Peg. I don't even want to lose the pain and the sorrow that were a part of our last months and days together. No! I'm not a masochist—I don't enjoy pain. But it was a part of our experience together—something I felt with her, part of us, some of our closest moments, and therefore worth keeping, at least the memory of it. And I admit, I don't see how God can preserve that for me and yet give me something new at the same time. I have to be willing to trust that God can bring on the new without losing what is of worth from the past.

Perhaps that is why Jesus kept the scars of His crucifixion in His resurrected body. God could have healed them and removed them from His sight and ours. We assume He left them for us to see as evidence of His suffering and crucifixion. But it just may be that they also serve to remind Jesus of His love and what it was like to die for the sins of the whole world. Perhaps when He sees them and remembers the pain, He also feels the depth of the love that made Him willing to receive them. If we look at His scars as evidence of His love, does He not see them as such too?

A second song that compounded the message of the first came along very shortly on the next tape. Amy Shreve beautifully interpreted Matthew chapter four in these lines of her song, *They That Mourn.*

> "Lost between numb and broken,
> Afraid that I'll fall apart.
> Battling grief and disbelief,
> I'm hiding a wounded heart....
>
> "Let the dew fall,
> Let the snow melt.
> Let all of the sadness pour.
> He will carry,
> He will comfort.
> Blessed are they that mourn."[31]

Blessed are they that mourn? That seems like an oxymoron—that the two are antithetical. But I can say that what Peg and I had that was precious came from the Lord. I have sometimes wondered what our lives would have been like had the Lord not brought us to faith—two strong-willed first-born children, one who functions very thoughtfully, cautiously, methodically, and slowly, the other who was very spontaneous, responsive to feelings, quick to respond, and vitally alive. We had some stressful adjustments and bumpy periods in our early years, but as we both came to faith, the Lord gave us a commitment to Him and to marriage that became our shock absorbers, until He was able to steer us onto better pavement (although there were still a few pot holes now and then, just to remind us to depend on Him).

Blessed are they that mourn? Yes, I suppose because they have something to mourn for. They either know there is something better than the moment because they have had it in the past or because they have been given a foretaste of it by God. And if God can give it once, He can give it again, by faith—or

---

31   © Amy Shreve Wixtrom 1998, G. B. Wix Publishing, ASC-00598, used by permission.

something as good or better. Besides that, in the loss of what is mourned, God, Himself, is the one who will "carry" and "comfort." And that should be sufficient.

I still cannot really grasp how God can retain all that is precious from the past and move me into the future without losing it, but I at least allow it may be possible. If with my God-given senses, on the way home from a funeral on a gray and dreary March day I can perceive spring is impending, perhaps I can sense with my God-inspired spirit this inner grayness can begin to lift as well.

This is my first weekend away on my own from active ministry. It is almost eight months since Peg's death and six months since I returned to work. I have been on one vacation for a week with Mike and family during that time, but this is my first real time off from the church on my own.

I worked it into the schedule several weeks ago because I knew I needed it periodically in the past—we both did when the two of us were working together. Early on in ministry we learned we needed to be out of town and generally unavailable in order to keep from being drawn into church-related business or activities. (I commend all the congregations we served for respecting our need for space and time away from our weekly duties. Once they learned our pattern for time off, they accommodated it very well.) Of course, there have been occasional emergencies and funerals that have involved Monday time, my usual day off, which we obliged and never resented. But we noticed when Mondays have been infringed upon for reasons other than those already mentioned, it has usually been by non-church people or denominational expectations. Certainly I need time off as much now, if not more. But I struggled with how and where to spend this weekend.

What we called a "weekend" was actually an overnight on Sunday with Monday as our day off. On Saturday, we would prepare to camp or take a short trip. When we got home from church on Sunday, we would finish up what preparations we couldn't complete the day before, and then drive to our destination. Usually we would have lunch on the road—sandwiches and other things we could easily eat while traveling—and then a bigger evening meal once we'd arrived at our destination. During the camping season, we would often take our little motorhome and I would cook something over charcoal, which Peg thoroughly enjoyed. During the colder months, it would be a motel at one of the not too distant cities. Mid-winter we would even take advantage of off-season rates at tourist centers less than an hour from home. Distance wasn't as important as just getting away. We would usually relax and read on Sunday evening, watch some TV if we were in a motel, and then the next day, after checking out of our accommodations, enjoy whatever activities might be in the area where we had stayed or along our way home. We would always eat out for supper and try to arrive home early enough to unpack and relax a little before bed, yet late enough so that we could stay disconnected from responsibilities for the whole day. They were only brief get-a-ways but we usually managed several each year, especially during the camping season, and they helped to distance us from the pressures of church and domestic life.

When the church started two Sunday morning worship services several years ago, I was granted two comp-time Sundays each year. So, in addition to the four weeks of vacation I already had, we could actually take two real weekends from Friday afternoon or Saturday morning, depending on the workload for that week, to include Monday. We would usually attend a church where we happened to be on Sunday morning, although sometimes when we were camping we would have our own worship with prayer, a song or two, Bible reading, and the thoughts that inspired—Peg especially liked our own worship times. That was a real blessing to have three full days off and we always took them as weekends away.

As I am writing this, I am on a comp-time weekend. I spent Friday night and Saturday morning with Mike and family, visited Peg's grave after I left their place, and traveled on to one of our favorite places for our get-a-ways. It is now late Saturday afternoon and I am parked along the St. Clair River in Port Huron near the Blue Water Bridge to Canada. Over the years, we have enjoyed watching the lake traffic as the freighters travel up and down the waterway, as well as the pleasure craft in season, where the river joins Lake Huron. I suppose watching the lake boats wasn't an interest Peg would have pursued on her own, but over the years, she learned about them through my interest, got to know some about them, and enjoyed seeing them come and go, especially the ocean-going vessels from other countries, as well as visiting the pleasant places where we went to see them.

Port Huron has a decent selection of restaurants, a great craft outlet Peg would sometimes like to visit, and main line railroading we would often check out a few miles southwest of the bridge. (When Amtrak came through, both of us would feel a yearning to get on board and go—we didn't care where.[32]) But we spent most of our relaxation time along the river enjoying the setting and the attractive view of the lake, the bridge, the truly aqua blue water from which the bridge gets its name, and Canada across the way.

---

32 On one occasion when we were at the station and a train arrived and departed and I saw Peg's genuine excitement and longing to ride the train again, it inspired me to work it out with her to move up the projected date on our last Amtrak trip. I am so grateful we did.

Over several years of coming to the same place, we developed little habits that became part of the experience. We would bring along our reading material, park in the waterfront parking spaces, and just sit in our vehicle to enjoy the pleasant setting, sometimes entering into conversation about our reading, the people and things we saw around us, or other things that just happened to come to mind. Takeout chicken from KFC became one of our traditions. We would pick it up on a well-timed run between passing freighters and bring it down to the river to eat in the car so we didn't miss any of the action on the river. We would walk the riverfront sidewalk under the bridge and past the historical light ship that has been made into a museum. Along the way we would greet the fishermen sitting there with their poles holstered in sockets clamped to the guard rails waiting for the bells tied to the tips to ring signaling a fish on the line. We would observe the people feeding the ducks that always congregate on the grassy inland side of the walkway. It afforded more than the half-hour of walking time we usually desired. All of these little routines and pleasures had enhanced what is to me now, the obviously greater pleasure, conspicuous by its absence, of our companionship and shared life together.

It may not be obvious at the time we are experiencing them, but I have learned that things we enjoy together take on a whole new level of meaning that exceeds the enjoyment they alone provide. The pleasure might seem to reside entirely in the experience, but when the togetherness is stripped away, the greater source becomes evident. That's not to say there are no such things as solitary pleasures, but it does seem that many things, when shared with others, are exponential in their enjoyment.

I think that's what Steve Brown was saying in his November 2003 newsletter for Key Life Network, when he wrote about the differing interests he and his wife have in music. He likes bluegrass and country. She likes classical. "I have grown to love Chopin and Beethoven for no other reason than I watched her love Chopin and Beethoven. I go to symphony concerts with Anna but would go even if she didn't. Do you know why? Because I've learned to love music Anna loves because Anna loves that music." [33]

I guess I haven't learned to love what my wife loved as much as Steve Brown has because I'm not inclined to attend concerts by the music groups she enjoyed. But I did learn to enjoy Peg enjoying her music just as I think she came to enjoy me enjoying my interests. And I do know, without her, even the particular things I enjoyed before are diminished and overshadowed right now and I'm having to work at pursuing them. So I can't say I'm as glad now as I have been in the past to be where we often came together, though I am glad to have the break from the daily grind of ministry.

---

33   © Steve Brown, *Keylife Network Newsletter*, November 2003.

Although I was here in the fall with my sister, Nancy, (she enjoys the lake boats too), and mother while Nancy was on vacation and I was on leave of absence, coming here now still feels like a first. I'm sure that's because it is my first comp-time weekend away. I wasn't sure I wanted to come to this place because I knew it is so closely associated with our past. But then even if I deliberately went somewhere we'd never been together, I would know why I was there. At least here I am in a familiar setting, not having to figure out new accommodations, locations, and routines.

For awhile I had thought I might just stay home for the weekend, especially since there are so many personal and domestic chores that I need to and want to get accomplished to improve my daily situation. That wouldn't be ministry related and would give me a break from work. Besides I thought I might find time for some of the recreational pursuits I enjoy at home but have even less time for now than before. But then Wednesday of this past week, when I was making the four and a half hour ride south from the Upper Peninsula and the funeral I had participated in there (which I wrote about in the previous selection), I observed it did feel good to be traveling and away from home. It reminded me of the benefit I received in our get-a-ways of the past. I took that as a sign I should take the weekend away despite my other inclinations and fall back on the things we had learned about the importance of getting away. Just because I am on my own now that hasn't changed. I decided the only way I will find out if doing the old familiar things will continue to be a benefit to me is to try them, as long as I don't have to unduly force myself. What I enjoyed and benefited from in the past should continue to do that for me in the future even though I know the most profound blessing in that, which I hardly understood at the time, is absent.

As I sit here watching the waters of the St. Clair River rush past, flowing under the Blue Water Bridge, the big Canadian and American flags across the way in the park on the Canadian side are unfurled against the gray sky by the damp cold breeze off Lake Huron. Two fishermen are getting set to try their luck in the deep turbulent waters just beyond the huge boulders and concrete rip-rap that keep the shoreline in place. The lights of the city and the traffic streaming across the bridge are beginning to appear. The laptop battery is beginning to show signs of depletion and I'm beginning to think about supper. The scanner doesn't report any river traffic due for the next several hours, and with the heavy overcast that is beginning to give the highest center span of the bridge a misty appearance, it's getting to be time to leave for the day. I guess it won't be take-out chicken tonight, but there's still tomorrow or Monday. I'll probably walk the waterfront in the next two days—I hope the weather permits because I desperately need the exercise. I have a couple of good books to read and this still seems like a good place for that. The laptop will charge up overnight and the Lord may give me more to work my way through by then. So what this experience will have amounted to by Monday afternoon when it comes time to head for home remains to be seen. But at least I will have given it a try, and God willing, I will know whether this is still a good way to get away.

Weekend Addendum:

I miss my car counter! The first train I saw leave the Port Huron yard headed west toward Flint was a long one with three engines. I always get out of the car to photograph them. Peg preferred to stay in the vehicle often counting the cars. When I came back, she would have told me how many there were and also would have commented on any of the railroad or company names on the cars that caught her attention, asked me if I saw the Wisconsin Central or other Upper Peninsula related cars, and mentioned the Dow Chemical tank car wondering if it might be going to Dow Chemical in Midland, near where we live. I would ask her if I missed anything on the scanner, which I would often leave in the car, and she would update me. I sure miss my car counter!

Late in the afternoon at the rail yard, I ate an orange. I ate the whole thing but if Peg had been here I would have shared it. I followed it with a couple of Milky Way miniatures. I'd have had room for more Milky Ways if she'd have eaten the other half of the orange. Of course, had she been here it probably would have been Carmello miniatures!

I wasn't sure I wanted to stay trackside 'til Amtrak was scheduled to come through, but I did. And it was just as emotional to watch it go by as I thought it might be. It's hard to observe the things you enjoyed with someone you love, knowing the other enjoyed them so much—it increased the pleasure—and you will never enjoy that other's enjoyment again.

It must be spring! Along the riverfront, I saw two seagulls, birds that usually fight avidly over scraps of food, sharing a bagel. One picked it up and carried it over to the other to take a bite. I thought of eating the orange and Milky Way miniatures by myself just a little while ago.

Well, I am home. In reflection, the time away was familiar and yet different. But then life is different. I followed the pattern we used to follow except that we often stopped at Mike and Becky's on the way home for a visit instead of for an overnight on the way out. I didn't eat inside at restaurants at all—everything was take-out. I spent more time at the railroad than I would have with Peg but that was mostly because the river traffic was very minimal. I know I wasn't ready to come home. I guess that's a good sign. There was so much good reading yet to do and I got into some interesting writing to explore—the article that follows—which I wasn't able to finish before leaving. I actually thought about staying on another day but have pressing things tomorrow. I trust it was beneficial to get away and I guess I would do it again.

"Therefore what God has joined together, let no one separate," (Mark 10: 9 – NRSV). Those words are Jesus' words spoken in response to a question by religious leaders about divorce. Jesus said even though the law of Moses allowed for divorce, it was not part of God's original design, and was a concession granted because of human hard-heartedness. God's design was for male and female to become intimately connected "So they are no longer two, but one flesh." (verse 8b.) [34]

Being "one flesh" has many aspects. The one that is most evident to me right now is shared identity. Peg and I took on an intimately linked identity. That is inescapable even today, though I am away from home. I attended worship at another United Methodist Church where I happened to know the pastor as a colleague in ministry. He recognized me and asked how I was doing, commented on what an adjustment I must be going through, and hoped the service would be meaningful to me. Obviously when he saw me, he thought about Peg and her death. I was immediately identified with her. Similar things continually happen because we were married and were no longer two but a twosome.

Prior to Peg's death, when friends and acquaintances saw one of us, they would ask about the other. If they knew one of us but not the other they might ask, "How's your husband?" or "How's your wife?" Sometimes it would be "How's your family?" That is simply an expression of interest and care about another person recognizing their identity and state of being is bound up with others. Sometimes, of course, when the acquaintance did know the other partner the question was asked out of genuine interest and concern for the one not present. But either way, it acknowledged the shared identity that goes along with marriage. Our society has traditionally formalized that by referring to couples as Mr. & Mrs. with the woman taking on the identity of the husband's family name.

Peg and I were "one flesh" in matters of health and well-being. When one was not well, the other was also distressed and concerned. Empathy is a sign of identifying humanly with the suffering and distress of another person. I have empathized with many parishioners in their illnesses. The same can be

---

34   See Appendix B for an exploration of the Biblical concept of "flesh."

said of death itself. I have empathized with others in the death of someone close to them and have sometimes felt the loss personally when the person was someone I was close too as well. But never have I been so deeply and lastingly affected by illness and death as I have with Peg's. I know that is because we were "one flesh." We were intimately linked by God so that we were no longer two, but one. What one felt, the other felt. What one suffered, the other suffered. What affected one affected the other as well. I believe that's God's intent and design.

I have already written much about shared interests—biking, camping, travel, reading, music, and others—but we participated in others because one of us was especially interested, like boats, trains, concerts, flea markets, and yard sales. Peg never went so far as to wear a railroad hat, which I do on my time off. I never learned to dance—something I know she would have liked me to do. Our becoming one was not a matter of becoming co-identical carbon copies of each other. Our oneness was more than mere "externally" shared activities. There was an essential spiritual oneness. I believe when we stood before God at our wedding and made the vows of marriage, God took those vows seriously, as He does in every marriage, and began a process of union binding us together as "one flesh."

When we think of flesh, we usually think of the human body, especially the soft tissue. In that sense, in the physical act and ecstasy of sexual union, husband and wife come closest to becoming "one flesh." And what are children but the one flesh evidence, which God intends to be conceived in the context of marriage, of the one flesh relationship of two people. Although all of that about the flesh relationship is true and valid, I believe that is only the sensual surface level of oneness. There are, of course, other motivators driving the physical relationship as well, since God does little that is one-dimensional. But that is why sexual union alone is inadequate as a binder in marriage.

Regardless of the faith of married individuals, I think that God's promise of the two becoming one becomes operative when two people enter marriage, or even if they begin to live together in a psuedo-marriage relationship. God's designs function as He intends regardless of our intent. As life is shared physically, socially, domestically, recreationally, parentally, and so on, the two individuals begin to take on a new identity, a new selfhood. God's designs and promises are operative whether we are aware of them or not.

That explains to me why divorce is often such a painful thing. It also explains why co-habiting has aftereffects on people, even if they do marry, because they entered into God's design without God's consent. In divorce, people are doing what God has forbidden, separating what God has been joining together—the souls of two human beings made in His likeness as complementary creatures intended to enhance and fulfill each other. But even if the divorce is what is sometimes labeled as "amicable," it only means the consequences of circumventing God's prohibition are not as obvious.

In the case of marriage partners who know God and believe in Him through faith in Jesus Christ, I think there is a union that takes place at an even more significant level than the flesh. This is the ultimate unity between human beings of any gender—the full and complete unity of spirit in the body of Christ. Add to that the unity of "one flesh" in marriage and you have two people who are soul-mates, bound not only by temporal marriage but eternal unity in Christ.

God's intent, however, is not that the unity of marriage last forever. It is a provision for this life that is a model, in many ways, for the greater unity of those who belong to Him in Jesus. Marriage in this world is temporal but it foreshadows the relationship on a greater scale that Jesus promises with His Church, which is called in Scripture, "The Bride of Christ." No other human relationship but marriage can adequately reflect the love that Jesus has for His Church and the deeply intimate nature of that union. This is the only thing that redeems what God eventually does to every human marriage. He promises to make two become a twosome, gives them a new identity, bonds them together in deepest commitment and intimacy, and then severs that relationship with the death and irreversible departure of one leaving the other behind abandoned with his or her identity shattered. Even in the reality beyond this world there is not the hope of marriage reunion with the former partner, for we are told by Jesus, "when they rise from the dead, they neither marry nor are given in marriage, but are like angels in heaven," (Mark 12:25). The marriage vows plainly state that marriage is effective "until we are parted by death." We have the hope of reunion, not as partners in marriage, but as children of God.

I do not think that diminishes our levels of intimacy in the reality of God's Kingdom. I think it actually upgrades human intimacy to the level of the relationship we will have with Jesus Christ. Human marriage only foreshadows the greatest intimacy we will have with Jesus and the intimacy we will enjoy with all other believers. But drive out of your mind any images of a free love commune where anyone can be erotically intimate with everyone who is consensual. This is not a possessive self-gratifying love driven by the motives of this world. This is what Paul described in 1 Corinthians 13:12 as he wrote about love. "Now we see but a poor reflection as in a mirror; then we shall see face to face. Now I know in part; then I shall know fully, even as I am fully known." (I find it interesting that the Greek word for "know" is the same basic word that is used for sexual intercourse in the New Testament.)

I think that is why God chose to describe Jesus' return for His people as the bridegroom coming for the bride. If God would design and implement something so potentially wonderful as marriage between the two genders He has created in His image that only stands to deepen and become more significant as life progresses, and then end it with no redeeming outcome, it would indeed be a cruel and heartless thing.

I believe it is for those reasons that God reserves to Himself what He has forbidden us to do; to put an end to the marriage of two people. His intent is not to elevate us to levels of joy and then take them away leaving us destitute, but to heighten our anticipation of an even higher level of joy, in kind, that is still forthcoming. If the highest joy I can humanly know in this life is complete and total intimacy with one who is designed and created in the complementary image of the Creator, then that foreshadows an even higher ultimate intimacy that is forthcoming through complete and total union with the Creator Himself, who is the source of the image of both genders.

Should that mean, then, that I should be satisfied in the loss of my partner, to live with the knowledge of what is forthcoming, and with whatever advances may be realized in me while I am still in this life? Perhaps at a rational level there is satisfaction in knowing that. But at a spiritual, emotional, experiential level, there is hunger for what once was fed, desire for what once was had, and yearning for what once was real. The degree to which my experience of those is forgotten with Peg, is the degree to which my anticipation of all that with the Lord is also diminished.

Just as God reserves for Himself the severing of what He has joined together, so only God can resolve this loss without diminishing the hungers for what He intends the loss to create. Though I can try to escape it, to numb it, or avoid it, I cannot heal what God has severed. "What God has joined together, let no one separate." I want to believe that God will treat and heal what He separates in His good time.

I am embarrassed to admit that last night I dreamed about Brooke Shields. Where did that come from? Over the years there have been a number of women I have thought were quite attractive, but Brooke Shields was not one of them. It's certainly not that she's unattractive, but Brooke Shields was not a woman I have ever been very aware of. In fact, I don't think I've even seen one of her movies.

I will say in my dream she looked very pretty with a warm smile and wavy brown shoulder length hair. We were going somewhere together—I have no idea where—and she was driving. I slid over across the seat toward her, told her I was going to snuggle up to her, then put my arm around her. She also put her arm around me—you can tell this was a dream because there were no preliminaries—and leaned her fluffy brown hair against my cheek. Then we kissed. I'm not sure who was steering, although I remember looking past her and handling the wheel for a moment. Then I held her close and began to cry. I cried because her feminine nearness stirred very pleasant feelings in me that gave me an awareness of Peg's absence. It was that mixture of joy and sadness that brought me to tears. Then I began to wake up becoming conscious that I had actually been making crying sounds that disturbed my sleep. I soon realized I was home in bed, it was 3:30 in the morning, and I needed to get up and go to the bathroom.

Since I'm commonly awake for at least an hour after those nighttime jaunts, there was a lot to think about. First of all, I had to tell myself there was nothing to feel guilty about. I was not deliberately fantasizing about another woman—it was only a dream, albeit I will admit, a very pleasant one to revisit. Secondly, I had to admit I am no longer intimately bound to Peg. I could say I am free to pursue relationship with another woman, but "free" sounds to me like I have been released from something that confined me or prevented me from something I wanted to do. But my marriage to Peg didn't confine or prevent me from any such thing. Any such inclinations had been lost some time ago, as I've already said elsewhere. Though I know with my mind that my marital status in society is now single, I still feel married and committed in heart to Peg.

It isn't like she holds some sort of expectation from the past over me. I don't remember what prompted the discussion or when it was—perhaps it was the death of a friend's partner or my health issues that involved surgery and a heart irregularity—but we had talked about just such a scenario. We both agreed that we would not want the other to stay single if one of us passed away and the other wanted to share life with a new partner. We couldn't see why the survivor should be alone and I certainly knew that Peg could be a real blessing to someone else as she had been to me.

I remember a pre-marital counseling session with a couple who raised that question. The prospective bride wanted her husband to promise that he would never marry again if something happened to her. I took them through the marriage vows and explained that was an unfair request, that God had designed marriage as an intimate relationship for this life only, and the promises they were making were only binding "until we are parted by death," is the way the vows state it. Both Peg and I understood that and offered each other our blessing in the event one of us died, leaving the other "free" to marry, if that was the survivor's desire. I am thankful we worked that through, but I still feel very much married to Peg in spirit.

No one has asked me yet, but I suppose it is just a matter of time before someone will want to know if I think I might ever marry again. I'm sure that people around me wonder. I do too from time to time. But I don't pursue that thought very far. It stirs a fear that such a thing would somehow diminish my memories and appreciation of Peg and the relationship we had—that it would push her into the past—and I don't want that. Then there's always the risk that I could end up going through another illness with someone else whose life had become intimately linked with mine, and I wouldn't want to go through that again. Just this evening at a community prayer service I talked to a man from another church whose first wife died 15 years ago after 41 years of marriage, who remarried, then lost his second wife only six months ago after more than ten years of marriage. That sounds like more grief and distress than I care to endure. Then there's the need to accommodate someone else's lifestyle, relationships, habits, and preferences that sounds like more adjustments than I care to consider. Still, I recognize that years of life with someone else could be a blessing to that person and to me.

The future seems very uncertain to me right now. I could conceivably retire in a year and a half. But I feel very unsure about what is best for me and what God wants. Whatever God wants *will* be best for me, and that's what I need to seek in everything. But even the seeking seems premature. I'm still trying to pick my way through the daily events that stir grief, knowing that in three days it will be the anniversary of Peg's first emergency hospitalization that was the beginning of the end. Dealing with that is more than enough.

One thing I will definitely take into the future out of my dream. I will be more aware of Brooke Shields. And though I don't know that it's necessary to apologize for dreams, I do offer her mine for being so forward with her on our first "date." I hope she will accept my apology and, if she's single, maybe we can go for a ride together again or even out to dinner sometime.

I have dreaded it happening and it did. It happened while Peg and I were at a holiday dinner with one of our church families in the fellowship hall. There were places for us at the somewhat large table prepared for the meal, but we sat back across the large room waiting for the bustle of activity to settle down with all of the food being brought and passed around. We expected to be invited momentarily to join everyone at the table.

As we sat patiently waiting, I realized how tired I felt, so I laid my head over on the table next to me just to rest a little. But I fell asleep. Then the thing that I dread happened. I began to wake up but I couldn't come out of it completely. My head was tipped slightly back and I felt like my tongue was back in my throat. I knew I needed to wake up and I tried calling for help but all I could do was make guttural noise—Ahhhhh! Ahhhhh!

Now and then I have this strange and scary experience if I sleep on my back. So I never sleep on my back deliberately. I'm careful to only go to sleep on one side or the other. But now and then I might end up on my back and this helpless suspension between sleep and awake comes over me. All I can do is make this guttural noise—Ahhhhh! Ahhhhh!—as a distress call. The sound would rouse Peg and she would gently wake me. Eventually I've come out of it on my own if she hasn't, though it is usually more prolonged and traumatic. It was reassuring to know she was there to bring me out of it whenever it happened.

There in the fellowship hall, I knew Peg was next to me, and I was able to touch her, so I squeezed and prodded her, thinking when she realized what was going on, she would wake me out of it. But this time she didn't respond, and I didn't know why. I could even feel her next to me and she wouldn't wake me. Finally I came out of it, awakened, I think, by my own noise and increasing anxiety. As I lay there, I realized I wasn't with a church family at a holiday dinner at all, and I wasn't with Peg. I was in my own bed and what felt like Peg was simply the way my arms were nestled in my pillow and bed covers. Even as I realized that, I avoided moving and the position of my arms gave me the sensation of her presence.

As I lay there with my heart pounding and anxiety elevated, I realized what had happened. The thing I had especially dreaded dealing with on my own had happened for the first time since I have been in bed alone. This time I wasn't really on my back, and that concerned me. My head might have been tipped back a little. Maybe I had moved before I was really conscious of my position but if I did it couldn't have been much. Yet for some reason, it didn't leave me as terrified as I feared it might, bringing to mind the saying, "We have nothing to fear but fear itself." That may be overstatement, but at least I wasn't as traumatized the first time I had to deal with it on my own as I feared I might be.

Then I remembered the familiar passage of Scripture from Ecclesiastes. " [9] Two are better than one, because they have a good return for their work. [10] If one falls down, his friend can help him up. But pity the man who falls and has no one to help him up! [11] Also, if two lie down together, they will keep warm. But how can one keep warm alone? [12] Though one may be overpowered, two can defend themselves. A cord of three strands is not quickly broken" (Ecclesiastes 4:9-12)

I had preached on that passage a number of times, especially at weddings. I called this the advantages of being a twosome. Peg and I were a living illustration of the passage. We had worked together most of our married lives in business and ministry and God had given a good return to us for our work. Our photography business flourished and our years of ministry together were full and productive.

If one of us was incapacitated, the other carried the load for both. She had done so for me through a back surgery, three eye surgeries, and with a heart irregularity, and I had done so for her through her battle with cancer. I recall in several wedding sermons illustrating verse eleven by saying that I discovered early in our marriage that the bed covers didn't work near as well when she was out of town. (And they haven't the past winter since she's been gone either. I've actually set the night temperature on the programmable thermostat higher since I've been alone.)

When we've had to face oppressive circumstances and difficult people, we learned by talking and commiserating with each other, and the Lord, we could gain strength and perspective to go on without being defeated or beaten down. It took me a long time to learn that one. Early on in our relationship, if Peg was having a struggle with someone, I tried to point out how she was coming across or what she could do differently in the situation. In typical male fashion, I tried to "fix it" by fixing her. She took that as criticism, which, I can see it really was as I look back—I was critiquing the way she handled things. Rather than trying to change the way she responded to others, I should have been affirming and supportive of her. She did that for me. She was always on my side, even if she might have thought I wasn't handling things in the best fashion. And if she ever did, she never betrayed it. Consequently, she didn't have the doubled defenses of the twosome of verse eleven, at least not 'til later in our marriage when I stopped trying to resolve her dilemmas with others and started joining forces with her.

In those wedding messages, referring to the last line of the passage, I pointed out something even better than a twosome—that indeed the Lord wants to be the third strand woven into every twosome making it a threesome. I often used a little illustration written by Catherine Paxton in which she describes marriage as a braid. Even though a braid only has two strands of hair, she says, you can't make a braid that way. It won't hold together without the third strand. Then she says that's the way it is in marriage. It takes God, woven into that relationship like that third strand, to hold the marriage partners together.

That reminds me again that God holds the prerogative of separating what He has joined together—in this case, the prerogative of unraveling the braid He has woven. Certainly we were woven tightly together, more and more so over the years. I trust the whole intertwining is not coming undone, even though the Lord has slipped out one strand. He must still be there if my recent night time episode is good for evidence. But certainly the weave doesn't feel as tight. There is a vacancy there where Peg was woven into my life and me into hers so that we were one life, one "flesh" together. The Bible is right—God is not quickly breaking our threesome into a twosome, and if He chooses to never tighten up the space that once was Peg's, I trust He'll help me live with that. It's His prerogative.

For the first time in quite awhile, I have most of an evening to write. We have come through a period of intense activity at the church with spring events and preparations for summer. I have finished cleaning up the kitchen after my evening meal, brought the finances up to date in the computer, checked E-mail, and I'm now able to settle down in the recliner with the laptop. I have sometimes been desperate for time to do this very thing, but tonight I do not have a sense of urgency. In fact, I could easily have pursued other endeavors if I let myself. I wonder what that means?

There are any number of things I could explore in writing but none seem ready to bubble over now that I've taken the lid off—I should say, raised the screen on the laptop and exposed the keyboard. I'm aware that it is just a year and two days since Peg was diagnosed with cancer. I thought that might be a traumatic anniversary to face, but it has come and gone without great ramifications so far and I don't feel inclined to go there now. I have had some thoughts about the nature of grief but that seems more cerebral than I care to be this evening. Then there is the biblical concept of "the flesh" in my previous writing I know I need to go back to and round out, but that feels more like sermon preparation than personal reflection. I suspect my difficulty in taking advantage of this personal time has something to do with the hectic pace of the spring and early summer schedule, then suddenly coming to a screeching halt here in the chair, feeling like I need to make something happen. Even grieving takes time and energy.

As I am settling down, I am noticing the sky through the sliding glass doors of the family room. I can see it in the opening between the evergreen trees that nearly surround the deck. It is striated bands of heavy gray and looks like it could rain. It brings to mind several evenings when Peg and I had settled into our camper for the night. I managed to cook the meat on the charcoal in the firepit before the heavy overcast in the west moved in. Peg made the rest of the meal on the stove inside and we set the dinette table instead of the outside picnic table knowing that the rain was coming. With the meat cooked, I battened down the outside things as the first drops of rain began to fall and we enjoyed our supper in the dry cozy surroundings of our little motorhome.

Back to the present—the rain has begun to fall lightly on the deck and a sudden flash of lightning and peal of thunder spurs me into action. I unplug the laptop, then I shut down the PC and unplug it. The lightning and thunder that follows seems more distant than that first flash and crash announcing its presence. Even though it's still an hour 'til sunset, the sky is very dark and the rain is steady. I am thankful for battery power that will allow me to continue writing with the laptop in the comfort of my chair despite the storm.

Those rainy evenings spent in our little camper were so pleasant. Being confined in that little RV by the weather made us feel even further removed from the demands of home and church life. We had thus far resisted purchasing a cell phone. (I still do not have one, though I'm weakening.) Occasional calls to "check in" with family and to "check on" answering machines had to be made on a campground phone, which became easier to do as more and more people acquired cell phones and fewer needed the public phone. But chances are we'd not venture out in the rain to make a call unless there was some pressing reason. So we were very much isolated from our responsibilities and everyone, except each other, which was just the way we wanted it.

After enjoying our charcoal cooked chicken, steak, ribs, or pork chops with potatoes charcoaled in tin foil, vegetables cooked on the camper stove, and salad, we would begin the cleanup. Well, not until I had dessert which might be packaged pudding or canned fruit cocktail, and definitely cookies—the best were Peg's chocolate chips brought from home. Usually I would wash the dishes and Peg would put away any leftovers and ingredients, then dry the dishes. When all was cleaned up, we would drop the table and fold down the seats to make the bed, lay out our big double sleeping bag, with pillows propped up at opposite ends making a sort of couch so we could recline on top of it facing each other and relax for the evening. If it was a Sunday and we had left home that day after church, Peg would probably have brought the Sunday paper to read. Since she liked to browse newspapers, sometimes she picked up a daily local if we were traveling. Otherwise it would probably be one of her romance novels. Depending on my mood, I might read a model railroad or boating magazine or one of the faith-related books I usually had going. Later, toward bedtime, I would switch to whatever recreational book I was reading at the time.

A variation of that might be to read whatever book we were reading together right then—we usually had one going that we would both enjoy. Often it was one of the classics. (We had been reading *Pride and Prejudice* by Jane Austen before Peg died, but never finished it. I lost interest in it after her death and didn't finish it.) Sometimes it was an adventure, fiction or non-fiction, like *Walk Across America* by Peter Jenkins, which we very much enjoyed. We would usually take turns reading facing pages out loud to each other, passing the book back and forth. Sometimes Peg would ask me to read to her while she did the entire cleanup. In that case, I would make up the bed for the evening then settle down to read while she finished up.

Now and then we would play *Trivial Pursuit*. Peg really liked old movies and had a movie version of the game. We didn't bother with the board game—we just asked each other the questions and kept score, usually playing to a particular number of correct answers to win. Neither of us were very competitive about it—we just liked to see how many we could get right and felt good if we could answer the questions or knew the answer to the other's question.

Those cozy quiet evenings inside were so restful and relaxing, the very thing that both of us needed with the kind of life we led in the day-to-day work of the church. I don't recall for sure, but I think our last outing with the camper was an overnight jaunt in September of 2002 to Lake Huron State Park near Port Huron. We usually went there in the fall, always with mixed feelings when we knew it would be our last one for the year. Of course, we had no idea it would be our last one ever.

So there isn't a "last camping trip" for me to clearly recall, which may be just as well. Instead there is a sort of general memory of camping that is a consolidation of the pleasant times we shared in our little motorhome. We had been looking for some time for a used replacement but couldn't find something within our price, features, and size range—something a little bigger to give us more space with a separate bed and dining area so we could have a place to lay down and a table to sit at simultaneously.

As it turns out, it may be just as well we didn't find one. I don't have any real desire to continue with a recreation vehicle right now. It sounds like more work to maintain, prepare, and pack than I have the time or energy for alone—domestic things and church work are more than enough to handle. And being alone in remote places doesn't sound very appealing either.

However, our little RV served us well for close to 15 years taking us more than 70,000 miles from Michigan to Florida, Maine, Texas, and the Grand Canyon, with numerous shorter jaunts to places like Oklahoma, Tennessee, Kentucky, and Pennsylvania. It would work pretty well for me alone I suppose, but it is getting tired and rusty, which is another reason we were ready to part with it, and I wonder about its reliability. Frankly, I just don't have the heart for it. It was ours. When we had everything packed inside, shut the doors, and headed out of the driveway, we were off adventuring together to someplace we had mutually agreed on. We had choreographed the ways we lived in its confined space, and above all else, just enjoyed wherever we went with each other, even those nights when it rained.

When bedtime would eventually come around, we would share an evening time of devotions, then enjoy a snack of crackers and cheese, popcorn, or a special treat of cheese curls or potato chips. (Snacks at home were usually more healthy.) Finally we would open up the sleeping bag and crawl in. It was pleasant to snuggle up, with good reading, next to each other—there was no retreating to your own side of the bed because you were already there. As it got harder to keep the eyes open and we turned out the light, we could lie there and hear the raindrops falling on the camper's thin outer shell. With such peace and companionship, sleep was usually not long in coming.

This evening is now at peace as well. The rain has stopped and so has the thunder, but only after the weather radio sounded a number of severe weather alerts, which I checked out on television. There were severe thunderstorms to the south and tornado warnings, although I don't think any tornados actually developed. It has all passed over for now. The laptop battery is still going but I think my battery is running down. This night won't be as peaceful and pleasant as those rainy nights in the motorhome with my very best friend, but I've made it through quite a few nights since the last one of those I spent with her. Somehow remembering those we did share helps with those we no longer share.

It's funny, but one of the things I thought I might explore when I had time to write was the idea that grief is the process of getting from the way things were to the way things are. I guess that's what I have been doing this evening without even knowing it. That thought deserves more exploration but not tonight, however. One last thought—if it is raining again as predicted when I get settled in upstairs, I think I'll leave the window open. I might be able to hear the rain in the evergreens outside the window and on the deck below. They don't amplify it like the shell of the motor home, but with everything else quiet and peaceful, I'll be glad to hear it just the same.

Today I completed an errand and got some exercise and an object lesson all in less than an hour. I needed to run into town to pick up a few groceries and a Fourth of July treat for the children's lesson in tomorrow morning's worship. It's only a mile, so I decided I would bike in, making a circuit through the country and stopping at the store on my way back. I usually haven't gone in that direction when I've biked on my own because the highway that runs through town and the main intersection are so busy. When I've biked just for exercise, I've gone the opposite direction out into the rural countryside.

Now and then, Peg and I would bike into town. She liked to ride the streets through the neighborhoods and sometimes we would head out into the rural area north of town just for a change of scenery. That's the area that I headed for today to extend my riding time, an area I haven't ridden through for at least two years.

I suppose I was a little more observant today than I might have been when Peg and I biked together because we used communicators and talked to each other as we rode. So even though I must have seen it a number of times before, a big oak tree standing all alone in a farm field caught my attention. It's not in the center of the huge field. It's about sixty feet from the road, so as I approached it I could see it quite well. I noticed how symmetrical in shape it was and how stately it looked featured there all by itself—quite a specimen of an oak tree.

As I got closer and began to pass by, my angle of view changed, and I noticed the tree seemed to have more branches and foliage on the west side, the direction from which I had come. It was still nicely shaped, like an umbrella, but the east side seemed much less full. Then I noticed a huge scar about a third of the way up where a big patch of bark was missing. Obviously at one time there had been a very large branch attached there. In fact, it might have been a fork in the main tree trunk. It had evidently been gone for quite awhile because the exposed wood was gray and weathered and the bark had rounded off and sealed over the way bark does along the edges of such a scar.

I wondered what might have happened to that old tree. Standing out there all by itself like that, it could have been a lightning strike, or perhaps strong west winds had broken away a part of it from the east side. As I continued on through the countryside, I thought with admiration about that old tree. It probably withstood a lot of storms until one day a disaster took down a large part of its structure. But it had survived, healing over from its loss, filling out the best it could, and resuming its shape so that it continued to be a substantial oak tree out there in that field.

As I rode on, I decided I had a lot in common with that old oak tree. I was riding past it alone because the storm of cancer had taken down a significant part of my life. Perhaps when Peg and I rode past that tree for the first time years back, that tree was full and complete too. Now neither me or that tree were the same. You can tell what it's been through because of the scar but, as old oak trees go, it was doing OK. It is living proof we can survive with scars. It is possible to go on after the storms and be what we were meant to be resuming a semblance of completeness, even though on close examination anyone can tell there is something missing. If the part of that tree that was lost was a substantial part of the trunk, what remained straightened up pretty well and it looks like it could go on being a substantial oak in that field for a long time yet. Of course, the next storm could ruin it forever, or so disfigure it that it would never be the same again—we never know such things—but in the mean time, it continues being what it was meant to be.

Many of the resources on grief I've consulted talk about healing and it taking time but I don't recall any that have told me what I observed in that tree—that healing doesn't mean there will not be a visible scar. In fact, I've been afraid there wouldn't. I don't want to move on and forget—I want to move on and remember. Just as the scar on that tree is a sign of what it's been through, the scars of grief and loss are signs of my life experience as well. I'm discovering I can function on my own with some semblance of the past, although there is much that is missing in what I do and the levels at which I do it. Peg was a main stem in ministry and life itself, functioning for us both in some things, and with me in others. I'm branching out to cover some of the void she left, but I'll never fill it all in, though I'm trying to keep the general shape of life intact. I'm continuing to stand where I am planted in my field of ministry doing what I believe I was meant to do. For how long, I do not know—I leave that to the Lord who put me here.

Although I only saw that tree for a few minutes as I biked past, I have gained a lot from it, so I'm sure I'll bike by it again. I'm sure the ride will bring Peg to mind because we usually only went that way together but now I have a kindred creature standing alone I may want to check on now and then—an object lesson I probably will need to see more than once to absorb. Besides, that tree seems to lend dignity to being older, and I guess, at my age, it wouldn't do me any harm to face facts and learn that either.

Chapter 8

Journey to Remove a Ring

Music has been a powerful influence in this process of grief. That shouldn't surprise me because it was something Peg and I shared in common, and a very significant part of her life. It happened again today as I was cruising along I-75 headed north on vacation.

This time it wasn't the radio, a tape, or CD, it was me. I planned to spend a couple of days at Sault Ste. Marie before going to visit my mom and sister. I had been diagnosed with sinusitis and pink eye and I certainly didn't want to bring that to them, especially my mom in her weakened health. Since I'm two days into the treatment and things are clearing up, I decided I could get away without risking spreading it in public if I'm cautious, and would spend a couple of days enroute. That would allow sufficient time to be sure I don't bring it to mom and give me a couple of reading and relaxing days on my own besides. The Soo, which is the shortened version of Sault Ste. Marie, seemed the logical midpoint—a place I'm familiar with and enjoy.

I didn't really round up much to listen to on the four and a half hour ride. A friend had given me a sermon tape from her church, I had some contemporary worship music to review for possible use in our services, and I had the ten or so favorite recordings I leave in the car and listen to all the time. With less than an hour to go, I'd listened to all the new stuff, and some of the old and nothing sounded appealing. But the Christian music I had just heard brought to mind a song I remember learning to sing for church years ago. So I sang it and it felt good. So I tried to remember other songs I'd sung in the past. The trouble is most of the music I sang, we sang, Peg and I, as duets. I didn't consciously think about that. I just started singing the next song that came to mind.

As I got to a line about shattered dreams I realized I always played guitar accompaniment on this one, sang the melody, and Peg sang counter melody. A flood of emotions ruined my vocalizing. Once they subsided, I did some internal debate over whether I was going to allow such things to ruin singing music I really liked from our past. I collected myself and in a few minutes began again. I got about as far into the song when I wavered again but pushed on into the chorus, which said to give everything to Jesus, even shattered dreams.

I was too devastated to keep singing. That song we had sung years ago had nailed me. My dreams, our dreams, are shattered. We had so many dreams for retirement. Some of them even were inspired in Sault Ste. Marie. We'd see places for sale along the river and fantasize about what it would be like to live there. There were plenty of other dreams too, some of them inspired by other places just as impractical and unlikely, but fun to think about and anticipate and wonder what it actually would be like. Now they're all impractical—no, impossible—entirely disintegrated.

The song also said to surrender our wounded hearts to Jesus. All the country songs I've heard about broken hearts never made sense to me. Oh, I'm not saying I doubted there is such a thing, but I just thought of it as sentimentality or emotionalism. Now I see it as more of a shade or shadow that comes over life that has something to do with losing something (someone) so significant that life doesn't have the same luster and appeal anymore. I can't say I feel my spirit is broken—life still has meaning and purpose—but there's a pervading sadness and loneliness that's like a smoky film on a dirty window. I see life through it and it's always there even when I'm not consciously aware of it.

I was very aware of it today. As I came into the Soo I decided to deliberately take the route along the Saint Mary's River we usually took when we went to the campground. I knew as we approached it we would be anxious to see how full it was and if we stood a chance of getting in (they don't take reservations). Today there were plenty of available sites, some even close to the river affording a good view of the passing freighters. But there would be no camping tonight, no supper cooked over charcoal, and no lounging together to enjoy our reading as we listened to the scanner to learn which boat to watch for next.

I went on to a motel we had stayed at a few years ago when we came to the Soo with my mother and sister. The only memory it held was Peg sending Nancy and I off to the ferry dock across the street so we could see the freighters more closely. She would stay with mom and could see the boats from there. We could tell her their names later.

When we lived at Newberry, just 60 miles west of the Soo, we would come on occasion after church or for a day, pick up Kentucky Fried Chicken, park by the Sugar Island Ferry dock, and watch the boat traffic while we ate, and of course, read. I did that tonight. Supper was good and so was the reading, but I confess I did wish Peg was in the passenger seat instead of the assorted containers from KFC.

Tomorrow, weather permitting, I will probably bike as we always did. I'll stop at the visitor center at the Soo Locks. I'll probably not go to the ice cream shop across the street and pick up a cone to eat on the visitor center lawn as we often did, though I guess I could. I'll go on to the railroad yard and follow the route we usually took—not because we took it—because those were the things we wanted to see and do then and I still do now. It's just the doing is so very different.

I was here last fall with my mother and sister. It was not this difficult then, but this is the first time I've been back here on my own. Maybe it's another "first" like so many others. I hope so, because it's now beginning the second year since Peg's death.

I've blamed it on the song, but maybe that too is the Lord's provision. I think what it did was name for me the sorrows I feel well acquainted with. I am aware that the song prescribes a remedy, but how to follow through on it, how to actually give these things to the Lord, I'm not sure. He'll have to help me with that too. I will continue to pray and trust that the Lord can do what the song says, and restore my joy, if not in this life, for certain in the next. Perhaps if it goes from being "our sorrow" to "my sorrow," there will be a difference. What has happened to me feels less important than what happened to her and what happened to us. So I guess I'm not that "individualized" yet. In the meantime, I am getting a bit wary of music!

I woke up this morning in a motel room on vacation "mellowed out." That was the term Peg and I used for being more than just physically relaxed in the morning. We never compared detailed notes, but for me it was a feeling of all systems idling in neutral, with a pleasant mild physical euphoria, mental contentment, and spiritual peace. A while back I read about something called "alpha brain waves," and that sounds something like this only it's more than a mental phenomenon. It isn't noteworthy this morning because of not experiencing it since Peg's illness and death. What was different was becoming aware of being without Peg and it didn't go away.

Since Peg's death, I have wakened in the morning with recollection of pleasant dreams about Peg and similar mellow sensations. But then as I have come to grips with reality, it has rapidly dissipated. Not so today. I realized where I was, my state of affairs, and still I felt mellowed out.

When we would experience it together, we might just lay there enjoying the peace and contentment. Sometimes we might be snuggled up together, other times barely touching, if at all. As we began to stir, we might talk a little but only casual conversation. Sometimes I might wake up before Peg and just lay there in that state with her sleeping. (If she ever did, she never mentioned it.) Eventually as our minds became active and engaged, or some other thing compelled us to "get going," it would diminish, although it might linger in vestige throughout a relaxing day. Often for Peg, it was the yearning for coffee that would compel her to get up and put the pot on if we were camping, or slip on her sweats and head for the lobby of the motel. Sometimes escalating need for the bathroom for one or both of us would force activity and induce decline.

This morning as I lay there, I deliberately avoided thinking too much about the day. The TV only had a remote to change channels and had to be turned on manually so I avoided the temptations to do that and check the Weather Channel or get out of bed and look out the window. I also deliberately did not turn on the scanner, though I could easily reach it, fending off curiosity about boat traffic on the river, afraid I'd hear something that I would just have to get up to see. I didn't have to head to the bathroom either, which is truly amazing given my increasing age. I lay there entertaining only casual thoughts and marveling that knowing my solitary situation didn't curtail it either.

After a half-hour, I ventured into a little reflection about what this meant. I always knew this was a blessing given by God for renewal and refreshing of energy, mind, body, and spirit. Usually it was contingent on being disconnected from responsibility and an immediate agenda. It could happen at home on a day off or on time away. Our part was to clear the calendar and arrange the schedule, making for a "sabbath" from our regular labors, but even that was only possible by the Lord's provision. I truly believe He mellowed us out with a sense of well-being and satisfaction as renewal and refreshing. I tended to see it as a recharging and respite in order to carry on the work and realize I haven't always just appreciated it as sabbath Presence.

The thing that pleased me most this morning was to discover that grief was not an impasse to this most pleasant sensation. Losing my life partner has curtailed or reconfigured so many other things. I take it from this morning that the Lord still intends to provide His physical blessings, mental contentment, and spiritual peace. And this morning leads me to believe even more this is indeed the Lord's provision—certainly not something I was even trying to rediscover, or capable of generating on my own. I'm sure I need rejuvenating and respite just as much now, if not more so than before. Its return reassures me that God hasn't curtailed everything that He provided in and through my partnership with Peg. He can provide the blessings I've lost in other or similar ways if He chooses. I don't expect He should but He can if they were truly from Him in the first place. I pray I'll not be so hindered by grief I won't be receptive.

I am torn, and music is the heart-rending cause once again. As I travel and drive for errands and ministry, I am listening to the cassette tapes we have accumulated over the years, sorting them out, determining what I want to keep and what to discard. Today, the day after my second Christmas without Peg, I drove to Saginaw for hospital visitation. So I put in the next tape from the collection, which was labeled in pencil, "July 20, 1980 – Mitchell Church Worship." I thought it would be nice to listen to a service from our home church, the church through which the Lord had brought us to faith and also launched us into ministry. What I didn't realize was the date was after we had moved away to Kentucky for me to attend seminary.

As the service began, I was pleased to listen to the man I still regard as my pastor, Rev. Bill Schoonover. He and his wife, Norma, were formative in the early years of our Christian faith and spirit, and we learned things about ministry and relationships with lay people from them that seminary never taught. It was good to hear his voice in liturgy, prayer, and the children's message. From the welcome and acknowledgments he did it was evidently the day after the wedding of our good friends, Jay and Beverly. We had returned to participate in their wedding. Then came a surprise in the order of service. Pastor Bill acknowledged our presence and would introduce us later when we were going to sing.

Going to sing! I knew we had some tapes with some of our duets in church from those years but I didn't know this was one of them. Now I was both stirred and intrigued. What had we sung? Had Peg played piano? Was I playing guitar? Did we do both? Who sang lead, counter-melody? I let the tape run through the other parts of the service anxiously anticipating. Then following the Scripture reading, it was time for us. After a brief greeting and comments on our situation, I said, "...I'd just like to remind you of the promises that God has given to us, or at least to emphasize one of them this morning, with this song in particular, the promise of His presence with us, and the help and comfort and all of those wonderful things that He offers us.

This song is called *For Those Tears I Died.*" Oh no! I had forgotten we sang that one. Just the title caused my feelings to rise.

I had just pulled into the garage as our part in the service began, so I shut off the engine, sat there, and listened to our song. Peg's voice and ours blending together found raw spots in me that are still tender when rubbed certain ways, while at the same time bringing her and our past together into present reality in a gratifying way. And the message of the song, nearly 35 years after the fact, has the same dual affect for it reminds us that Jesus would be with us each day sharing our sorrows. Little did I know as we sang that song that the greatest sorrow of my life would be the tragic loss of the one who was singing that song with me. I needed to hear again the Lord's promise to share my sorrows.

We sang on about Jesus dying because of all that brought sorrow and tears to us. There have been plenty of tears—still are from time to time—in the darkness of Peg's absence. Not that there are not joyful and significant moments, but the lustre of daily life is gone without her. Just like shadows only appear in the sunshine, sadness casts a shadow across what might otherwise be life's cheery landscape now and then. But the song assures me Jesus feels my tears, the sorrow of mortality and separation, and that it was because of the pain-causing distresses of life that He, out of His great goodness, gave Himself sacrificially for us.

Truly I do not understand God's goodness. I have reflected previously on the potential for goodness out of Peg's premature death—still I do not see it. I can only trust it is another of those promises I spoke about when introducing the song. However, God did loose Peg from the disease that had taken her body captive. Death set her free from her misery and illness. Still, I wonder why her in the first place? She asked that very same question as she dealt with her disease, "Why me?" The answer that came to her was, "Why not me?" And so I have to ask the same question. Though my mind may have to allow her answer, my heart has a lot of reasons why it shouldn't have happened to her.

As the song urged us to do, Peg did give herself to Jesus. She praised Him with delight and joy, not only with her musical talent, but with her words and actions. She truly was His child and He took her from this earth to the realm of heaven.

The reminder I had shared with the Negaunee congregation, God had preserved through modern technology to minister to me in my own words and voice more than three decades later. I stopped the tape, deciding to listen to the rest of the service on my next drive somewhere—that was enough for now. I would take time to record my thoughts and experience, reflecting on what I had heard. As I began, I needed to listen again to the tape to be able to accurately report my own words. So I went back out to the garage and brought it in. As I was finishing up the transcribing, the tape ran beyond the song, and suddenly Peg began to speak. There was another song, and she was introducing it!

"Seems like there's been a lot of tears shed the last three weeks. Some of them have been from joy with two very special weddings. Some of them have been from some worry. One of the men that I work for has had very serious heart surgery and we were very concerned about him while I was gone. But praise the Lord, he's doing well, and the next song we're going to sing is called *Give Them All to Jesus*. It's one of my very favorite songs. And in the last three weeks, having so many joys and so many sorrows all at the same time, it's just really neat to know that we can give them to the Lord and He's going to take care of them. No matter what His will is it's always right and we can never second-guess Him. Amen for that!"

She was doing it again, just as she had done in introducing the song we used in her funeral service, the one she had introduced one Sunday morning with the Praise Band, that we happened to have on video. Again her message was to trust and rely on the Lord, no matter what. Only this time, my voice was mingled with hers singing, of all things, the very same song I had struggled with awhile ago on my trip north to Sault Ste. Marie!

My shattered dreams are wrapped in the previous pages, so there's no need to write them again. It seems the only place to put them where they will not putrefy and permeate the present is at Jesus' feet. He has not yet turned them to joy, and perhaps He never will in this life, but I must confess I am looking now and then to see what He might do.

It seems to me it truly would be miraculous if, as the song promises, the Lord would ever make it possible for me to sing about these things that have been so painful. I just can't imagine making music without pain out of death, grief, and loss. That's why I am so torn, and why music is so heart-rending for me.

Folk music, gospel songs, and the guitar were a part of my life before I ever met Peg. But since we shared that interest, much of our musical activity became blended together. Our singing at the Negaunee Church was public culmination of that. Probably because music so engages the emotions and the spirit, it is one of the most difficult areas in which to become an individual again, especially since it had become a dormant interest for me before Peg died.

I have a gift certificate from Peg she made up several years ago for a new guitar. And the Christmas season before she died, while she shopped in music stores for gifts for the grandchildren, I looked at guitars, thinking maybe it was time to pick it up again. But after Peg's death, I lost any inclination to sing and play.

But I am beginning to miss it. Every now and then as I ride here or there, I find myself singing with the music tapes or CDs I listen to. Not long ago I sang as many of the songs as I could remember from the folk music era while I was driving somewhere. Sometimes I only make it to certain songs and then I'm overwhelmed by memories of singing with her. But I'm beginning to wonder if music isn't welling up in me and getting ready to seep out. I just might redeem that certificate from Peg and see where it goes. I think I can imagine that, although singing about everything that caused such pain would truly take a miracle.

I knew I needed to remove it but how and when? Peg had placed the wedding ring on my finger more than 38 years ago. It has been there ever since. Oh, I had taken it off now and then for various reasons, but never for long, and never for anything relating to our marriage. Essentially it remained in place from the time she put it there in our wedding ceremony at the Calumet Methodist Church. As I pondered removing the ring, it occurred to me that I would be back in Calumet, where we were married, on vacation. Perhaps I would have opportunity to remove the ring in the same place she had given it to me. That sounded like an appropriate thing to do.

I arrived at my family home on Thursday evening. The next day was my mother's 84th birthday. Then my sister began her vacation on Saturday and we spent the weekend doing things together and getting ready to be away the following week. On Monday, Nancy and I traveled to Duluth, Minnesota, and spent the week vacationing there. We arrived home on Saturday and spent Sunday doing things together as a family. My sister went back to work on Monday morning and I would be traveling home on Tuesday. If I was going to visit the church where we were married, it would have to be Monday. With some anxiety, I began to feel the possibility was slipping away.

When Monday morning came, I slept in 'til just before nine o'clock. I lay there feeling quite relaxed and rested contemplating the day when the next thing I knew, I was waking up again and it was quarter after ten! I knew the church secretary was in the office for a few hours during the week but I didn't know which days or at what time—I imagined probably in the mornings. I didn't want to call and get into explanations for my inquiry. I just wanted to walk in and ask to sit in the sanctuary for awhile. My first instinct was to jump out of bed and get going. No, I needed to trust the Lord and His timing on this, if this whole thing was His provision for my desire. My devotional reading for the day was from Isaiah 43 and verses 18-19a jumped out at me. *"Forget the former things; do not dwell on the past. See, I am doing a new thing!"* Was this the Lord's way of telling me I should just forget the whole business of the ring, take it off, and get on with it? Maybe going to the church and taking the ring off there was just foolish sentimentality?

By the time I finished my devotional time, showering and getting ready for the day, it was almost 11:30. I spent a few minutes saying good-morning to mom, then told her I was going on an errand and would be back in a little while. The church is less than two miles from my family home, but as I got almost to it, I was stopped by construction. Calumet Avenue was being renovated. The pavement was being removed all along the street in front of the church and the side street next to the church was inaccessible. As soon as my lane of traffic was allowed to go, I pulled into the vacant lot across the street from the church thinking I would just walk down the road a little to cross to the opposite side of the street. But when I got out and looked for a place to walk through the construction, I could see there was a trench several feet deep and the equipment operators surely would get excited if I tried to get through. I would have to drive a quarter mile back the way I came, take the street behind the church, and come up the side street. I could see there was a car in the church's side parking lot so surely someone was there. But it was now getting close to noon and I hoped they wouldn't leave before I could work my way back around.

Soon I was pulling into the side parking area just before noon. To my great relief, the side door to the church was open and I walked up into the area behind the sanctuary to the office and greeted the secretary. I told her who I was and that I would like to spend a little time in the sanctuary if that was OK. She didn't question my desires, said that was fine, she would be leaving shortly after noon, and if I was still there, would set the door so it would lock when I left. I thanked her and walked out of the office into the hallway that led into the front of the sanctuary. I walked across the front and sat in the front pew on the right side.

As I settled down, I was relieved and encouraged that the Lord had arranged for me to be there despite all the uncertainties of the circumstance and my own desires and doubts. It was a familiar setting. Peg and I had been there for morning worship several years ago and I had preached there for a pulpit exchange when I served a church on the same district. Yet things were a little different than I remembered, not quite as spacious and the platform wasn't as elevated as it was in my memory. I looked around readjusting my recollections of the space and the décor. Two banners on the wall of the sacristy encouraged worshippers to give glory to God. One behind the lectern quoted Psalm 1:3, "He is like a tree planted by streams of water... and its leaf does not wither." I needed to be like that tree planted in the living water of Jesus and not wither in what I was about to do.

As I sat on the front pew absorbing where I was and why, I visualized Peg and me standing on the platform with our wedding party. I began to picture all who had been a part of our special day. Peg's oldest brother was a groomsman and my cousin was best man. He was the one who introduced me to Peg.

My cousin and I had become good friends in my last year of high school. So when I came home on leave from the Army before going overseas to Japan for two years, I looked him up. He was hanging around with a group of kids from his class and got especially interested in one of the girls he was helping get through chemistry class. Several of them were going out to do some target practicing on a Saturday afternoon and he invited me to go along. (They were all either in ROTC[35] or in the school's Rifle Club, so were well acquainted with firearms.) That's when I first met Peg—she was the girl my cousin was hoping to date. The group of about eight of us spent part of the afternoon together, and I really don't remember much about it, except that Peg was an attractive bubbly little blonde but off limits since my cousin was interested.

Later on, since he didn't have a car, my cousin wondered if I would drive them to the movies that evening, if Peg would agree to go. I said I would, thinking that one of them might arrange for another girl to go as well. But when I picked him up, I discovered it would only be the three of us. He gave me directions to Peg's house and I believe she sat between us on the way to the movies. (This was in the days before bucket seats.) When we got to the movie, my cousin ushered her into the seats first, he sat next to her, and I sat next to him. I will always remember Peg finding some reason to adjust the seating arrangement and sit between us—I've often smiled about that since and it still tickles me! Now I am sometimes a little slow, but I confess I was paying very close attention to her and I began to pick up that she was interested in me. Before I took them both home that evening, I felt she had given me the green light to pursue things further. That made for a very awkward conversation with my cousin, to say the least.

That Sunday, Peg and I went riding together, and spent as much time with each other after that as we could when Peg was not in school. In what remained of the two short weeks of leave I had before going overseas, we became close enough that we carried on a relationship by mail that lasted almost the two years I was stationed in Japan. We broke up by mail a few months before I came home but got back together within a few days of my arrival and, as they say, the rest is history.

---

35   Besides colleges, high schools have offered ROTC—Reserve Officers Training Corps programs.

I did apologize to my cousin for the way things went with Peg and tried to assure him I had no intentions for things to develop as they did. It was just one of those things that happen between two people. I truly do thank him for introducing us and being gracious about the developments. Subsequently he did meet a very nice girl whom he married and they have had a fulfilling life together.

Peg's attendant was a high school friend and her maid of honor a good friend who lived across the street, who was married and a little older than Peg. It took me a little while to sort out exactly who had been in our wedding party, and as I did, I remembered others of our family, and friends who had been close to us. Then I thought about each one in the present. I was astounded to realize that three of Peg's close friends had lost husbands in death. Her maid of honor lost her husband to cancer while only in his late 30's. I believe her other attendant was divorced from her first husband and lost a second husband to cancer not long ago. One of her other circle of close friends lost her husband to heart disease in his 40's. Only one of the four she had been close to is still with the husband she married as a young woman. In addition, Peg's youngest brother died of cancer just two years before her and one of our two ushers died of cancer within the last two years. Three of our four parents are deceased as well. It was sobering to think of all that had happened to the people closest to us in the 38 years since our marriage, all of them, except for our parents, well under age 60.

With a more profound sense of the time that had passed, I got up and went to the platform, sitting on the step just forward of where I had stood for the wedding. I looked down the aisle and could picture Peg and her dad coming through the doorway at the entry to the sanctuary. It was somewhat dim without the lights on and my colorless mental images of Peg in her white wedding gown and her dad in his dark suit were influenced, I'm sure, by the black and white candid pictures in our wedding album. No matter—I knew very well Pegs' hair was blonde and her eyes were blue. I saw her smile widen as our eyes locked on to each other's and she came closer and closer. I know her smile wasn't only for me. She was thrilled to be walking down the aisle on her dad's arm. When we decided to be married in the Methodist Church, she wasn't sure if her dad could walk her down the aisle. He was from staunch Catholic background, though he had married a Lutheran, and there was some question about what his Church might think if he participated in a Protestant wedding. But when she asked him if he would give her away, there was no question in his mind. Of course he would escort his little girl down the aisle at her wedding.

This was a dream come true for Peg. She had always admired the Calumet Methodist Church. She had attended various activities there with a girlfriend who was from that church and she always thought she would like to be married there. My family were members at the Laurium Methodist Church, a church in a neighboring community that bordered Calumet. That is where we were planning to be married. But Providence intervened to fulfill a young girl's dreams and the January day of our wedding, the furnace in the Laurium Church broke down and the wedding was moved at the last minute to the Calumet Church. I like to think Peg's smile and obvious delight as she came down the aisle was in part for me but I know it was also because she was walking down that aisle of that church on the arm of her dad, who she knew, without a doubt, loved her very much—indeed he did.

As I relived the wedding processional in monochrome I could see beyond Peg the whiteness of the blowing snow through the windows in the church's exterior doors. It wasn't a crippling snowstorm, thankfully, but it was still a pretty good January storm even by Upper Michigan standards. No matter. We would soon be off to Chicago, where I was attending photography school, to begin married life together. I was proud to extend my arm and take her to my side to become my wife.

I don't remember much of the ritual of the ceremony. I repeated the vows I was supposed to make and said "I do" or "I will" at the appropriate parts. I was there to claim my bride and take her with me off into the city and the great adventure of life. But as I sat on the step nearly 40 years later, I thought about those vows—vows I was now very familiar with after nearly 25 years of wedding ceremonies as well as pre-marital review of them with wedding couples. (One of the reasons I review the vows with them is because Peg and I had no such preparation or introduction to the promises we were making.)

I could recall most of the ceremony from the current Methodist ritual, which has been revised slightly since 1966. So even though I couldn't quote verbatim the older version, I knew the essence of it. The part that really stood out says "until death do us part." If I even heard that in our wedding, I undoubtedly thought of it as something so far off that it didn't seem real. It was just another one of the romantic promises of marriage. But now, 38 years later it was very real—death had parted us, but not only us, it had visited many others who had been there as well.

"With this ring, I thee wed," was in the concluding statements we made in the ceremony. Our rings stood as tangible reminders of the intangibles of the marriage commitment. We placed them on each other's fingers with all the hopes, aspirations, and good intentions I'm sure every couple has at that point, not knowing or even imagining what might be ahead. Peg wore her ring faithfully. It stayed where I placed it until the funeral director removed it before her burial. (I have since thought it might have been significant for me to have removed it at that point myself.)

As I said at the outset, mine was still where she had placed it as I sat there on the platform, on the very spot I had been standing when she said, "I give you this ring..." I looked at it still there on my finger. I had been wearing it solo for just over a year. Its partner had been residing in a little zipper case, given to us by the funeral director, with the other jewelry we had removed from her body before closure of the casket. I rotated the ring around my finger as I looked at it once more, reviewing my decision to remove it.

Awhile back as I thought about my ring, I appreciated that in our society a wedding ring is a sign that a person is in a committed relationship with another. If I continued to wear mine it was not a true indicator of my marital status. But I decided if people in our society saw it and assumed I was currently married, that didn't matter. It was mine given to me by Peg and if I wanted to continue wearing it, that was OK. Besides, I still felt our marriage was a very significant factor in my life and the ring still represented that. And if people who knew I was widowed wanted to wonder why I was still wearing it, I would be glad to tell them. (In the year that I wore it since Peg's death, no one ever asked or commented!)

But I also came to realize the ring wasn't just my private possession, it was ours, one of a pair, given to each other in solemn vow. Yet the vows they represented in token had been lived out and fulfilled. They were now null and void because death had "put asunder" what God had joined together. For awhile I thought perhaps I would move the ring to another finger and wear it as a memorial to our marriage. But that seemed sort of like trying to let go of something while trying to hang on to it at the same time. By removing the ring and putting them together, they would no longer be in the places they had been created and consecrated for but would at least be together as a sign of our union until its end.

As I continued to rotate the ring around my finger, I knew I was delaying what I had come to this place for. And I knew I was now alone because, a little while before, I had heard the secretary walk down the steps of the exterior side entry to the church, latch and close the door. I now felt free to let my feelings well up and overflow, thankful that I could do so without self-consciousness or distressing anyone else. Slowly I slid the ring from my left hand ring finger with the fingers of my right hand and held it between them. I realized I had reversed what Peg had done—she had put it there—I had removed it. It was not my wish to do so. It was just an admission of what life had already done in more traumatic ways.

The sense of intense loss I feared might overwhelm me never came. Instead the Lord said to me, "Your marriage may be over but it still is of value." I understood God was saying death did not take away all that was precious and worthwhile in our marriage. What God had done in us and through us, for and with each other, will continue in who and what we became together. That would not suddenly disappear with the removal of a ring. That will continue for me while I still have life, and though I do not believe we will be marriage partners in God's eternal Kingdom, its effect will last "forever and ever, and then some." That came as great consolation and comfort.

I just sat for awhile holding the ring, letting the feelings ebb and the new thoughts soak in. I looked at the ring and noticed it was no longer perfectly round. In the process of some project(s) it had been squeezed out of shape. The handyman in me knows it was one of the car repair jobs or construction projects I indulge in from time to time that made it that way. But the poet in me wants to say it was the suffering of Peg's illness and the grief of this past year without her that squeezed it out of its once perfect shape just as I have been squeezed and stressed by all that happened.

I looked at my ring finger expecting it would evidence where the ring had been. It did. There was a slightly lighter band of skin protected from the little bit of sun I've been exposed to this summer, but the skin was also shiny and smooth from the movement of the metal against it. I know it will soon fade and lose its distinctness from the other fingers. I suppose it needs to in my return to a solitary state. As that happens, I will cling to those words for reassurance, "Your marriage may be over but it still is of value."

I looked up from the platform in the direction that we had taken from that place, down the aisle and out into the world. Our 37 years had been full and meaningful years—not without hard times in our marriage and otherwise—but not without adventure, joy, and purpose either. They were anything but mundane and monotonous—the Lord had seen to that—even though we didn't know Him then as we would later on.

I have often thought how the course of Peg's life might have been different had she walked down the aisle with someone else from the local community and lived out her years there. I don't think she would have been the person she had become. I like to think she needed the expanded horizons, the broadening experience, and sense of adventure that our independent pursuit of self-employed business and, later on, full-time ministry supplied. It challenged her and inspired the vitality and energy that came to characterize her as a unique person. I like to think I had a part in opening those horizons to her.

When I wrote to Peg about my travels in the service and we talked about them on my return, Peg dreamed about traveling and seeing the world. She stirred something in me that gave me a deep desire to take her to all those places and to new places neither of us had ever seen. Though we never traveled overseas, I am thankful that we were able to see so much of this country. I feel grateful that I was able to fulfill so much of that desire, as though I was able to make good my romantic promises to her in those innocent days when we were fascinated with each other, discovering each other, and beginning to move from infatuation to genuine love.

Yet I know it was not me who was opening her up to life and her potential. I was only one of the instruments used of the Lord to expand her horizons and her possibilities. All that, and so much more, really began for both of us more than 38 years ago where I was now sitting as we were pronounced "husband and wife, together, with the joining of hands and the giving and receiving of rings."

As I continued to look down the aisle toward the door opening into the world, the door we had walked through into that January blizzard and day one of our marriage, I noticed a banner above the entry to the sanctuary that said, "Go In Peace." There are still raw spots on my heart and even my spirit—I know that. But I did feel at peace for the most part. Our marriage was over, but it was not lost, not without meaning and significance in the present, nor would it be in the future. How could I ever have feared it would be, if indeed it was a gift from God to both of us? Though I may not have known the Lord when we made those vows in His name, He knew us, He knew me, and eventually He would bring us to know Him as well. That is the greatest comfort—the knowing Him together, and now on my own. Indeed, I could go in that deeper peace.

Then I noticed a banner over the main exit door. It said, "Serve the Lord." Some churches remind their people that way that we go into the world for ministry and service. It wasn't there, I'm sure, when Peg and I walked beneath its place many years ago. But even so, that was our destiny and our great blessing, first to know the Lord, and then to continue knowing and serving Him in the upward spiral of a unique partnership I believe few couples have the privilege of sharing.

I believe that is still my calling and my purpose though my experience of it alone has been radically altered. I took that banner as the Lord's reaffirmation to continue following His call and claim upon my life. It was prophetic retrospectively of our marriage as together we passed beneath the place that it later was to occupy. This time, I would not leave by that door, and the ring Peg had given me was not on my finger where she had placed it as a sign of marriage vows made in hope and the innocent love of youth. It was in my hand as a memento of more mature love, a token of vows not always perfectly kept but forgiven, and a marriage ultimately fulfilled and completed, until we were parted by death. As a newlywed, I had left that place with my life companion through the front door, unaware that the God I had hardly noticed was with us. This time I left by the side door, without any human companion, knowing that I had been in the presence of the Lord, and that He was with me.

From the perspective of a few days time since visiting the church, I can't say that my grief is gone, nor did I expect it to be. The third finger of my left hand feels naked. And I never realized I had developed a habit of touching my wedding ring with my thumb. I reach for it and when I don't find its solid smooth presence but pliable flesh instead, it startles me for an instant. Just as it once made the reality of marriage real, its lack now makes the reality of singleness the same. Whether touching my ring was something I started doing subconsciously since Peg's illness and death or something I used to do before, I do not know. All I know is now its absence is a reminder of my solitary existence and the occasion the Lord arranged for me to be in the Calumet Church to take it from my finger.

My ring is now in the little zipper case with Peg's ring. I believe that's where it belongs and will be kept with important papers and a few other valuables under lock and key. What will become of them on into the future, I can only imagine. Others will ultimately decide that. Right now, I thank the Lord for His provision in the giving and the taking. He has taken a dreaded moment and given it meaning and significance with comfort and great mercy.

APPENDICES

A: Illness and Death

Throughout this whole period of Peg's illness, death, and aftermath, I realize I am moving through various phases. The first phase was getting her through her illness. I can honestly thank God that He made it possible for me, for family members, or others close to her to be with her throughout her ordeal of misery and suffering and that she did not have to endure it alone. Indeed there was much to endure.

It all began with muscle pain late last year. It was common for Peg and me to walk for a half-hour for exercise two or three times a week in the subdivision behind our home. In December Peg's back and legs began to bother her and so we slacked off the walking. We thought it was perhaps a reaction to a new medication she had begun taking to lower her cholesterol level. Muscle pain was one of the possible side effects. She had an appointment for an annual check up in late January, and so she postponed dealing with it 'til then. It was easy to skip walking in the winter anyway.

Her doctor didn't think it was the new medication that was the problem so she continued taking it, and began taking other medication to ease the pain and reduce any possible inflammation. In the meantime, she had an X-ray of her lower back and had blood tests looking for possible causes. The pain medications seemed to be working and she had things to do and places to go.

In the middle of February, our son, Mike, was conducting a week long seminar on counseling in Toronto that Peg wanted to take in. Then we had a week of vacation planned for South Carolina in the middle of March. In addition, she was slated for jury duty for the weeks before and after Easter. She was concerned about being able to handle that with the discomfort she was experiencing sitting on some chairs, but she managed to get by without being selected for a jury and with minimal pain from the waiting area seating. Because of all that, she did not schedule appointments in close succession throughout March and April.

We were not extremely concerned for several reasons. I had been through an ordeal with a back problem that took several months to resolve culminating with back surgery. We also knew that back pain is a common ailment and usually not life-threatening. In many instances it clears up without ever knowing what the cause was. As an active involved grandmother, musician, church employee and volunteer, it was more of a nuisance than a worry to her.

By the first part of April she had no diagnosis, the pain was escalating, and she had been referred to a rheumatologist. He ran a series of tests that were inconclusive and decided that she needed to be on pain medication that would be easier on her digestive system than the over-the-counter one she had been taking for some time in increasing amounts. He put her on a new medication and within two days she had an adverse reaction that started out as hives. They began to spread and cover her whole body with a red inflammation becoming so severe that I brought her to Emergency the Friday night of the Mother's Day weekend. By the time it was full blown, her torso was the color of a lobster's and her arms and legs were mottled so they looked like a red leopard's. The itching was intense. I admired her restraint at not making it worse by scratching.

After five days in the hospital, with steroids and a different type of pain medication, it was under control enough for her to go home. Coincidentally the steroids she was given improved her back and leg problems and she was able to start walking half the distance we used to walk in the neighborhood. But as the steroids were reduced, the pain returned. Eventually she was taking the maximum dosage of her prescribed pain medication as often as possible. She would go to bed, sleep anywhere from two to four hours, and then be up with pain, sometimes waiting intently for the time to elapse so she could take her next dosage. Then we would watch the clock waiting for the pain medication to take effect. Often she would leave the bedroom to come downstairs and sit in a swivel rocker that was the most comfortable place for her to be. She would use a heating pad and sometimes a cold pack, whichever seemed to work at any given time. She also found she could lay on the couch in the family room and the pressure of the back against hers helped. Rubbing her back often helped as well. It seemed to relax the muscles and provide relief. We tried putting the mattress from a bunk bed on the floor at the foot of our bed so she could put her back up against our bed and I could lie on our bed and rub her back. Very often it would settle her pain so she could sleep a little. That worked for awhile.

The Friday night of the Memorial weekend she was awake about two hours after going to sleep. She was in obvious agony, grimacing in pain, going from one position to the next, from the bed to the floor, looking for any position that would give her relief. We tried everything that had helped before but nothing worked. There was nothing else I could think of to do. I knew she needed medical attention. She reluctantly agreed to go to the ER. When we went in, she was in obvious misery and the medical people promptly responded. She was given a shot of morphine which soon took effect and she began to get some relief. She was put on stronger oral medication and admitted. After several days, things seemed to be under control and she was sent home. She was referred to a physical therapist who did an assessment and determined that there was a problem with her pelvis. She began therapy the next week and doing exercises at home to stretch out her legs and realign her pelvis as well as a belt to wear when she was active.

On the Friday of the Father's Day weekend, she was again in severe pain in the middle of the night. Reluctantly she agreed to go to ER, was given stronger pain medication again by injection and got enough relief to go home. Again, a stronger oral medication was prescribed. She felt well enough on Sunday after church that we rode the hour to our son's place for a visit.

That week on her appointment with her rheumatologist he admitted he was stumped. He had ruled out every possible muscle related disease he could think of and was referring her to a hematologist. In follow up with her family doctor, he began to talk about scheduling an MRI but deferred that to the specialist to decide. But once again, the back pain began to escalate, especially at night. She would sleep for two to four hours and then have to get out of bed, forcing herself to do her exercises even though they often hurt her considerably, sometimes finding temporary relief.

At the end of that week, on Friday, she didn't feel well enough in the morning to go to work. She went in the afternoon, but struggled to complete her work, having to come home and take a break mid-way through. After she got home, I could see it was getting worse and encouraged her to go to ER and avoid another late night trip. She again reluctantly agreed. That was the last day she worked.

The doctor in ER reviewed her previous hospitalizations and gave her another shot of morphine. It began to provide some relief and she was discharged within a couple of hours. But by four in the morning she was up again in intense pain–exercises, medication, hot pad, cold pack, nothing helped, and we headed back to ER. She said she knew as we were going home from ER earlier that it wasn't as effective as it had been the previous time. This doctor gave her another shot of morphine to get her some relief and put her on a morphine pump. He obviously began to sense something extreme was going on and within an hour and a half he had her undergoing an MRI. It was also determined that her hemoglobin was low (7.0 with 12 being normal) and she needed transfusion. Needless to say, she was admitted again.

Sometime during mid-morning, I left her room to go to the cafeteria to get something to bring back to the room. As I came in, a nurse met me at the door and said, "The doctor came while you were gone and we've had some bad news." Peg was obviously distressed and the nurse closed the door. Then Peg told me, "The doctor said its cancer." She went on to explain they had found bone cancer on her spine in the MRI. That probably explained the low blood because the bone marrow was affected. Once they had a chance to study things more thoroughly someone would be back to go over the details. The nurse then left us alone.

I don't remember much about that except we hugged and cried and were scared together. The "C" word is one that none of us want to hear. If you have ever been told you or someone close to you has cancer, you know what I mean. All this time we had been hopeful that a diagnosis would mean finding the right medication, the right therapy, perhaps surgery, or some other fix that would get things turned around for her. But now that we knew what it was there was no sense of hope, just dread.

Peg and I both agreed that we learned what dread is. In the course of her illness there were times when each of us had this intense feeling of despair, an overwhelming feeling of alarm centered in the pit of our stomachs, that things were not OK and not going to turn out well. I remember it lingering on though it would eventually diffuse and I would lose my awareness of it. What it must have been like for Peg who was suffering the physical trauma of her illness as well, I can hardly imagine.

That was a dark day for us as we lived with the knowledge that she had bone cancer, knowing little about it and imagining what that might mean. I had a wedding that day and realized I had to muster the strength to talk positively about marriage when the future of my own was uncertain. It gave me a whole new sense of the vow "until we are parted by death." That vow used to sound like an admonition to stay together until some day in the distant future when death would take one of us in old age. Now it sounded like an impending threat. You may be able to imagine what was going on in me as I read those words to the happy couple.

More than three weeks after Peg's death, as I read the *Afterword* to the 1976 edition of C. S. Lewis' *A Grief Observed,* written by Chad Walsh, it struck me how similar to the circumstance between C. S. Lewis and his wife ours was. The first diagnosis for "H," as he called her in his book, was acute rheumatism. Peg had been referred to a rheumatologist. "H" developed cancer that ate through her thigh bone. Peg's cancer had metastasized on her spine and pelvis. Of course, "H's" cancer went into remission which made it possible for her and C. S. Lewis to have the four years together that they did. Peg's never relented but spiraled downward quickly from the point of diagnosis on. Of course, we had 37 years together. Still as I read about "H's" going into remission, I envied them. Oh, to have time together with the perspective that facing serious illness provides, with the sense of value that it spreads over life and relationships. But then we all know in our heads we are mortals. Still, when it hits you in the pit of the stomach, it has far greater impact.

Peg's family doctor called in an oncologist who came to see her on Monday. We learned that bone cancer is not a primary cancer and that they would be doing further tests to determine the primary source. The preliminary indications were lymphoma. He would have a surgeon visit her to determine from where he might take a lymph node for pathology. A diagnosis could then be made as to the kind of cancer so a treatment regimen could be determined. It would likely be radiation and chemotherapy. At this point, things began to sound a little hopeful. Lymphoma was usually a slowly progressing disease and often very treatable.

So the next procedure that Peg underwent was surgery on Tuesday to remove a lymph node from under her arm. She was taken to the surgical floor, anesthetized, and spent an hour or more in recovery. The surgeon was satisfied that he had a good sample for pathology and we would hear the results as soon as possible.

By Thursday the oncologist confirmed the preliminary diagnosis. It was follicular lymphoma, low grade, and stage four. But there was a complication. Because Peg had been taking the steroid, Prednisone, since her reaction to pain medication, the diagnosis was difficult. Prednisone is a medication that is also used in chemotherapy because it works on cancer cells. Because she had been taking it for awhile, it may already have begun to affect the cells and analysis was more complex than usual. The doctor was going to send the biopsy to the University of Michigan for an independent report. In essence it would be a second opinion and that sounded fine to us. Meanwhile, the doctor reviewed with us what the treatment would likely be, he would consult with the radiologist on a treatment schedule, and he planned to get started as soon as practicable. She was given a mammogram, echocardiogram, and additional X-rays as precautions.

While we were waiting for the pathology to come back, the pain was once more brought under control and by Thursday she was transitioned to oral medication. She was given the option to go home and when she felt confident the pain was under control, she decided to leave. Her physical therapy was discontinued, now that the real cause of her pain was identified.

People of the church helped to get the house ready for her return and a single bed was moved from upstairs into the family room so she would not have to regularly climb the stairs. Our son's wife, Becky, came and stayed with us for a week, something she would do several more times during Peg's illness. She is very skilled at food preparation and nutrition, and she planned a menu that provided healthy and nourishing foods and food supplements that would help Peg's body to resist the cancer. She and Peg had a very close relationship so her being with us was great encouragement to both of us as well as extremely helpful to me with care-giving and domestic responsibilities.

Once more the pain began to escalate. I called her family doctor and he prescribed a pain patch we hoped would make a difference until she could get on track with the treatment. But again, on a holiday weekend, she was overwhelmed by the pain and we ended up taking her to ER. She was admitted early in the morning on July 4th and put back on a morphine pump again to keep her comfortable. We were both glad she was getting relief and it was just a matter of time until her treatment could be put in motion.

That weekend, my sister, Nancy, and mother came from the Upper Peninsula to visit—it was the last time they would see Peg before her death. I had tried to be with Peg overnight at the hospital to help her as much as possible since she was tethered to the morphine pump and IV. She often urged me to go home at night telling me she would be OK, but I was concerned that under the influence of the medications she didn't always think clearly. In addition, she was often hesitant about summoning the nurses, feeling like she was prevailing upon them when, in fact, she really did need assistance. Besides that, given the gravity of what she was facing, I just felt like someone close to her needed to be with her. With Mike and Nancy's help, she spent only a few nights of her hospitalizations without someone of the family with her, and those were in her early stays.

Nancy stayed two nights during the extended weekend she spent with us. One of those nights she woke up to find Peg on her hands and knees crawling back into bed. She was whimpering as she tried to settle down, but was obviously having troubles. Nancy helped her get unraveled from her tubing and bedding and get comfortable. Before bed they had been watching a baseball game on TV. Peg said she had been dreaming that she was with a baseball team but they wouldn't let her play, that she was tangled up some how or other. Actually, she said it was not a dream, it was a nightmare. Later that night she woke up again needing medication because she was hurting and needed her long acting oral medication. Then when she got up to go to the bathroom they found her bed was wet and blood-stained. One of her IV connections had separated, leaked fluid, and bled back from the site in her hand. All of that confirmed my dedication to seeing that she was not alone.

Mike and Nancy not only gave me relief but it gave them extra time together with her. Peg and Nancy regarded each other as sisters, something neither of them had in their own families of origin, and Nancy was the only one of Peg's close family not with her when she died.

We were very surprised on the evening of the 4th of July, a Friday evening on the holiday weekend, when a radiologist came to her room to see her. We thought she would just be kept comfortable until Monday when things would begin to happen. He reviewed her case and said he was going to look over her X-rays. In an hour he was back. He explained that he was very concerned because she had a collapsed vertebrae, T-12, the lowest of the thoracic vertebrae, above the lumbar region. The cancer had been eroding it and it was extruded. It was very close to impinging on her spinal cord. If that happened, she could lose motor control of her lower extremities and body functions. He felt that the cancer that was destroying it needed to be stopped immediately. He was ready to call in his crew and begin radiation right away. He explained the possible side effects as well as the benefits, one of which would be eliminating the source of the intense pain Peg had been dealing with for so long. We were stunned. But it did not take us long to determine she needed to receive the treatment. Relief from the back pain alone made it appealing.

The first thing to happen would be an assessment to determine the area to be radiated, then the treatment would take only a few minutes. There would be one more treatment Saturday morning, which the technician would come in special to do. Then she would resume treatments again on Monday and receive 12 more for a total of 14.

Within a few days, she began to use less of the morphine, and she seemed to be tolerating the radiation rather well. She did begin to use some medication for nausea after awhile and was quite drained of energy, but that was to be expected with the radiation. She even began to venture into the hall for short walks.

About Tuesday of the next week, Peg's hematologist/oncologist stopped to see her. When he learned that she was already receiving radiation he indicated he would have to wait to begin the chemotherapy. Her body would not be able to tolerate both. She would need a couple of weeks to recoup and then she could start the series of six chemo treatments three weeks apart over the next several months. She should schedule an appointment with him right after her radiation was completed.

In the meantime, he began preliminaries, one of which was a heart assessment with a special test using injected dye to check the strength of her heart to withstand the chemo and her heart was found to be strong and healthy. She was, however, taking a medication to reduce her heart rate which was elevated when she was admitted, probably because of the stress on her system of the pain and disease, and her heart rate remained somewhat elevated thereafter.

By the time Peg went home from the hospital, she had seven of the fourteen radiation treatments done. She was beginning to feel somewhat worn, but that was to be expected from radiation and all that she had been through, as well as the side effects of the medications. The back pain was now gone completely and she was starting to wean off of the morphine using it in an oral form that she reduced every three days in order to avoid any withdrawal symptoms. She was given morphine in a liquid form that she could take orally with a syringe if the daily dosage of tablets was not sufficient and she had any "break through" pain, but she never used any of it.

Peg had to work at eating but she knew that it was essential to her recovery. We kept assuring her that eating difficulty was all part of the side effects of the treatment and medications as well as a result of the disease itself. She did work valiantly at eating, even when everything in her didn't want to. Usually the first few bites were the hardest. Sometimes she would eat a little, then head for the bathroom, and lose some of what she'd eaten. But she would come back to the table, sit there for awhile, and then manage to eat a moderate portion of her food. I can hardly express the admiration I felt for her resolve. It brings me to tears now to remember it, though I offered encouragement and assurance at the time.

By the time she completed the radiation, it was evident that she was losing strength and body mass. She had been going upstairs every other day for a shower since there is only a half-bath on the ground floor of the parsonage. But it was getting to the point where she had all she could do to climb the steps and by the time she got upstairs she would have to lay on the bed to rest. She would then shower by sitting on a chair covered with a plastic lawn bag. On one of the last trips she was able to make up the stairs, she lay on the bed and said, with obvious distress, "I think I'm getting worse instead of better." It was hard to know what to say because I thought so too, but then I expected that for reasons I've already stated. The refreshing warm water always felt so good to her (she couldn't use very hot water because it might irritate her skin where she'd received radiation) that it was hard to see her come to the point where she couldn't climb the stairs. She would then sit on the stool in the downstairs bathroom and wash up with a wash cloth and I would shampoo and wash her hair while she held a basin in her lap. It was hard to fathom that her condition was coming to the point where she could not longer care for some of her own basic needs. But we were counting down the days until her radiation was finished and she would begin to recover.

The day she finished radiation, I tried to make a sort of celebration out of it. I had hoped in some small way to make it special. I knew any sort of food for a treat was not a very attractive thing to her, so while we were riding home, I tried to convey excitement about this phase of her treatment being finished, but she was just very tired. When we got home, she headed for the bed and went to sleep.

She did a lot of sleeping as her illness progressed and that distressed her. I remember saying to her that sleep was good medicine and thinking that sleeping time away was not a bad thing considering what she was going through. The worst part of that was she would eat and then sleep so it seemed to her like life was one endless meal. At least she was not suffering with the terrible back pain any more even though she was increasingly tired.

Even more distressing than the tiredness was the continuing loss of strength and body mass. She was obviously losing muscle. I could see it especially in her legs, particularly her thighs. That distressed me because she was eating moderate amounts of food. I thought she should be drinking more, that perhaps she was dehydrating and that had something to do with it. But drinking wasn't appealing to her either. Becky began giving her ice chips and chips of frozen juice, which she would often take, but it didn't seem like enough volume to me. My concern continued to increase.

In order to try to keep up some physical activity, she would do "laps" around the house, through the hallway past the bathroom, into the living room, then the dining room, around into the kitchen and back to the family room, usually when she had to get up to go to the bathroom anyway. Three laps was her common goal. On a couple of occasions she stopped and did brief E-mails to the grandkids on the computer, which is on the far side of the living room. But gradually the laps grew less in frequency and number and getting back to the bed became her only destination.

Early on, when she had been spending part of the night downstairs with the back pain, I had hauled out the foam pads we had used for camping and the sleeping bag and laid them out on the family room floor. If she was able to settle down on the couch or in the chair for the rest of the night, I would just crawl into the sleeping bag and be there with her. By the time she came home after the radiation, I realized there was not going to be a quick turnaround and that I needed to make better provisions for my own sleeping. So I had the second single bed moved down to the family room so I could be more comfortable and readily available when she needed anything.

Two days after she finished her radiation, Peg was to have an appointment with her oncologist. He didn't plan to start chemotherapy until two weeks after the conclusion of her radiation, but he wanted to meet with her to review his plan. When that day came, she felt absolutely "crummy," is the word we used. She did not feel at all like riding the 25 minutes to her appointment, a ride she had been tolerating for her daily radiation. By this time, Becky was back with us for several days and we both strongly suggested that we see if she could meet the following week with him since he wasn't going to be starting anything 'til at least the week after that. She was reluctant to ask for postponement but finally the prospect of staying home to rest won out. I called and got the appointment delayed for a week. That was a mistake.

Instead of finding some recuperation, she continued to feel worse, generally even more "crummy" than before. We blamed it on adjustments to reduced levels of morphine and the after effects of radiation. Finally, I called her family doctor to see what might be done to help her, but he was on vacation and the nurse practitioner I spoke to was not especially helpful. Peg suggested I call the radiologist and see if they thought she should be feeling any better yet since her radiation was over. The nurse I spoke to in that department listened to me describe her symptoms then pulled out Peg's file. She discovered that Peg had not had her blood checked once radiation had ended. Evidently radiology had dispensed with that when her treatment was completed since she would be seeing her oncologist/hematologist in two days. That was the appointment we postponed.

The nurse in radiology said if I could get her in right away, they would do a blood test immediately and the radiologist would be able to look at the results promptly. We got her into the car immediately, and with a wheelchair I had borrowed from the church, into the mini-lab at the hospital right away. Just sitting in the wheelchair in the waiting room was miserable for her. She looked very sick—her color was not good, the way she held her head, sometimes in her hand, betrayed her misery as did the expression on her face. I tried to convey a sense of urgency to the personnel behind the counter without getting pushy. I could tell by the way others who were coming and going were looking at her that her sickness was obvious.

After about 20 minutes, a nurse came for her, and immediately recognized she was very ill. She was super accommodating and sympathetic. Within a few minutes she had the blood drawn and determined that once again Peg's hemoglobin was very low at 6.2. She said no wonder Peg felt so miserable. With our approval, she took extra vials of blood to do workups in the event a transfusion would be necessary, which she was sure would be the doctor's order. That would save Peg having to come back again to the mini-lab for more blood work. We then went into the waiting room while the test results were prepared, which she said would be not more than three minutes. I didn't time it, but she wasn't far off. She sent us on our way to radiology with assurance that Peg would feel much better after a transfusion.

We delivered the report to radiology and I asked if there was any chance that Peg could lay down somewhere while we waited for the doctor. The girl behind the counter went to find a nurse and soon one came and took us to an examining room. Peg was helped to an examining table where she lay on her right side, which was becoming her most comfortable position, and felt a little better.

In less than a half-hour, the radiologist came in to see her. Radiation over as large an area of the spine and pelvis as she had received would retard the blood producing ability of that large bone mass, he said. There was no question that she needed a blood transfusion. He would set it up for her to be admitted as an outpatient to receive two units of blood right away. She should come back in two days for a blood test and if another unit were necessary, he would order that for her on the weekend so she would be ready to see her oncologist the next week. Within three hours of the time we had come, she was on the fifth floor, in the same room she had been in for her previous admission, receiving the blood she desperately needed. The medical people all assured her that the new blood would make her feel like a new woman.

Although she did begin to feel better several hours into the transfusion, she did not have the quick recovery we had hoped for. Some of the staff said it takes the body a little while to fully recover from the trauma of the blood loss. By 10:30 that evening we were on our way home. Over the next couple of days, she was still not feeling very perky. By the time she went back for her follow up blood test, her hemoglobin was up to 10.2 and when she met with her oncologist, he said that was above the minimum level of 10 that he wanted to see in order to administer chemo. He reviewed her case and set a date for a week away to begin her treatment stressing it was imperative to begin attacking the disease that was the root cause of everything else she had been dealing with.

All the while, Peg was wondering how well she was going to be able to tolerate the chemotherapy and, frankly, so was I. She was very depleted from all she had been through but several people who had received treatment assured us that radiation was much more exhausting for them than chemo. Besides, she would have another week of recovery time, her blood level was now up and being monitored, she was managing to eat, and she was getting off the morphine.

When she first came home while the radiation was still in progress, she was having a problem with constipation. She hadn't been eating much in the hospital, which seemed to be a contributing factor, but after awhile of eating at home, the problem persisted. She had been using stool softeners in the hospital and continued to do so at home, along with a diet that was intended to help. Again, we understood that the morphine, as well as radiation, could contribute to sluggishness, although some experienced the opposite problem. Obviously different people were affected in different ways. We then decided to resort to enema. Since she was not very mobile at this point, we placed one of the foam pads on the floor near the bathroom door so that if there were any urgency, she would be close. The first one was very successful and so was another the next day. That got her back to regularity. We were very encouraged that finally something seemed to be going right.

After awhile, she began to have more frequent bowel movements and they were becoming more like diarrhea, and sometimes urgent. That was a concern because she was getting less steady on her feet and she was having difficulty negotiating the one step up from the family room to the main level of the house. Early one morning, I was startled awake by her sounds of distress when she reached the step, trying to hurry from the bed to the bathroom as she struggled to maintain control with only partial success. Even though it was minimal, she was horrified that I had to clean up after her. Again, as she leaned on the sink and I helped her to clean up, I noticed how depleted and weak her leg muscles had become. Even though she tried to tell me she was trying to let me sleep, I lectured her about calling for help whenever she needed to get up.

After that, I noticed she was hanging on to furniture and the walls as she went back and forth so I was sure to help her to the bathroom. Her laps were becoming fewer and she needed support in order to be steady and might stop to rest twice on a single round.

At the same time, she was having trouble getting comfortable in bed or sitting up. We had been using many pillows to prop her up at various angles for quite some time. We had talked about a hospital bed, but she preferred the pillows. No matter what configuration of pillows we used, she couldn't lay very long on her left side because it seemed hard to breath and then it became difficult to be on her back for very long. There was some pain, though it was unlike the pain she had before the radiation. As each day passed, she would awake hoping that the corner had been turned, but the weakness increased and the discomfort intensified.

Finally one Saturday morning, as I helped her to the bathroom, I had to lift some of her weight for her to get up the single step. That should have been a clue. When she got back to the step returning to bed, I was with her to steady her. But when she stepped down to the family room level, I wasn't ready for what happened. Her legs gave out, and she went down on the floor. She assured me she wasn't hurt, at least physically, but I know it damaged her confidence, not only in her physical ability, but in the way that things were going altogether. She crawled over to the bed on her hands and knees, which wasn't far, and I helped her up into bed. Getting comfortable was now a major concern as well and I realized I was needing to help her position her legs. She couldn't lay on her left side because of pressure and laying on her back was increasingly intolerable. I sat on the bed with her and we talked. She didn't feel good at all and she knew she was only getting worse. Though I didn't say it, I felt helpless and was increasingly concerned about my ability to care for her. I said I thought we needed more medical attention. She pondered it for a little bit and agreed. I was concerned that she didn't seem to have the will to resist another trip to ER as she had usually done before.

As I helped her into the car and we headed for the hospital, I didn't have a very good feeling about it at all. Sometimes on our previous trips, I felt like we were going to get the help she needed that would make a difference. This time I just felt a heavy resignation that we were doing something that was necessary to deal with the needs of the moment. I don't recall that either of us said much. She just lay back in the reclined seat with her eyes kind of looking blankly out the window and I held her hand as we rode. Both of us must have been wondering if this was a last time. It was.

After reviewing her condition and history in ER, the doctor decided to once again put her on a morphine pump to give her relief from the discomfort which meant that she would be admitted. X-rays were taken of her abdomen and pelvis as well as a CT scan of her chest, then she was sent again to the fifth floor. Once again it was a weekend, though not a holiday. Because she was so weak and unable to navigate on her own, a device was put in her bed to alert the nursing staff if she got up, the bed side-rails were raised, and she was to call for help to go to the bathroom. On her previous hospitalizations, I had often helped her, especially when she had an IV pole to deal with. This time, even without the bed alarm, I knew the staff needed to help her. The changes from her previous hospitalizations did not bode well to me and I'm sure they weren't beyond her notice either. She was still most comfortable on her right side with the bed at about a 30 degree angle. The morphine was once again a blessing that began to take effect creating a fogginess that eased her general discomfort.

After awhile, the reports from the X-rays, CT scan and other tests came back. Her sodium and minerals were down. In addition her lipase, a test associated with the function of the pancreas, was much too high, 1,000 when normal is 150. The on-call doctor had diagnosed her with pancreatitis. He noted that her abdomen was tender and that there were enlarged lymph nodes around the pancreas. One of them might be pressing on the duct from the pancreas. His remedy was to take her off of solid food to rest her pancreas and to administer nourishment through IV and to see what that would do. He would have all the necessary tests run for her doctors to have a team conference about her condition on Monday.

In addition he noted there was fluid in her chest cavity which explained the shortness of breath and although her oxygen levels tested fine, he put her on 2.5 liters of oxygen to ease her breathing. The fluid explained her difficulty laying on her left side and back and the pressure she was feeling. By now she weighed 111 pounds and her weight held at that level for the duration. (She weighed about 135 pounds during the winter.)

By Sunday, her lipase was returning to normal—down to 300. Because she was having problems with fluid, she was started on a diuretic and her IV was decreased. Her hemoglobin was down to 8.2.

Monday morning we anticipated a visit from Peg's family doctor as he made his rounds before office hours. When he wasn't in by 9:30, we were surprised. By early afternoon, I was getting concerned. I asked one of the nurses if he often came in after office hours, and she said, no, he usually came in before. She would call his office. Before very long, he came. The hospital had contacted the on-call doctor from his group practice on the weekend but, through someone's error, word didn't get to him. He was very apologetic. He was very sorry that she was not feeling well again. He reviewed her tests and condition. He was very concerned about the fluid and tenderness in her abdomen. He could feel swelling there as well, which he thought to be lymph nodes. Her blood pressure was running around 90 over 60 and her temperature was as low as 96 degrees. The good news was her lipase was normal so her pancreas seemed to be responding and the other lab tests showed improvement. He would contact respiratory medicine and someone would see her yet that afternoon.

By late afternoon, a doctor was there. He told Peg that he would be able to remove the fluid through a relatively simple procedure. He would plan to do it on her right lung, which was about 100 percent filled, within an hour there on the same floor. (Her left lung had fluid too but not, of course to that extent.) Because she was so exhausted, one of the nurses said she would sit facing her, they could put their arms around each other, and she would hold Peg in the necessary upright position for the fluid to drain. As soon as preparations were made, Peg was taken to another room next to the lounge. Mike and Becky were with us, and we could wait there and see her being returned to her room when the procedure was finished.

After about 45 minutes, we saw her being brought out of the room on a bed. She had been brought there in a wheelchair but the staff had brought her bed down to the procedure room because she was so exhausted by the time the tapping was nearly through. When it was about 90 percent complete, her blood pressure began to drop and she began to feel much worse, so they curtailed the procedure. Back at the room, she was made comfortable, the pressure she had felt earlier was gone, and she was able to lay on her left side and back again. The nurse who had held her spoke with us and commended her for how well she had handled it, calling her "a real trooper." We would hear that same phrase to describe her from others of the medical staff over the next few days.

Mike and I saw the bottles of fluid that were drawn sitting on the counter at the nurses' station and went to look at them. They were an opaque rusty brown in color, a one liter bottle full, and another almost full, 1.8 liters in all, almost the same amount as a two liter bottle of pop. They looked ominous. I stared at them as though they were an enemy, a manifestation of her disease, thankful that the fluid was no longer a threat to her. They would be analyzed and a report forthcoming.

Again there was hope. Surely removal of the fluid would increase her ability to breath and her range of comfortable positions. Her pancreas had responded, she was receiving oxygen to ease her respiration, saline solution which was necessary with the morphine was replenishing her body after experiencing some dehydration, medication was easing the burden on her heart, and IV fluid was now supplying energy in lieu of the solid food she was having difficulty eating. Perhaps this was the corner we had been waiting to turn.

The next day, Peg's interest in taking fluids was on the increase. She had a cup of broth, Jell-O, applesauce, a can of the supplement called Boost, and several small containers of cranberry juice. (This is the juice I found so hard to deal with later.) She was also permitted to go back on solid food. But then the nurses began to be concerned that her urine output was diminishing. After some time passed without any real significant output, they called her doctor and he increased her diuretic to try to restore their function. At the same time she was put on a catheter. After more time passed, and there was still no urinary output, her doctor ordered another medication but by Tuesday evening, nothing had changed.

Tuesday evening her oncologist stopped to see her to review the schedule for chemo. (He had been in on Monday evening as well right after her lung was tapped, but said he was on his way home from one of his satellite offices, just wanted to look in on her, and would be back tomorrow to review the game plan. In retrospect, I think when he saw her condition, he decided not to go over things with her at that point.) He reported that her blood level of 8.2 was probably a result of rehydration now that she was receiving fluid. That meant she would need more blood. But his greatest concern was the fact that her kidneys were not functional. Their job in the chemo treatment was to remove the waste products resulting from the chemical destruction of the cancer cells. Without their operation, the cancer could not be effectively treated. It would be necessary to deal with that problem before proceeding. He said dialysis would be a possibility but since her kidneys had stopped functioning after removal of the fluid, he wondered if something internally had shifted and might be closing off the ducts between organs. He didn't actually use the word "surgery," but it was implied as he talked about exploring what was going on internally.

At that point, Peg was laying on her back listening to him as he stood at the bottom corner of her bed. I was at the other corner. With her eyes very intent on him, piercing blue, and wide open, she shook her head deliberately from side to side. By this time, her voice was beginning to show some signs of weakness but she said very strongly, "No! No more. I've had enough." He said to her there was still the possibility that the medication might take effect and restore function. She said then that would be fine, but she wasn't going to have surgery or anything else done. She couldn't take anymore. With great composure, she said, "Every time I have something done, something else goes wrong," and she was right.

It started as far back as the summer before. She had a swollen lymph node in her neck over some length of time. (That was probably a symptom of the lymphoma even then.) She was given an antibiotic and if it didn't clear up, her doctor would follow up on it. But it did clear up even though she had a reaction to the antibiotic for which she was given Prednisone. In the fall she began taking a statin medication to reduce her cholesterol and within two months the muscle pain began. When she was given a prescription drug for the pain that would be easier on her system than the over-the-counter stuff she was using, she reacted to it and ended up in the hospital. She began physical therapy and the pain only continued to get worse. She had the radiation which eliminated the source of the back pain, but then her blood level dropped and she needed transfusion. She did everything she was supposed to do to eat nutritionally and nourish her body, but her body began to deplete, become weaker, and her pancreas began to malfunction. She had the fluid removed in order to ease her discomfort and restore her breathing capacity but now her kidneys had shut down and their function was essential to treating her disease. It seemed like a door was repeatedly slammed in her face and she didn't have the heart to pound on it any longer.

Her doctor did not press the issue. He affirmed that her choice was certainly a legitimate option. She had the support of her family and her church. He, along with the medical staff, would do everything possible to make her comfortable. In addition—he had come to know some about her— she had her faith and that would see her through. With those very wide, still intent blue eyes, she raised her eyebrows and said to him, "God is an awesome God!" He agreed and said he would continue to look in on her.

I don't remember much of our conversation at that point or even what transpired between us. It seems like we hugged and held each other for awhile. I do remember her again assuring me she couldn't take anymore. Earlier, I had told her it was OK to do what she needed to do and she thanked me again for understanding, which I've said more about elsewhere. There seemed little else to say right then. I know I was trying to come to grips with what this meant. I still hoped that the medication might take effect. Over the next few days I would look at the collection bag, hoping and asking the Lord if by some miracle it might begin to fill, but as time went on, I became resigned to the fact that it wouldn't. If God were going to spare her there were already plenty of opportunities to do something that would have been nothing short of miraculous.

I called Mike and Becky that evening. They had been back and forth a number of times during that time period, were trying to salvage some family time from the fragmented summer, and were camping with the children. He would come the next morning and Becky and the children as soon as possible. I called the church office in the morning to have the news circulated and the prayer chain contacted.

Our family doctor visited her in the morning. He examined her and noted that her abdomen seemed firm, that fluid was probably accumulating there as well, and he felt the cancer may have spread. He understood and respected her decision to simply let the disease take its course. He also expressed his admiration for her, remembering how she had sometimes challenged him especially in the matter of the cholesterol medication, and how he had come to appreciate her as a person over the years he had been her doctor. She thanked him for the care he had provided and for all he had done in trying to help her overcome the illness. He encouraged her to use the morphine, that there was no reason to hurt. She said she would but that she was comfortable and she was at peace with her decision and her Lord.

Indeed she was. I have not experienced anyone dying an agonizing death, but hers certainly was not. Her disease and its treatment had caused her considerable misery, but death came steadily, gently, and quietly to her. From that point it was a matter of keeping her as comfortable as possible. We would sometimes call the nurses to turn her in the bed and sometimes we would do it the way we had seen the nursing staff do so using the pad that was underneath her. We used pillows to bolster her so she could be on her side for a change of position, but by the end she was content to be on her back. We were assured after she could no longer speak that we would be able to read her expression to tell is she were uncomfortable. We could then administer the morphine, but she seldom needed it.

Eventually her breathing began to become more labored. She was working to take each breath, but her oxygen level remained high until just hours before her death. Her eyes began to become heavy and her jaw dropped with her mouth open as I had seen happen with my father who died of chronic obstructive pulmonary disorder, a respiratory illness.

Those last few days were a very precious time and I have written about some of those moments elsewhere in my recollections. On that Wednesday, her brother Frank, her only surviving immediate family member came to be with her. They had opportunity to spend some precious time together and to deal with some matters that had come between them in recent years. (Another prayer of hers that God answered.) That same afternoon, many of our church family came to see her and us. It was hard to deny some of them the opportunity to speak with her but she was becoming so exhausted that we had to limit some visits to talking with us in the hall. On the Thursday many of Mike and Becky's friends and some of her family came as well. Ministry colleagues also called during those final hours. In the evening a youth group of about seven young people from a church Mike and Becky had worked with on a mission project came and gathered around her bed and quietly but beautifully sang praise songs. She must have thought she was already in heaven with the angels singing. We ended the evening by holding hands and praying before saying goodnight.

She seemed to sleep for hours at a stretch through the night while her brother, Frank and I stayed with her in the room, Frank managing to sleep some on a chair and myself on a recliner. The hospital staff very graciously made accommodations for Mike, Becky, and the children so they could also be nearby. Every time we checked on her during the night, she seemed to be resting comfortably and the hospital personnel didn't bother her anymore than necessary.

In the morning, her doctor stopped by again on his morning rounds. He noted that her breathing was becoming more shallow and it was longer between breaths. He thought it wouldn't be long, not more than hours. The nurses were unable to read her vital signs with their equipment. She was no longer showing any signs of responding to us as we spoke to her and touched her, but we continued to do so trusting that she knew we were there, and we all were when the end came. Gradually it became longer between each breath. Then the next one didn't come, and she was gone at 9:00am.

The thing I remember most about standing there looking at her now lifeless body was just a deep sense of sadness. There would be stronger emotions later and more distressing thoughts to come, but for the moment,

I think we were all just very sad and filled with sorrow. Yet there was also a sense of relief that she was set free from this body that had been devastated in so many ways by disease and could no longer sustain her life in this world. Though God had not postponed death as we desired, He had granted some blessings in it. The pain had ended—actually it seemed to have ended several days before—she had come to the end of her life in this world at peace, and we had all been able to be with her and to see her through.

The hospital staff respected our need to be alone with her in her room behind closed doors, but as soon as we began to stir, one of them came to find out who they should call to come for her body. We gathered together her personal things and the things we intended to keep from her hospital stay. We had prayed as a family with Peg and for her before her death and after; now the hospital chaplain came and led us in prayer again. Before leaving, we decided to wait for the representative from the funeral home to come for her.

As we waited, I observed how much her body evidenced what she had been through with her face pallid in color and narrower than I'd ever seen it, her jaw drooped open and head tipped back for breath, her eyes almost closed. I reached out and closed them the rest of the way so it looked more like she was sleeping though I recognized even deep sleep conveyed more life than this. I wondered how she would appear when we saw her body next at visitation.

When the man from the funeral home arrived, we took one last look and stepped into the hall. Through the partially open door, I saw them lift her from the bed to the gurney, then cover her body. As they brought her out into the hall, her brother went with her and the man from the funeral home to a service elevator and down to the funeral coach, and the rest of us went the other way to the public elevators and out into a world that had changed forever. In the aftermath of her death, as we planned her funeral and burial, notified family and friends, visited with friends and neighbors who also mourned her loss, and dealt with the necessary business and financial matters that follow someone's demise in our society, I would begin to discover just how different that world was.

B: The Biblical Concept of Flesh

In the Old Testament, there are several Hebrew words that can be translated with the English word, "flesh." The most common one, *basar*, refers basically to animal musculature, the soft fleshy part of the body. As such, it is one of several elements in the Old Testament comprising a human being, others being the heart, soul, and spirit.

The "flesh" is often presented as contrasting with the nature of God, who is spirit. While God is all powerful and eternal, "flesh" is weak and mortal. But the idea that sin somehow resides in the flesh is a later development coming from the period between the Old and New Testaments.

Still, there is more resident in the Old Testament term than mere physical body. By extension, this word can also mean the entire human body, people who are blood relations, the human race, living things in general, or life itself. And to say that a man and a woman become "one flesh" in sexual intimacy implies much more than just physical union.[36]

In the New Testament, the predominant Greek word translated "flesh" is the word *sarx*, with only one other word with similar meaning used twice. While *sarx* has all the meanings of the Old Testament word, *basar*, its range of meaning is much broader. It also can mean: the sensuous or animal nature of humanity, with or without incitement to sin; the earthly nature of humanity as opposed to God and prone to sin. That latter meaning is especially present in the writings of the Apostle Paul who attributes nothing of value to the "flesh."

This feature of life with its tangible and intangible dimensions expressed with these two primary biblical words is translated not only with the English word "flesh" but with many other words and phrases, to name a few: man; mankind; all people; body; physical; human passion; will; natural limitations; natural self; old nature; sinful nature; evil nature. Since the range of meaning is so broad, some Bible versions trying to convey a sense of meaning in the context sacrifice consistency of translation in order to convey meaning and use different English words in different passages. In these instances the reader has no indication the word *sarx* was present in the text and has little sense of the scope of it. Other translators, remaining faithful to the original language, are consistent using the word "flesh" wherever *sarx* appears, but are then unable to convey the layers of meaning inherent to this word that is laden

---

36   Theological Wordbook of the Old Testament, no. 291a – *basar*, p. 292.

with so many. In these instances the reader is left with sometimes conflicting impressions of what it is to have a flesh-nature. Classic example would be the formal religious attitude of previous centuries that saw sex as a concession to animal passions to be overcome by rigorous spirituality, while in actuality this capacity of the flesh is God's good provision for human life when indulged within the parameters of His design.

The multi-dimensional nature of the "flesh" as a feature of life in this world is evident when the broad scope of usage for these biblical terms is examined and summarized. The first thing that is evident is that flesh is not inherently evil or sinful. Jesus entered the flesh in His incarnation, which is sometimes appropriately called His en-fleshment. Therefore, if Jesus, the holy Son of God, became a living person in flesh and blood, it is not inherently evil or sinful. God used it as a wardrobe He could don to reveal Himself. To use another metaphor, it became a curtain He could pass through between two realities, allowing Him access in kind to humanity.

Accordingly it is not something to be naturally hated but to be nurtured and treated with tender care like that Jesus has for His Church.[37] Indeed much of life's time and energy is devoted to the care and nurture of the flesh-life, not only in the sense of caring for the tangible body with things like shelter, clothing, food, and health, but in caring for the intangibles connected with it that involve social life and emotional needs arising out of body-life with its passions and yearnings.

It is precisely at this point that a zone exists—and I deliberately call it a zone rather than a line because precise lines are difficult to draw in these matters—between legitimate and illegitimate flesh-needs and desires. Flesh is only one of the dimensions of our humanity, for along with a physical nature we also have a spiritual, psychological, emotional, willful, and social nature (although the flesh-nature is integrally interconnected with them all). So the flesh has desires, passions and power—human urges that drive it to sustain its existence to its satisfaction—the intangibles of the flesh-nature that make it more than musculature. But those very things that sustain flesh-life are also a precise point of human weakness for they are deficient to fulfill us as the holistic creatures God designed us to be.

It is through this inadequacy of the flesh that evil and sin gained entry into the human realm, separating us from God and plunging us into our fallen human condition. Under the influence of evil and the devil, the assertive nature of the flesh takes on a mind and will that is basically hostile to God. It will not submit to God of its own accord. Therefore, because of sin, the person living only in response to the flesh-nature is as good as dead—that is, dead to God and therefore to eternal existence. (Though our struggle is

37   See Ephesians 5:29-32.

lived out in the flesh it is not actually with the flesh but with evil and the devil, since the flesh can be made compliant to God's will with God's power asserted over it. Yet the flesh is the "battle ground" on which the struggle over the souls of people is fought.)

So the flesh is weak and deficient when it comes to living in ways that please God and that realize the God-given human potential and eternal life. Despite the best willful intentions of the human spirit living subject to the flesh-nature influenced by the devil, the result is defilement of the body by sin and impurity. That means, as is, the mortal body of flesh and blood, even though devised and created by God, is an unacceptable vessel for entrée into the presence of a holy God.

To reveal the inadequacy of the flesh to meet God's expectations, He devised the law of commandments, which He gave to the people of the Old Testament, as the criteria for life as He designed it to be lived. In fact, under the influence of the flesh-mind, do's and don'ts seem like the way to fulfill our purpose and to please God, but they really illustrate the inherent weakness of the flesh. When God explains that His standard is keeping those laws perfectly, not only in practice, but in the inner life of thought and motive, we have to admit the flesh is weak, and we are not able to measure up to that expectation. Thankfully He has revealed that, even though the commandments are His standards, He gave them to us so we would discover we couldn't attain to His standards that way.

If God has given us a standard and packaged us in a way that makes our measuring up impossible, there seems to be injustice in that. But what keeps this from becoming injustice is that this is not just a matter of nature, but of mind and will. The flesh is assertive in nature with a mind and will of its own that is basically hostile to God. It will not submit to God's ways of its own accord. But God, in His scheme of things, intends it that way. His design is such that the flesh cannot self-regulate to His satisfaction. What satisfies God is not self-effort but cooperative effort, with Jesus as the major player. And so the Holy Spirit has a distinct role in conjunction with the flesh.

First of all, the flesh is of little significance to God who is willing to turn over a person's flesh to defeat at the hands of Satan in order to save the spirit, the essence of that person. And so living according to the leading of the Spirit won't gratify the flesh. Faith is not a work-around to get God to give legitimacy and gratification to the passions, desires, and yearnings of the flesh-life. Secondly, the Spirit plays a correcting role in making us pleasing to God. Bringing the Christian to perfection is initiated by the Spirit of God and cannot be accomplished by the flesh which is inclined to make us pleasing to God through law-keeping, as we've already seen. The Spirit keeps the outcomes of the flesh in check for when they go unchecked, they produce things like sexual immorality, hatred, jealousy, etc. (see Galatians 5:16-21). God even uses ailments and deficiencies of the flesh to reign in the spirit curbing things like over-enthusiasm, according to the Apostle Paul, who was denied healing of some sort of flesh-problem to keep him humble and dependent.

At this point it might almost seem that flesh is a throw-away that God has devised to contain us as persons in this life for the purposes of bringing us to faith and then growing us to His liking for eternal existence beyond this life in the flesh. But Jesus' purpose is not simply to accomplish salvation from this flesh-reality, it is to salvage all that God has designed and created, redeeming it forever. He not only entered human flesh in the incarnation, He took it to the cross where it was crucified and put to death, and then brought it out of the grave reinventing body life, resurrecting it to a whole new category of existence. The nature of the new body is beyond the scope of this writing, but it is parallel to life in the flesh except with exponential immortal functions, without the influence of evil and the offensiveness of sin.

Jesus' death in the flesh is a sign that He truly became like us, co-identical with us, and just as we have to die in the flesh because of sin, so did He, albeit not His own sin. This was necessary for Jesus to destroy the power of death the devil held over God's human creatures through the flesh that had become the arena of rebellion against God. But Jesus didn't just live above the flesh with spirit keeping it in check, He redeemed the flesh from its fallen condition under the influence of evil and sin. We have hope because Jesus' flesh did not remain in the grave and undergo the deterioration and decay common to all mortals. Instead His resurrection displays His victory over death of the flesh, which was only possible because He surmounted sin and evil. Through His flesh, He has given a new lease on life as well as a new category of life to the world.

In the meantime, we continue to live in the flesh, until we too shall become like Christ in His resurrection, beyond death and the grave. That means Christians can expect to suffer in the flesh-life because Christ did. Suffering is a way God has made to counter the inclination to sin. When a believer suffers in the flesh for his or her faith, it actually completes the suffering of Christ for the Church. Certainly Christ's suffering as Savior was sufficient for salvation, but God in His grace allows the sacrifice and suffering of believers to augment Christ's suffering for the Church—another of God's ways of redignifying His human creatures following the indignity of sin and failure. It is God's gracious way of allowing us who were a major factor in the problem to have a part in the solution.

This multi-dimensional life of the flesh is the arena of marriage. It is a microcosm in which the many facets of flesh-life are given opportunity to play out on an interpersonal plane. The Old Testament in Genesis says two people of different genders become so integral in marriage that they become "one flesh." Upon seeing Eve for the first time, Adam describes Eve as not only "flesh of my flesh" but "bone of my bone." They share a core commonality prior to any distortion of the relationship resulting from falling into sin. So there is a unity of substance between the genders as well as a unity of origin in God's creative design and act. Becoming one flesh is evidenced and actualized in the conception and bearing of children, for what are children but "one flesh" evidence of the union of a male and female?

The nature of this essential union is further strengthened by the use of the word translated as "cleave" in some versions. This somewhat uncommon English word captures the meaning of the Hebrew better than words like "united," "clings," and "joins" used in other translations. A man is to "cleave" to his wife. Things that are united, joined, or that cling to each other, can often be seen as distinct entities that can be separated into their component parts without damage to either. Not so with things that cleave. To cleave is to be united in essential union in the way that parts of the body are attached to one another. There can be no separation of one part of the body from the others without intense distress.[38] Such separation results in death to at least one part if not both, for human bodies do not have the ability to divide and for both parts to continue to live as some lesser life forms do. (Note: in meat cutting, a "cleaver" is an instrument that is used to violently split apart flesh and bone into separate cuts or pieces that otherwise naturally adhere in unified wholeness.) To "cleave" expresses a deep essential union. This is the same word used for the kind of relationship we are to have to God according to Deuteronomy 10:20 and other verses.

Even in this biblical passage that introduces flesh as commonality for the genders, there are connotations of "flesh" signifying more than just the physical. This one flesh relationship is of such significance that it is cause for the two to leave their families of origin and establish their own separate social unit.

The New Testament further strengthens the depth of this bond between the genders. Jesus quotes it without changing the meaning of the passage, probably speaking the words in Aramaic, with the Gospel writer giving us the Greek transliteration. The word Mark chose, translated as "cleave," tells us something of the perception of the Hebrew that Jesus must have conveyed to His disciples. This word for becoming one flesh was also used of metals

---

38   In the experience of sexual intimacy, the conjoining of male and female to become one flesh operates whether it is a God sanctioned conjoining or not—thus God's prohibitions of sexual relations outside of marriage.

bonded together, like copper and tin in the making of brass, so that they become something new.

What Jesus adds to the Genesis passage that is unique is first of all elaboration, that "they are no longer two but one flesh." Surely that means that their physical lives are now substantially linked together. (We recognize that in civil society expecting that a marriage, to be valid, must be "consummated.") Secondly, Jesus says this "yoking" is to be terminated by no one (presumably no human being), implying particularly the parties involved. Then the New Testament word translated "cleave" adds the idea of sticking together in the sense of devotion.

It is no wonder the Bible calls becoming one flesh in marriage a profound mystery. That is because God has created the one flesh nature of marriage to be a worldly parallel to the kind of bond He desires to have with His Church, His people, as "the bride of Christ." That does not mean, however, that the marriage relationship can function as a closed circle for the flesh-life. Just as individual life in the flesh must be under the control of God, so marriage with its highly flesh-oriented nature must also be. Though it is legitimate as a fleshly expression, it does lead to stresses in the flesh because of the stirring of its passions, desires, and powers. This points to the necessity of God as the third partner in marriage to not only keep the relationship centered on the legitimate aspects of the flesh nature and to overcome its illegitimate expressions, but more importantly to deal with their source in the human heart.

All of this serves to illustrate the intense trauma that results when two people who have been conjoined in one flesh, one new self, in marriage are "put asunder" through the death of one. God forbids such dissolution to anyone, except to Himself, as divine victor over death. Presumably only He is qualified to disengage and disentangle the two selves so intertwined without damage to either partner in the reality of this world or the reality of His eternal Kingdom. That does not mean, however, that the two revert back in any way to what they were prior to their marriage. Rather it means that who and what they have each become is significantly the product of their "one flesh" life together as refined by the Holy Spirit, like stones tumbled in a lapidary process, giving shape and polish to each other. For the one remaining in this world, this individuation is experienced as grief with its mixture of memories, feelings, and adjustments. Nevertheless, it is God's prerogative and His provision at the cessation of the two being one and becoming two again in different realms of existence for a time and then forever, since marriage does not carry over into eternity.

Printed in the United States
by Baker & Taylor Publisher Services